Thomas Alfred Davies

Gospel Christianity

Thomas Alfred Davies

Gospel Christianity

ISBN/EAN: 9783337285333

Printed in Europe, USA, Canada, Australia, Japan

Cover: Foto ©Lupo / pixelio.de

More available books at **www.hansebooks.com**

Gospel Christianity:

BY

THOMAS A. DAVIES,

NEW YORK CITY.

AUTHOR OF

Cosmogony or Mysteries of Creation.—Genesis Disclosed.—
Adam and Ha-Adam.—Answer to Hugh Miller.—
An Appeal of a Layman to the Committee on
the Revision of the English Version of
the Holy Scriptures, to have Adam
restored to the English Genesis
where it had been left out
by former translators.

LIBRARY EDITION.

Press of E. H. Coffin,
49 John Street, New York.

PREFACE.

This work, now published under one cover, was written in Sections and by Subjects, either in book or pamphlet form, and scattered by sale and gratuitously by thousands throughout the country. The object of this course was to elicit valuable criticisms from Theologians and learned men, that corrections could be made if any untenable grounds had been taken. But one adverse criticism has been received, and that one was on a point of Theology, which was answered, and nothing further was heard from that source. Whether the answer was satisfactory or not is not known.

There are at least four different kinds of gospel taught from pulpits of the different Christian denominations in the United States. The first is the pure gospel of Jesus Christ. The second is an inferential gospel derived from self-interpretation and construction. The third is when the pure gospel is coupled with matter not found in it, and which is antagonistic to it. The fourth is when there is no distinction made in teaching the Jewish religion from the Old Testament and the Christian religion from the New Testament.

Declamation on any subject outside the gospel that will please or amuse an audience and bring notoriety to the speaker has become quite common of late years, but have nothing more to do with Christianity than that such harangues are made from pulpits consecrated to God.

The Christian religion is the highest limit of Science, as it is a result which satisfies the great equation of man's creation and the universe for his use. Hence to understand the gospel we must understand the laws of God, and as they are immutable and unchanging, so is the gospel immutable and unchangeable. If people do not understand the laws of the gospel, the fault does not lie in the gospel, but in the people who read it in the original Hebrew and Greek. These laws cannot be interpreted or construed; they are just what they are, no more and no less. It cannot be helped that men will draw different conclusions from the Law facts of the gospel, but this does not change the laws or their binding effects.

The first point discussed was the Theology of the unity of the race under the title of "Am I Jew or Gentile?" This was inspired by the Theology that ADAM and EVE were our first parents. In following up the discussion through the work, it is shown that no such single man was created as ADAM, but the single man created was called in the Hebrew HA-ADAM or THE ADAM—Ha in the Hebrew meaning "the" in English. That ADAM was not the husband of EVE, nor was EVE created on the day of creation among the two classes of male and female then created, but was made from the rib of THE ADAM, her husband, some time after he was placed in the garden of Eden. ADAM was the *name* of a created class of male and female, Gen. v. 2, (the Gentile races). THE ADAM was the name of EVE's husband, so that THE ADAM and EVE were not our first parents by the Hebrew record, nor was there a unity of a race in them, as they were Hebrews under a distinctive title of Jews.

These conclusions and assertions were read by some with holy horror as the prattlings of a disbeliever in the Scriptures. But when they came to examine the inspired Hebrew account carefully, they found the diversity of the races clearly set forth, and that ADAM and EVE were not the first parents of the human family, and were not even the heads of any type of that family, and that the unity of the race is an error of Theology, and that the Hebrew account being part of God's inspiration was a law of God and part of His Gospel, by reason of being part of His Organic Laws.

This is clearly supported by the following which took place at the establishment of the Christian religion. That religion required acknowledgment and obedience to all the laws of God then existing and in operation. What then was the condition of the human family? There were six types then in existence, the Caucasian, the Mongolian, the Hebrew, the Malay, the Indian, and the Negro, and their varieties, each with distinct form and character, have remained so to the present day, and are reproduced persistently in type and varieties. Are these results caused by laws of God? The answer will be yes, and hence are *part* of the Christian religion and of Christ's gospel. These two theologies that ADAM and EVE were our first parents, which made a unity of the race, are now considered by those who have made a careful examination of the subject, as passed numbers. As a logical conclusion, those who accept and teach these two theologies do not teach the whole gospel of Jesus Christ.

This Theology of the unity of the race was the foundation of St. Paul's theology of original Sin in ADAM. This Theology is not found in the gospel. Sin is treated there as a free-will act, as an act of thought or body, and responsibility for it is direct, and extends to lineage only to the third and fourth generations of those that *hate God.* Sin is a specific act, not a hereditary universal quality, and we are to be judged according to the deeds done in the body,—in other words, according to the acts done in the body.

Another misfortune to the Bible is the garbled translation from the Hebrew of the object and extent of the flood. The Sin of THE ADAM in the garden of Eden in disobeying God's command, and the sin of his daughters in marrying the Gentiles and having children by them, were the causes of God's bringing on the flood, which, according to the Hebrew account, was to destroy every descendant of THE ADAM whose lineage was to evolve the Saviour, in order that Noah, being a just man and walking in the ways of God, should be a worthy ancestor of Jesus Christ. Instead then of the destruction extending only to the descendants of the Jews, THE ADAM and EVE, except Noah and his family, leaving the Gentile races and the other Hebrews unharmed, the translation destroys *every man and beast on the whole earth,* except those saved in the Ark. It is pleasant to know that this translation is gradually losing hold upon the intelligence of the nineteenth century. This will be seen from the initial action taken by Yale College in its

Divinity School, where students are now required to understand Hebrew, that their teachings as ministers shall be upon the Hebrew and Greek as a basis. The result of this will be a more strict adherence to the Scriptures in the original languages, and not bind them as heretofore to theologies based upon incorrect translations on certain points.

It must be apparent to every one reading the Old Testament, that the so-called people of God were not prepared to receive the enlightened Christian religion. It was requisite to have them informed what the organic laws of God were, and the mode and manner of obedience to them. God in his wisdom established the Jewish Religion, not as a permanent religion for the world, but as a Kindergarten School, to teach His Organic Laws and obedience to them, giving the people just enough insight into the future that their prophets could blindly foretell the coming of a Messiah, but in no wise enabling them to define his exact position and relation to the world.

The Incarnation of Jesus Christ is the most important single fact of the Christian religion. It was the first initial manifestation of the perfect will of God in its establishment. Here was laid the first foundation stone of that religion, of the gospel, of Christ's Church, and of our salvation. All Christians admit that this religion was the creation of God's mind, and still some, claiming to be Christians, deny that He did create the child Jesus in the womb of Mary His mother, to have two natures, the Divine and human. How can these Christians reconcile this denial with this fact, when it is stated over and over again in the gospel and affirmed by Christ Himself. While these misguided people admit that all individual separate existences were created by God, amounting in numbers beyond computation, they single out this particular act of creation as impossible.

There seems to be great confusion in the Christian world as to what Christ's Church is, and this is more particularly due to the Roman Catholic organization, one that is the strictest observer of all the cardinal principles of the gospel, while some of its disciplines cannot be found in the gospel, nor are they consistent with it, but are antagonistic to its spirit and the record. It is not surprising that an organization having such a long list of points of discipline should not have some few errors in it.

There is, however, a difference of opinion among the clergy of that denomination on this point, some holding that Christ's Church is a spiritual kingdom on earth extending to heaven, while others claim that the Roman Catholic Church is the only true Christ's Church. The Rev. Father Thomas Burke, the most famous Catholic lecturer of the world, and admired by all Catholic readers, says of Christ's Church:

"Christ, therefore, is the true head of His Church, the unfailing, ever watchful head of His Church, and is as much to-day the head of the Church as he was 1800 years ago. Christ to-day is the real head, the abiding head." He also said in the same lecture, Christ's Church was a spiritual kingdom established on the earth. Page 452.

Catholics generally call their organization Christ's *Visible* Church on earth, that is, that a Spiritual existence is visible. If this theology is sound, we should be able to see God, Jesus Christ, and the inside of heaven, from earth.

From this it appears that Father Burke did not recognize Peter as the head of Christ's Spiritual Church, nor does he recognize the Pope as the spiritual head, because that there cannot be two heads. Peter was the first head of the organization that was called a church in imitation of the name Church given by Christ himself to His Church. From the time of the Apostolic

Era to the present day, the Roman Catholic organization has, by writings and teachings, endeavored to weld Christ's Spiritual Kingdom, His Church, into one continued form under the title of Roman Catholic Church. The attempt has been a signal failure, for they can no more weld spiritual existences with material forms to be the same, as either than they can weld oil and water to be either oil or water separately.

It would be unjust to charge that this welding process was commenced and carried on in the making of the Catholic creeds, by neglecting to put in them Christ's Church, instead of these various names, the Holy Catholic Church, One Catholic Apostolic Church, and One Holy Catholic Apostolic Church. Every one of these names require construction and interpretation, whereas if they had used Christ's Church, the name He gave to it, no construction or interpretation would be necessary. No one can come to any other conclusion than that the catholics supposed and intended to point to the Roman Catholic organization as Christ's spiritual kingdom on earth, a simple point of judgment in language. Neither of these names for a church used in these creeds can be found in the Gospel, and hence we are justified in saying that the Catholic organization, under these names, is not the only true Christ's Church in name, and this point of discipline is antagonistic to the gospel.

Another point of discipline is the assumption that the apostolic succession, with the same Divine powers which Christ conferred upon His eleven active Apostles, exists now in the Catholic Clergy. This assumption cannot be found in the gospel. The claim is made, however, upon the ground that because Peter and the other apostles had Divine powers conferred upon them, that they, by a discipline of their own, had the Divine right to confer upon others those powers, without any authority from Christ to do so. Not one word can be found in any one of the four gospel books, that Christ gave His apostles the power to confer Divine power upon any one.

This claim belongs to the class of inferential gospel made by men, that has brought the Christian world almost into a state of anarchy between denominations, which state need not be described for it is well known. The Catholic is not the only denomination which has indulged in these inferential gospels, but is the first to appeal for Christian unity of faith. This appeal is well founded in alarm, if it is intended to be a unity of faith and discipline combined, as that is an impossibility on the announcement. There is Christian unity of faith to-day in all denominations which accept and teach the pure gospel of Jesus Christ. But when the effects of teaching as gospel what is not in the gospel, but antagonistic to it, is spread through the land, it is time to sound the tocsin of alarm.

The appeal for christian unity comes logically from the Catholic organization, and underlying it may be a desire to get back in language to the gospel instead of reaching it by construction and interpretation. This would cover a vast field of discord and unchristian feeling which is now, and has been for some time past, cropping out in this country in various forms and organizations, certainly not christian organizations. In this Republic there ought not to be any aristocracy of religion or of civil rights. If those civil rights or religion are interfered with by any considerable body of men with unfounded claims, the certain result is, as it has been in all times past, resistance, which comes first in the shape of conciliatory arguments, and when they are of no avail, then—History repeats itself.

These two points of discipline, as has been said before, are not religion or inspirers of christian love, but are open elements of discord. They have no place in the gospel as requirements of salvation. They may be potent means of making converts and riveting their belief, that through their merits is the only way to God's kingdom.

The Catholic appeal for christian unity does not define the grounds of unity except to be of the same faith, hence the faith intended is the Catholic faith. Other christian denominations have no faith in these points of discipline, and therefore the following quotations from the gospel would seem to be pertinent, except as to "hypocrisy."

Luke VI., 41. And why beholdest thou the mote that is in thy brother's eye, but perceiveth not the beam that is in thine own eye?

42. Either why canst thou say to thy brother, let me pull out the mote that is in thine eye, when thou thyself beholdest not the beam in thine own eye? Thou hypocrite, cast out first the beam out of thine own eye, and then shalt thou see clearly to pull out the mote that is in thy brother's eye.

It is to be sincerely hoped that these two points of discipline in the Catholic organization will soon be publicly abandoned in the United States at least, that no cause shall exist in our population for protest. In this Republic of equal rights and equal liberty to all, any invasion of them easily excites to retaliation, the masses. One kind word from good Pope Leo XIII. would do away with these two points of discipline and make a Comparative Millenium on earth, and especially in the United States, and make Christ's XII. Commandment, " Thou shalt love thy neighbour as thyself," (in a christian sense), a living entity instead of as it is now, almost a dead letter. There is no estimating the change of Christian feeling that would come over the world ; it can be more easily imagined than foretold, as then christian unity might be possible on the gospel and discipline in christian organizations.

CONTENTS.

	PAGE
AM I JEW OR GENTILE? Read and See	3

FIRST ADDENDA.

Genesis not Understood	51
Genealogy of Jesus Christ, Proving His Divinity	57
Biblical and Scientific Proof of the Genesis Creation, as from the Hebrew	65

SECOND ADDENDA.

Alleged Errors in the Bible	89
Errors of Translation in the King James Bible	97
Postulates in the Genesis considered as Settled on the Basis of the Hebrew Inspiration	101
SONG OF CREATION	107

    Invocation—Nothingness—Creation's Dawn—Throne of God—Mysterious Form of God—Angelic Hosts—Light of Heaven—God's Attributes—Seal of Heaven—God—Creation—Time—Installation of Time—Time Returning the Universe to God—Return of Time—Godhead—New-Born Light—Space—Day and Night—Evening and Morning—Night of the Fourth Day.

THIRD ADDENDA.

	PAGE
Inevitable Conclusions	141
The Bible of Nature	143
The Two Bible Systems	147
The Bible of Inspiration	149
The Translators' Bibles	157
Cause and Effect	167
Creation Makers	177

FOURTH ADDENDA.

Obey the Laws of God	187
The Christian Religion	207
Belief and Faith	221
Conscience, the Rudder of Life	227
The Higher and Upper Plane of Christianity	233

FIFTH ADDENDA.
READING THE BIBLES BY CO-ORDINATES OF TRUTH.

Read the Bibles by Co-ordinates	243
What is a Co-ordinate?	249
What is Inspiration?	257
Establishing the Christian Religion	269
The Jewish and Christian Religions Co-ordinated	283
The Birth of Jesus Christ	289
Conception of Mary, Mother of Jesus	293
Rewards and Punishments	299

SIXTH ADDENDA.

How to be A Christian by the Gospel of Jesus Christ.

	PAGE
Road to Salvation	307
Preface	309
Appeal for Christian Unity	313
Christ's Church	347
Laws that Christians must Obey	355
Christian Organizations	359
Composition of Christian Organizations	369
God's Organic Laws	375
Catholic and Protestant Laymen	399
Apostolic Era	407

AM I JEW

OR

GENTILE?

INTRODUCTION.

This work is the resume or corollary from various publications on the same general subject by the author which have extended through a period of over forty years, and can be stated succinctly as the misuse of two English words in the King James Bible—The one word being "Man," used indiscriminately for Adam and The Adam in the Genesis, and the other is the word "So," at the head of Gen. I., 27, in the place of "And," the proper Hebrew word. In the Oxford Revision lately published, one of these errors has been rectified by returning the Hebrew word "And" to its long lost place and deposing the usurper "So" from its high and commanding position for mischief. The other error still remains in our Bible and in the Oxford Revision, as there is no equivalent word in the English language for Adam "male and female" created (Gen. I., 26,) or The Adam a single "male" created (Gen. I., 27.) By restoring these Hebrew terms to their proper places, it becomes apparent that the first verse records the creation of a class of human beings, while the second records the creation of the Hebrews, and that The Adam was a representative Hebrew and the created head of the Jewish line, which evolved the Saviour of mankind. This would seem to prove the Divinity of Jesus Christ and Christianity as being an original design of the Creator. By restoring these terms the flood only destroyed the descendants of The Adam, except Noah and his family, leaving the descendants of Adam unharmed by that punishment.

The author invites the most searching criticisms on the positions taken, for if he is right, truth should be inscribed on the portals of the Gateway to Divine Revelation in the English as contained in the Hebrew.

AM I JEW OR GENTILE?

This important question has been substantially raised by the Oxford Revision of the Holy Scriptures, completed a short time since and published to the Christian world. It arises from the fact, that the Revisers have dropped the word "So" at the head of Gen. I., 27, which appears in our Bible, and have placed in its stead in the Revision, the proper Hebrew word "And." The true understanding and proper rendering of "Man" in both, Gen. I., 26 and 27, would seem to settle the vexed question of the creative origin of mankind.

The word "So" in our Bible, to the general or careless reader, made the creative act in Gen. I, 26, a declaration of God's intention to create what he did create in Gen. I, 27. While the word "And" indicates, as it does in every other Verse of the First Chapter, an additional something, and in this case an additional act of creation. By the replacing of Adam in the 26th Verse, and THE ADAM in the 27th Verse, which are the corresponding terms in the

Hebrew for "Man" in the Bible and in the Revision, it becomes strikingly apparent that these two verses record two separate and distinct creative acts, of two separate and distinct portions of mankind.

By looking over the rules established for the guidance of the Oxford Revisers, we can see why they did not replace Adam and THE ADAM in the Revision, if they desired ever so much to do so. These were the rules by which they were to be guided.

1. To introduce as few alterations as possible into the Text of the Authorized Version consistent with faithfulness.

2. To limit, as far as possible, the expression of such alterations to the language of the Authorized and earlier English Versions.

3. That the Text to be adopted be that for which the evidence is decidedly preponderating, and that where the Text so adopted differs from that which the Authorized Version was made, the alteration be indicated in the margin.

From this it will be seen that the power and scope of the Revision Committee to make changes from the Authorized Version were limited, and the knowledge of this fact will be gratifying to the whole Christian world. Nothing is more repugnant to Christians than radical alterations in the Bible Text, while there is nothing more searching than desires for clear explanations of obscure portions.

While this is so in the general, we are all interested in having the account of the creation of our ancestors as clearly stated as it is possible to obtain it from the Hebrew, and if the Hebrew terms themselves are not used, any true explanation relating to the English terms will unquestionably be hailed as true Bible teachings.

It may be interesting to the English reader to whom this little work is more particularly addressed, in the hope of making clearer what has been regarded as obscure, to know the history of our various Versions of the Bible, which we take from the Oxford Revision.

"The English Version of the New Testament here presented to the reader, is a Revision of the translation published in the year of Our Lord 1611, and commonly known by the name of the Authorized Version.

That translation was the work of many hands and of several generations. The foundation was laid by William Tyndale. His translation of the New Testament was the true primary Version. The Versions that followed were either substantially reproductions of Tyndale's translations in its final shape or revisions of Versions that had been themselves almost entirely based on it. Their successive changes may be recognized in this continuous work of authoritative revision : First, the publication of the Great Bible of 1539-41, in the reign of Henry the VIII ; next the publication of the Bishops Bible of 1568 and 1572, in the reign of Elizabeth ; and lastly, the publication of the King's Bible of 1611, in the reign of James I. Beside these, the Geneva Version of 1560, itself founded on Tyndale's translations, must here be named, which though not put forth by authority, was widely circulated in this country and largely used by King James' translators."

We can all see from this that our King James Bible was framed from manuscripts, claimed to have been written by inspired writers.

The general account of the creation in Genesis is founded upon the application of God's Laws, called Natural Laws, to matter. The inspired, in writing this account, handles all these laws in creating, combining, in reproducing and in setting the heavenly bodies of the Universe in motion, which the most skilled scientist or philosopher of to-day would use in the lecture room before his students. Most of these laws have been discovered since the translations of these manuscripts, while the scientist and philosopher have unearthed these manuscripts and their inspiration, by developing God's Acts in Nature.

While the Genesis is the gate-way to Divine Revelation, it is a purely scientific account and the record of Divine law as applied to matter. It is a simple and concise statement of facts. No dogmas or religious creeds are referred to or hinted at, so that the explanations of the principles laid down there, while they give strength to the Christian faith, are to be tested more by discovered natural laws than by simple faith in their truth.

Without a further and clearer explanation of this English word "Man," used by translators in our Bible in the creative account, (as there is no explanation of the term given there,) our belief naturally takes a wider range from actual knowledge and experience, than the imprint can hold us to. We see and we know, and we would like to read as we see and know; but we cannot, from the fact that we are unable to compass the meaning of "Man" in that connection.

This has aroused the author to a research to see where the truth lay. The result of that research, although continued diligently for many years, has never till quite lately crystallized into a consistent and satisfactory form, which he is now willing to give to his fellow readers, and if it produces an effect on any other class, he will be so much the more gratified.

The conclusion arrived at is, that the Hebrew record of the Creation of Mankind is exactly correct, and in accordance with the developed laws of God, the most prominent of which is His Divine law of reproduction, "after its kind," so persistently repeated in the First Chapter of Genesis. That the record explains itself clearly and needs no manisms of construction, and that it accords harmoniously with the present received opinions of mankind, if read in the Hebrew.

In reading any language, when we come to a term which we do not understand, or its meaning is doubtful, we refer to the standard dictionary of the language for information. In reading the Genesis as it is usually read, the ordinary reader would probably find nothing to criticise; but if he is an accurate reader and desires to understand what he reads, he will ask himself what "Man" means in the creative account, as used in the following verses in our Bible and in the Oxford Revision.

GENESIS I.

* * * * * *

26. And God said, let us make "Man" in our image, after our likeness, and let "them" have dominion over the fish of the sea, and over the fowl of the air, and over the cattle, and over

all the earth, and over every creeping thing that creepeth upon the earth.

27. And God created "Man" in His own image, in the image of God created he him, male and female created he them.

* * * * * *

The reader takes up his Webster's Dictionary and turns to "Man," and finds the following definitions:

> MAN. An individual of the human race; a human being; a person; a grown up male, as distinguished from a woman or boy; the human race; mankind; the totality of men; sometimes the male part of the race, as distinguished from the female; one possessing in a high degree the distinguishing qualities of manhood; one of manly strength or virtue; a servant of the male sex; a vassal; a subject; a married man or husband; a piece with which a game as chess or drafts is played.

Which of these definitions is the reader to apply to the term "Man" in this creative account? He is puzzled and perplexed; but a Hebrew scholar steps in here and comes to his assistance. He opens the Hebrew Dictionary and finds that the Hebrew term for Man is Ish, as pronounced in English, and the Hebrew scholar is still more perplexed when he finds no word Ish in the creative account. He then begins to examine the record itself, for being acquainted with

Scriptures, he finds in Gen. V., 2, just the definition which he desires, and in the creative account, the corresponding place of the term defined. He then reads in Gen. I., 26, the account of the making of Adam, and the definition of this term Adam in Gen. V., 2.

GENESIS I.

26. And God said, let us make ADAM in our own image, after our likeness, and let THEM have dominion over the fish of the sea, and over the fowl of the air, and over the cattle, and over all the earth, and over every creeping thing that creepeth upon the earth.

The Hebew Scholar now begins to investigate. He reads the mosaic definition of ADAM used in the creative account thus:

"Male and female created he THEM, and blessed THEM, and called THEIR name ADAM in the day when they were CREATED." Gen. V., 2.

Here, then, is the name "Adam" in the creative account and its definition "male and female," created, not born of a woman, but brought into complete existence like all other things in the Genesis, without parents, or in other words by fiat.

All the various meanings attached to "Man" in English and Ish in the Hebrew are people with parents, born of a woman and grown up from birth to manhood. There is no one word in the English language, and but one word in the Hebrew, and that is the word ADAM, that signifies "male and female," created, complete, and not born of a woman.

In like manner there is no one word in the English language, and but one in the Hebrew, and that is THE ADAM, that signifies a single male, created, complete, and not being born of a woman.

In like manner Adam is used to denote the descendants of Adam "created," in the Scriptures, and then its meaning can be correctly defined as "Man," because they are people born of a woman.

The same applies to THE ADAM and his descendants.

We now pass to the Second Division of the Creation of mankind, as stated in the Hebrew.

GENESIS I.

* * * * * *

27. And God created THE ADAM in his own image, in the image of God created he him, male and female, created he them.

The Hebrew Scholar will inform the reader, that in this Verse where Ha the Hebrew for "the" is used in connection with Adam, it is THE ADAM, being the identification of an individual governed by "him" in the same sentence.

The usual rendering of THE ADAM in all translations has been "the man," while in many places clearly indicating THE ADAM, it is rendered "man," "men," "man's" and "men's." In our Bible and in the Revision, in Gen. I., 27, it is rendered "man," simply without the designating article "the."

The same reasoning as to the use of this term "man" instead of Adam in the 26th Verse, will equally apply to the use of "man" in the 27th Verse, instead of THE ADAM, except as to the omission of "the."

It would undoubtedly be clearer to the English reader to have used the Hebrew terms in these two Verses, rather than take him through the circumlocution of a special education on the subject. Still, he might not compass the real meaning of the Hebrew terms without some explanation. But when he reads further on in the Genesis and finds this term THE ADAM used almost continuously, he would himself be put upon his enquiry as to its true meaning in Gen. I., 27.

Having thus stated these two creative acts, let us now analyze them as compared the one with the other, and ascertain if possible wherein they differ. The language used in Gen. I., 26, is: "And God said, let us make ADAM in OUR image, after *our* likeness." Whatever US and OUR mean in this connection is not explained by the record itself, but one thing is certain, it means something. The expression, "in our image after our likeness," is distinctly a different quality as a whole from that of THE ADAM, created in Gen. I., 27, when it says: "And God created THE ADAM in his OWN image, in the image of God created he HIM."

Comparing the language and terms of the two acts, and the subjects of them, it must be admitted that they differ essentially in terms. It would take more knowledge than we possess on the subject of the Creation, to point out the exact differences in these two Divine Acts; but if language means any thing, there is a difference, and that difference alone is sufficient for any one to say, without fear of contradiction, that there are as recorded, two separate acts of making and creating, to say nothing of the fact, that in the one act Adam means "male and female," while in the second THE ADAM was a single "male."

These slight differences in rendering the original terms of the Hebrew into English, does not in the least effect the account in the Hebrew, as that is a fixed inspired record, which some may conceive, and others misconceive, and it is only by applying the microscope of exact knowledge that its truths are gradually developed The reader will observe in the Second Chapter of Genesis, and 19th Verse, that ADAM is there used for the first time in our King James Bible. If he had been confused before, he would be still more confused at this sudden introduction of an unexplained name or term.

The Oxford Revision has delayed the introduction of ADAM to the reader, to Gen. III., 17, for what reason cannot be imagined. It is, however, equally abrupt in the narrative and equally without explanation of meaning to the reader.

We now give to the English reader the two Verses, Gen. I., 26, 27, as they are in our Bible, in the Oxford Revision, and in the Hebrew, that he may see for himself that all three mean the same, when he knows what "Man" means and stands for in these English Versions.

GENESIS I.

* * * * *

THE CREATION OF ADAM.

BIBLE.

26. And God said, let us make MAN in our image, after our likeness, and let THEM have dominion over the fish of the sea, and over the fowl of the air, and over the cattle, and over all

the earth, and over every creeping thing that creepeth upon the earth.

REVISION.

26. And God said, let us make MAN in our image, after our likeness, and let THEM have dominion over the fish of the sea, and over the fowl of the air, and over the cattle, and over all the earth, and over every creeping thing that creepeth upon the earth.

HEBREW.

26. And God said, let us make ADAM in our image, after our likeness, and let THEM have dominion over the fish of the sea, and over the fowl of the air, and over the cattle, and over all the earth, and over every creeping thing that creepeth upon the earth.

THE CREATION OF THE ADAM.

BIBLE.

27. So God created MAN in his own image, in the image of God created he him, male and female, created he THEM.

REVISION.

27. And God created MAN in his own image, in the image of God created he HIM, male and female, created he THEM.

HEBREW.

27. And God created THE ADAM in his own image, in the image of God created he HIM, male and female, created he THEM.

❋   ❋   ❋   ❋   ❋   ❋

We have referred before to the fact, that in our Bible the word "So" appears at the beginning of Verse 27, while the Revision has dropped that word and given the correct Hebrew word "And" in its place, which word indicates that something additional was to be recorded as created, not before recorded.

The conclusions to be drawn from these names, ADAM and THE ADAM, as to what was created under them, are not constructions, but are facts. While no one can tell how many of mankind were created under the name ADAM, we can with certainty say that there were more than was created under the name THE ADAM. Another point we can be certain of, and that is, that all of mankind created were created under one or both of these names.

We will now proceed with the Hebraic history, which more particularly, as will be seen by the reader, relates to THE ADAM, and continue it to the Ninth Chapter of the Genesis, when the THE ADAM's were dispersed among the Isles of the Gentiles and the nations of the earth.

In order that this work shall not exceed certain limits, those Verses only will be quoted which contain Adam or THE ADAM, leaving the reader to refer to the Bibles for further information.

GENESIS, CHAPTER II.

* * * * * *

BIBLE.

5. And every plant of the field before it was in the earth, and every herb of the field before it grew; for the Lord God had not caused it to rain upon the earth, and there was not a man to till the ground.

REVISION.

5. And no plant of the field was yet in the earth, and no herb of the field had yet sprung up; for the Lord God had not caused it to rain upon the earth, and there was not a man to till the ground.

HEBREW.

5. And no plant of the field was yet in the earth, and no herb of the field had yet sprung up; for the Lord God had not caused it to rain upon the earth, and there was not an ADAM to till the ground.

NOTE.—The reader can put his own construction of the meaning of ADAM in this Verse. As the meaning to us is ambiguous, we do not pretend any explanation. The Bible has it Man, and the Revision has it Man.

* * * * * *

BIBLE.

7. And the Lord God formed man of the dust of the ground, and breathed into his nostrils the breath of life, and man became a living soul.

REVISION.

7. And the Lord God formed man of the

dust of the ground, and breathed into his nostrils the breath of life, and man became a living soul.

HEBREW.

7. And the Lord God formed THE ADAM of the dust of the ground, and breathed into his nostrils the breath of life, and THE ADAM became a living soul.

> NOTE.—The manner of making THE ADAM is specific and plain to the reader, and needs no comment. The Bible has "the man," and Revision "the man," while the Hebrew is THE ADAM.

* * * * * *

BIBLE.

8. And the Lord God planted a garden eastward in Eden, and there he put the man whom he had formed.

REVISION.

8. And the Lord God planted a garden eastward in Eden, and there he put the man whom he had formed.

HEBREW.

8. And the Lord God planted a garden eastward in Eden, and there he put THE ADAM whom he had formed.

> NOTE.—The Bible and Revision each render THE ADAM as "the man," while the Hebrew is THE ADAM.

* * * * * *

BIBLE.

15. And the Lord God took the man and put him into the garden of Eden, to dress it and to keep it.

REVISION.

15. And the Lord God took the man and put him into the Garden of Eden, to dress it and to keep it.

HEBREW.

15. And the Lord God took THE ADAM and put him into the Garden of Eden, to dress it and to keep it.

NOTE.—In this verse, the Bible has THE ADAM "the man," and the Revision the same, while the Hebrew is THE ADAM.

* * * * * *

BIBLE.

16. And the Lord God commanded the man, saying, of every tree of the garden thou mayest freely eat.

REVISION.

16. And the Lord God commanded the man, saying, of every tree of the garden thou mayest freely eat.

HEBREW.

16. And the Lord God commanded THE ADAM, saying, of every tree of the garden thou mayest freely eat.

NOTE.—In this verse, the Bible has THE ADAM "the man," the Revision the same, while the Hebrew is THE ADAM.

* * * * * *

BIBLE.

18. And the Lord God said, it is not good that the man should be alone; I will make him an help meet for him.

REVISION.

18. And the Lord God said, it is not good that the man should be alone; I will make him an help meet for him.

HEBREW.

18. And the Lord God said, it is not good for THE ADAM should be alone; I will make him an help meet for him.

NOTE.—In this verse, the Bible has THE ADAM "the man," and the Revision the same, while the Hebrew is THE ADAM.

* * * * * *

BIBLE.

19. And out of the ground the Lord God formed every beast of the field, and every fowl of the air, and brought them unto ADAM, to see what he would call them; and whatsoever ADAM called every living creature, that was the name thereof.

REVISION.

19. And out of the ground the Lord God formed every beast of the field, and every fowl of the air, and brought them unto the man, to see what he would call them; and whatsoever the man called every living creature, that was the name thereof.

HEBREW.

19. And out of the ground the Lord God formed every beast of the field, and every fowl of the heaven, and brought them unto THE ADAM, to see what he would call them; and

whatsoever The Adam called every living creature, that was the name thereof.

Note.—In this verse, the Bible has The Adam "Adam," and the Revision has it "the man," while the Hebrew is The Adam.

* * * * * *

BIBLE.

20. And Adam gave names to all cattle, and to the fowl of the air, and to every beast of the field; but for Adam, there was not found an help meet for him.

REVISION.

20. And the man gave names to all cattle, and to the fowl of the air, and to every beast of the field; but for man, there was not found an help meet for him.

HEBREW.

20. And The Adam gave names to all cattle, and to the fowl of the air, and to every beast of the field; but for Adam, there was not found an help meet for him.

Note.—In this verse, the Bible has The Adam "Adam," while in the second instance it has "Adam," and the same appears in the Hebrew.

The Revision has The Adam "the man," and in the second instance, for Adam in the Hebrew it has "man," while the Hebrew has The Adam in the first instance, and Adam in the second. The term Adam in the Hebrew seems somewhat obscure, and no explanation is given, except it refers to The Adam, the individual.

* * * * * *

BIBLE.

21. And the Lord God caused a deep sleep to fall upon Adam, and he slept; and he took

one of his ribs and closed up the flesh instead thereof.

REVISION.

21. And the Lord God caused a deep sleep to fall upon the man, and he slept; and he took one of his ribs and closed up the flesh instead thereof.

HEBREW.

21. And the Lord God caused a deep sleep to fall upon THE ADAM, and he slept; and he took one of his ribs and closed up the flesh instead thereof.

NOTE.—In this verse, the Bible has THE ADAM "ADAM." The Revision has it "the man," while the Hebrew is THE ADAM.

* * * * * *

BIBLE.

22. And the rib which the Lord God had taken from man, made he a woman, and brought her unto the man.

REVISION.

22. And the rib which the Lord God had taken from the man, made he a woman, and brought her unto the man.

HEBREW.

22. And the rib which the Lord God had taken from THE ADAM, made he a woman, and brought her unto THE ADAM.

NOTE.—In this verse, the Bible has THE ADAM "Adam." The Revision has it "the man," while the Hebrew is THE ADAM.
It will be observed by the reader that "man" ends the verse in each instance. This is the translation of the Hebrew term Ish, which has no necessary connection with either ADAM or THE ADAM.

BIBLE.

23. And Adam said, this is now bone of my bones, and flesh of my flesh; she shall be called woman, because she was taken out of man.

REVISION.

23. And the man said, this is now bone of my bones, and flesh of my flesh; she shall be called woman, because she was taken out of man.

HEBREW.

23. And THE ADAM said, this is now bone of my bones, and flesh of my flesh; she shall be called woman, because she was taken out of man.

NOTE.—In this verse, the Bible for THE ADAM in the first instance it has "man," in the second instance "the man." The Revision in the first instance has "the man," and "the man" in the second, while in the Hebrew it is THE ADAM.

* * * * * *

BIBLE.

25. And they were both naked, the man and his wife, and were not ashamed.

REVISION.

25. And they were both naked, the man and his wife, and were not ashamed.

HEBREW.

25. And they were both naked, THE ADAM and his wife, and were not ashamed.

NOTE.—In this verse, the Bible has THE ADAM "the man," and the Revision the same, while the Hebrew is THE ADAM.

GENESIS, CHAPTER III.

* * * * * *

BIBLE.

8. And they heard the voice of the Lord God walking in the garden, in the cool of the day; and ADAM and his wife hid themselves from the presence of the Lord God, amongst the trees of the garden.

REVISION.

8. And they heard the voice of the Lord God walking in the garden, in the cool of the day; and the man and his wife hid themselves from the presence of the Lord God, amongst the trees of the garden.

HEBREW.

8. And they heard the voice of the Lord God walking in the garden, in the cool of the day; and THE ADAM and his wife hid themselves from the presence of the Lord God, amongst the trees of the garden.

NOTE.—In this verse, the Bible has THE ADAM "ADAM," the Revision has it "the man," while the Hebrew is THE ADAM.

* * * * * *

BIBLE.

9. And the Lord God called unto ADAM, and said unto him, where art thou.

REVISION.

9. And the Lord God called unto the man, and said unto him, where art thou.

HEBREW.

9. And the Lord God called unto THE ADAM, and said unto him, where art thou.

NOTE.—In this verse, the Bible has THE ADAM "ADAM," the Revision "the man," while the Hebrew is THE ADAM.

* * * * * *

BIBLE.

12. And the man said, the woman whom thou gavest to be with me, she gave me of the tree and I did eat.

REVISION.

12. And the man said, the woman whom thou gavest to be with me, she gave me of the tree and I did eat.

HEBREW.

12. And THE ADAM said, the woman whom thou gavest to be with me, she gave me of the tree and I did eat.

NOTE.—In this verse, the Bible has THE ADAM "the man," and the Revision has it "the man," while the Hebrew is THE ADAM.

* * * * * *

BIBLE.

17. And unto ADAM he said, because thou had hearkened unto the voice of thy wife and hast eaten of the tree of which I commanded thee, saying : Thou shalt not eat of it ; cursed is the ground for thy sake. In sorrow shalt thou eat of it all the days of thy life.

REVISION.

17. And unto ADAM he said, because thou hast hearkened unto the voice of thy wife and hast eaten of the tree of which I commanded thee, saying : Thou shall not eat of it ; cursed is the ground for thy sake. In toil shalt thou eat of it all the days of thy life.

HEBREW.

17. And unto ADAM he said, because thou hast hearkened unto the voice of thy wife and hast eaten of the tree of which I commanded thee, saying : Thou shall not eat of it ; cursed is the ground for thy sake. In pain shall thou eat of it all the days of thy life.

NOTE.—In the Bible, in the Revision and in the Hebrew, the same term Adam is used. Why the article "The" is dropped from the Hebrew body-term ADAM cannot be explained; but the identity of THE ADAM, the individual, is so unmistakable, that ADAM in this place is the exact equivalent of THE ADAM. Other instances of this kind will be found as we go on.

* * * * * *

BIBLE.

20. And ADAM called his wife's name Eve, because she was the mother of all living.

REVISION.

20. And the man called his wife's name Eve, because she was the mother of all living.

HEBREW.

20. And THE ADAM called his wife's name Eve, because she was the mother of all living.

NOTE.—In this verse, the Bible has for THE ADAM "ADAM," and the Revision has "the man," while the Hebrew term is THE ADAM.

BIBLE.

21. Unto ADAM also and to his wife, did the Lord God make coats of skins, and clothed them.

REVISION.

21. And the Lord God made for ADAM and for his wife, coats of skins, and clothed them.

HEBREW.

21. Unto ADAM and to his wife, did the Lord God make coats of skins, and clothed them.

NOTE.—In this verse, and also in the Revision, each have ADAM for ADAM in the Hebrew. The individuality of THE ADAM is unmistakable as the husband of Eve.

* * * * * *

BIBLE.

22. And the Lord said, behold the man is become as one of us, to know good and evil. And, now lest he put forth his hand and take also of the tree of life, and eat and live forever.

REVISION.

22. And the Lord God said, behold the man is become as one of us, to know good and evil. And now, lest he put forth his hand and take also of the tree of life, and eat and live forever.

HEBREW.

22. And the Lord God said, behold THE ADAM is become as one of us, to know good and evil. And now, lest he put forth his hand and

take also of the tree of life, and eat and live forever.

NOTE.—In this verse, the Bible has for THE ADAM "the man," and so has the Revision, while the Hebrew is THE ADAM.

* * * * * *

BIBLE.

24. So he drove out the man ; and he placed at the east of the Garden of Eden, cherubims and a flaming sword, which turned every way to keep the way of the tree of life.

REVISION.

24. So he drove out the man ; and he placed at the east of the Garden of Eden, the cherubim and the flame of a sword, which turned every way to keep the way of the tree of life.

HEBREW.

24. And he drove out THE ADAM ; and he placed at the east of the Garden of Eden, the cherubim and the flame of the sword, which turned every way to keep the way of the tree of life.

NOTE.—In this verse, the Bible has for THE ADAM "the man," and the Revision has the same, while the Hebrew is THE ADAM.

* * * * * *

GENESIS, CHAPTER IV.

* * * * * *

BIBLE.

1. And Adam knew Eve his wife ; and she conceived and bare Cain and said, I have gotten a man from the Lord.

REVISION.

1. And the man knew Eve his wife ; and she conceived and bare Cain and said, I have gotten a man with the help of the Lord.

HEBREW.

1. And THE ADAM knew Eve his wife ; and she conceived and bare Cain and said, I have gotten a man with the help of the Lord.

NOTE.—In this verse, the Bible has for THE ADAM "ADAM," the Revision has "the man," while in the Hebrew it is THE ADAM.

* * * * * *

BIBLE.

25. And ADAM knew his wife again, and she bare a son and called his name Seth ; for God, said she, hath appointed me another seed instead of Abel, whom Cain slew.

REVISION.

25. And ADAM knew his wife again, and she bare a son and called his name Seth ; for, said she, God hath appointed me another seed instead of Abel, for Cain slew him.

HEBREW.

25. And ADAM knew his wife again, and she bare a son and called his name Seth; for, said she, God hath appointed me another seed instead of Abel, for Cain slew him.

<small>NOTE.—In this verse, the Bible, the Revision and the Hebrew have "Adam" in the place of THE ADAM, his individuality being unmistakable.</small>

* * * * * *

GENESIS, CHAPTER V.

* * * * * *

BIBLE.

1. This is the Book of the generations of ADAM, in the day that God created man, in the likeness of God made he him.

REVISION.

1. This is the Book of the generations of ADAM, in the day that God created man, in the likeness of God made he him.

HEBREW.

1. This is the Book of the generations of ADAM, in the day that God created ADAM, in the likeness of God made he him.

<small>NOTE.—In this verse, the Bible and the Revision each have ADAM in the first instance and "man" in the second, while the Hebrew is ADAM in the first instance and ADAM in the second instance. There might be some doubt as to what ADAM meant in the Hebrew without the word "him" in the same sentence governing its meaning; but as it reads in that connection, it is a clear identification of THE ADAM.</small>

BIBLE.

2. Male and female created he them, and blessed them, and called their name ADAM in the day when they were created.

REVISION.

2. Male and female created he them, and blessed them, and called their name ADAM in the day when they were created.

HEBREW.

2. Male and female created he them, and blessed them, and called their name ADAM in the day when they were created.

NOTE.—In this verse, in the Bible, in the Revision and in the Hebrew, the Hebrew term ADAM is correctly rendered and stands for "male and female" of the human races, created by fiat.

* * * * * *

BIBLE.

3. And ADAM lived an hundred and thirty years, and begat a son in his own likeness, after his image; and called his name Seth.

REVISION.

3. And ADAM lived an hundred and thirty years, and begat a son in his own likeness, after his image; and called his name Seth.

HEBREW.

3. And ADAM lived an hundred and thirty years, and begat a son in his own likeness, after his image; and called his name Seth.

NOTE.—In this verse, the Bible, the Revision and the Hebrew each contain ADAM properly, in place for THE ADAM, the identification of this individual being unmistakable.

BIBLE.

4. And the days of ADAM after he had begotten Seth, were eight hundred years, and he begat sons and daughters.

REVISION.

4. And the days of Adam after he had begotten Seth, were eight hundred years, and he begat sons and daughters.

HEBREW.

4. And the days of ADAM after he had begotten Seth, were eight hundred years, and he begat sons and daughters.

NOTE.—In this verse, the Bible, the Revision and the Hebrew each contain Adam properly rendered in place for THE ADAM, the identification of this individual being unmistakable.

* * * * * *

BIBLE.

5. And all the days that Adam lived were nine hundred and thirty years, and he died.

REVISION.

5. And all the days that ADAM lived were nine hundred and thirty years, and he died.

HEBREW

5. And all the days that ADAM lived were nine hundred and thirty years, and he died.

NOTE.—In this verse, in the Bible, in the Revision and in the Hebrew, each contain ADAM properly rendered, in place of THE ADAM, the identification of this individual being unmistakable.

* * * * * *

GENESIS, CHAPTER VI.

* * * * * *

BIBLE.

1. And it came to pass, when men began to multiply on the face of the earth, and daughters were born unto them.

REVISION.

1. And it came to pass, when men began to multiply on the face of the ground, and daughters were born unto them.

HEBREW.

1. And it came to pass, when THE ADAM began to multiply upon the face of the earth, and daughters were born unto them.

NOTE.—In this verse, in the Bible and in the Revision, THE ADAM is rendered "men," while in the Hebrew it is THE ADAM.

* * * * * *

BIBLE.

2. That the sons of God saw the daughters of men, that they were fair ; and they took them wives of all which they chose.

REVISION.

2. That the sons of God saw the daughters of men, that they were fair ; and they took them wives of all that they chose.

HEBREW.

2. That the sons of God saw the daughters

of THE ADAM, that they were fair; and they took them wives of all which they chose.

NOTE.—In this verse, in the Bible and in the Revision, THE ADAM in each is rendered "men," while in the Hebrew it is THE ADAM.

* * * * * *

BIBLE.

3. And the Lord said, My spirit shall not always strive with man, for that he also is flesh; yet his days shall be an hundred and twenty years.

REVISION.

3. And the Lord said, My spirit shall not strive with man forever, for that he is also flesh; yet shall his days be an hundred and twenty years.

HEBREW.

3. And the Lord said, My spirit shall not always strive with Adam, for that he is also flesh; yet his days shall be an hundred and twenty years.

NOTE.—In this verse, in the Bible and in the Revision, in each, ADAM is rendered "man," while the Hebrew term ADAM is equivalent to THE ADAM, the individual, governed by "he" in the same sentence.

* * * * * *

BIBLE.

4. There were giants in the earth in those days, and also after that, when the sons of God came in unto the daughters of men, and they bare children to them; the same became mighty men, which were of old, men of renown.

REVISION.

4. The Nephilim were in the earth in these days, and also after that, when the sons of God came in unto the daughters of men, and they bare children to them; the same were the mighty men, which were of old, the men of renown.

HEBREW.

4. There were giants in the earth in those days, and also after that, when the sons of God came in unto the daughters of THE ADAM, and they bare children to them; the same became mighty men, which were of old, men of renown.

NOTE.—In this verse, in the Bible and in the Revision, THE ADAM in each is rendered "men," while in the Hebrew it is THE ADAM.

* * * * * *

BIBLE.

5. And God saw that the wickedness of man was great in the earth, and that every imagination of the thoughts of his heart was only evil continually.

REVISION.

5. And God saw that the wickedness of man was great in the earth, and that every imagination of the thoughts of his heart was only evil continually.

HEBREW.

5. And God saw that the wickedness of THE ADAM was great in the earth, and that every imagination of the thoughts of his heart was only evil continually.

NOTE.—In this verse, in the Bible and in the Revision, THE ADAM in each is rendered "man," while in the Hebrew it is THE ADAM.

BIBLE.

6. And it repented the Lord that he had made man on the earth, and it grieved him at his heart.

REVISION.

6. And it repented the Lord that he had made man on the earth, and it grieved him at his heart.

HEBREW.

6. And it repented the Lord that he had made THE ADAM upon the earth, and it grieved him to his heart.

Note.—In this verse, in the Bible and in the Revision, THE ADAM in each is rendered "man," while in the Hebrew it is THE ADAM.

*   *   *   *   *   *

BIBLE.

7. And the Lord said, I will destroy man, whom I have created, from the face of the earth; both man and beast, and the creeping thing and the fowls of the air; for it repenteth me that I have made them.

REVISION.

7. And the Lord said, I will destroy man, whom I have created, from the face of the ground; both man and beast, and creeping thing and fowl of the air; for it repenteth me that I have made them.

HEBREW.

7. And the Lord said, I will destroy THE ADAM, whom I have created, from the face of

the ground ; from ADAM unto beast, and the creeping thing and the fowl of the air ; for it repenteth me that I have made them.

NOTE.—In this verse, which controls what was to be destroyed by flood, is wonderfully distorted from the Hebrew, both in the Bible and in the Revision.

In the Bible, in the first instance, THE ADAM is rendered "man," and in the second instance is rendered "man ;" also in the Revision the same; while in the Hebrew, the first is THE ADAM and the second ADAM. This is not all. In the Bible and in the Revision is inserted the following: "both man and beast," while in the Hebrew it is " from ADAM unto beast," a very decided difference as to what was to be destroyed. See explanation in Note to Gen. VII., 23.

* * * * * *

GENESIS, CHAPTER VII.

* * * * * *

BIBLE.

21. And all flesh died that moved upon the earth, both of fowl and of cattle, and of beast, and of every creeping thing that creepeth upon the earth, and every man.

REVISION.

21. And all flesh died that moved upon the earth, both fowl and cattle, and beast, and every creeping thing that creepeth upon the earth, and every man.

HEBREW.

21. And all flesh died that moved upon the earth, both of fowl and of cattle, and of beast,

and of every creeping thing that creepeth upon the earth, and every THE ADAM.

NOTE.—In this verse, in the Bible and in the Revision, THE ADAM is rendered "man," while in the Hebrew it is THE ADAM. The reader will notice that every THE ADAM died, not every ADAM.

* * * * * *

BIBLE.

23. And every living substance was destroyed which was upon the face of the ground, both man and cattle, and the creeping things and the fowl of the heaven ; and they were destroyed from the earth ; and Noah only remained alive, and they that were with him in the ark.

REVISION.

23. And every living thing was destroyed which was upon the face of the ground, both man and cattle, and creeping thing and fowl of the heaven ; and they were destroyed from the earth ; and Noah only was left, and they that were with him in the ark.

HEBREW.

23. And every living substance was destroyed which was upon the face of the ground, both ADAM and cattle, and the creeping things and the fowl of the heaven ; and they were destroyed from the earth ; and Noah only was left, and they that were with him in the ark.

NOTE.—This verse, to the exact reader, is the most important one in the Genesis, as determining the extent of the flood, and is the only one casting a shadow upon the otherwise consistent account, by the use of Adam as being the subject destroyed. In the Bible and in the Revision, Adam in the Hebrew is rendered "man." We would accept Adam readily as the proper term, even though it destroyed all of humanity, were it not that the term is so hemmed in, that its true meaning is THE ADAM.

1st, Because the designating article "the," or prefix to Adam, is frequently dropped, as has been seen, when the individuality of The Adam is plain.

2d, God said he would destroy THE ADAM by flood for cause, and we accept his word as truth.

3d, In declaring what he would destroy in Gen. VI., 7, he said: "I will destroy THE ADAM from the face of the ground, *from* Adam *unto* beast. Here Adam is the boundary line on the one side, and beast on the other, and THE ADAM, the subject destroyed, within them. This is equivalent to recording that Adam was not to be destroyed.

4th, All terms used in connection with the flood, such as all flesh died, and others of like import, are not to be taken as human flesh, without the record so defines it.

5th, In Gen. VII., 23, "All flesh died * * * and every THE ADAM. This was the stated result, to which we are not authorized to add anything more of humanity.

6th, The rendering of Adam in this verse, is substantially explained in Gen. VIII., 21, when the Lord said, he would not again destroy THE ADAM.

It would seem clear that the preponderance of evidence is overwhelming, that Adam in this verse is THE ADAM, the subject to be destroyed, and which was destroyed, while there is not a word in the entire record indicating that Adam was to be destroyed, or any reason hinted at that they had committed any offence towards God deserving such punishment.

We therefore conclude, that the record is clear, that only THE ADAM, except Noah and his family, were destroyed by the flood, leaving on earth what remained of Adam unharmed.

* * * * * *

GENESIS, CHAPTER VIII.

* * * * * *

BIBLE.

21. And the Lord smelled a sweet saviour; and the Lord said in his heart, I will not again curse the ground any more for man's sake, for the imagination of man's heart is evil from his

youth; neither will I again smite any more every thing living, as I have done.

REVISION.

21. And the Lord smelled a sweet saviour; and the Lord said in his heart, I will not again curse the ground any more for man's sake, for that the imagination of man's heart is evil from his youth; neither will 1 again smite any more every thing living, as I have done.

HEBREW.

21. And the Lord smelled a sweet saviour; and the Lord said in his heart, I will not again curse the ground any more for THE ADAM'S sake; for the imagination of THE ADAM'S heart is evil from his youth; neither will I again smite any more every thing living, as I have done.

NOTE.—In this verse, in the Bible and in the Revision, for THE ADAM, in the two places in each, is rendered "man's," while in each of the two places in the Hebrew it is THE ADAM.

* * * * *

GENESIS, CHAPTER IX.

* * * * * *

BIBLE.

5. And surely your blood of your lives will I require; at the hand of every beast will I require it, and at the hand of man; at the hand of every man's brother, will I require the life of man.

REVISION.

5. And surely your blood, the blood of your lives, will I require ; at the hand of every beast will I require it ; and at the hand of man, even at the hand of every man's brother, will I require the life of man.

HEBREW.

5. And surely your blood, the blood of your lives, at the hand of every beast will I require it ; and at the hand of THE ADAM ; even at the hand of every man's brother, will I require the life of THE ADAM.

NOTE.—In this verse, in the Bible and in the Revision, in two places in each, THE ADAM is rendered "man," while in the Hebrew in each it is THE ADAM.

* * * * * *

BIBLE.

6. Whoso sheddeth man's blood, by man shall his blood be shed ; for in the image of God, made he man.

REVISION.

6. Whoso sheddeth man's blood, by man shall his blood be shed ; for in the image of God, made he man.

HEBREW.

6. Whoso sheddeth THE ADAM'S blood, by Adam shall his blood be shed ; for in the image of God made he THE ADAM.

NOTE.—In this verse, in the Bible and in the Revision, THE ADAM in the Hebrew is rendered "man's." In the second, Adam in the Hebrew is rendered in each "man." In the third, THE ADAM in the Hebrew is rendered in each "man."

GENESIS, CHAPTER XI.

* * * * * *

BIBLE.

5. And the Lord came down to see the city and the tower, which the children of men builded.

REVISION.

5. And the Lord came down to see the city and the tower, which the children of men builded.

HEBREW.

5. And the Lord came down to see the city and the tower, which the children of THE ADAM's builded.

Note.—In this verse, in the Bible and in the Revision, THE ADAM is rendered in each "men," while in the Hebrew it is THE ADAM.

* * * * * *

The reader has now seen for himself the account of the creation of THE ADAM, and male and female, in Gen. I., 27; the experience of THE ADAM in the Garden of Eden, and the commission of his only recorded sin, that of eating the forbidden fruit, and his consequent expulsion from the Garden.

The crowning sin which brought on the flood, and destroyed every THE ADAM except Noah and his family, was committed solely by the daughters of THE ADAM. That account reads: "And after that, when the sons of God came in unto the daughters of THE ADAM and they bare children to them, the same became mighty men, which were of old, men of renown." Gen. VI., 4.

Such a severe and terrible punishment would indicate the violation of some highly important command. The simple fact of the daughters of THE ADAM marrying and having children, could not possibly be the cause of such severity, since God's command was in Gen. I., 28: "Be fruitful, and multiply and fill the earth."

These acts of the daughters of THE ADAM have been regarded as an unexplained portion of Scripture, and we believe it is due, as in numerous other cases, to the fact, that God's laws of reproduction in the human family have been grievously neglected. But give force and vitality to these laws, and a key is furnished that will unlock many obscure passages. Turn to your first chapter of Genesis, and you will find these laws repeated again and again; and if the reader will pause for one moment and reflect, he will see the necessity for them.

Without these laws, reproduction would be a chaos; woman might bring forth cattle and cattle bring forth men; the white woman a black child, an ape, a baboon or a snake; the acorn an elephant, a horse or an apple tree.

When we plant, sow and reproduce in the vegetable or the animal kingdom for food, we see how uniform is the result, and that like always reproduces like; can we deny that it is the result of Divine Law? No man can point to a case of one type of the human family producing another, while we know that these types will assimilate and make hybrids; but hybrids reproducing hybrids will run out in three or four generations, while the pure types will survive, for it is a Divine law.

Bearing in mind these principles, let us return to the acts of the daughters of THE ADAM. Is there any possible reason to be assigned, within the ingenuity of man to conceive, for

God's anger, other than their violation of the Divine law of reproduction in bearing children that were hybrid Hebrews and hybrid Gentiles? The proposition would seem to prove itself in all directions, if God had cause for his anger. If the proposition be admitted, it shows in what high veneration God holds his laws of reproduction.

The lineage of THE ADAM, through Noah to Jesus Christ, is plainly and distinctly laid down in Scripture. But for the Laws of reproduction, the line could have been broken at any point, and other peoples or something worse have been substituted instead. By sound analogical reasoning, do not these laws equally apply to other races of mankind? Whatever status we find to-day in these persistent reproductions, by following back these lines, we will land in the creative account in ADAM.

Therefore, Jesus Christ, having been a Hebrew and a Jew, Noah was a Hebrew and a Jew, and THE ADAM was a Hebrew and a Jew. So with the Caucasian, Mongolian, Malay, Indian and Negro races, all to-day reproduced in pure type before our eyes ; and taking the lineage of THE ADAM as Scriptural proof and applying the same law to them, we are constrained to say that they, too, run back in continuous lines to Adam, "male and female," which name stands with THE ADAM in the day of creation, for the heads of all created humanity.

As has been seen, we have the account of the creation of one male, being apparently selected from among the "male" created, and particularly identified as THE ADAM. Is there nothing in this fact that should arrest the attention of the reader? The Creator, having made ADAM and brought into existence all of humanity necessary to carry forward all of his works, there was still with him the knowledge that something more was required. Whatever God has done, he designed to do, and hence he designed to give Christ to the world as the Saviour of mankind. Is it not reasonable to infer, that he would create a distinctive individual to go through the desired test of obedience to his laws, and to be the father of the line of humanity that should be his chosen people on the earth, and evolve his only Son, the Redeemer of mankind? This would seem to be the top round of the ladder of sound reasoning and judgment.

We then regard the creation of THE ADAM as a special providence of God, having in view the grand ultimatum of Christianity. Instead then of dropping, eliminating or giving substitutions or equivalents for THE ADAM in our Bibles, the name should be printed in letters of gold, from the creation, to the Cross of Jesus Christ.

As the Jews killed Christ by reason of the truths he was disseminating, so THE ADAM has been unwittingly killed by translators.

The Jews, as a race, have been jeered at and almost despised by other races of men, on account of some of Christ's immediate kindred having crucified him. This we think to be unchristian, and a great injustice to those Jews who had no hand in the matter. All Jews are relatives of Jesus Christ, and Christians should not despise them or be ashamed of them on that account.

The reader's mind will naturally revert to the reason why THE ADAM has never appeared in our Bibles. He has seen that the translation from the Hebrew was made in the year 1611, and the Great Bible, which is generally followed, was translated in 1539-1541. If the inspiration of the translators had equalled the inspiration of the Hebrew writers, there would have been no corrections to be made thereafter, nor would there have been any omissions. But this is not supposable, and being human, they were not perfect in knowledge ; neither were the astronomers, philosophers or chemists of that time perfect in like manner. Great discoveries have been made since ; the world has become more enlightened, and many controlling laws of God have been discovered in the material world. In the universe of inspiration, revolving and shining in the inspired writings, think you that no discoveries are alike possible in them? Could humanity grasp the whole subject in every detail in the year 1539-1541 ? We think not, and we are just as likely to make discoveries in recorded inspiration, as the astronomer of to-day is liable to discover an asteroid or a distant star.

Much more could be said on every branch of this subject, but the limits of this little work are reached. The reader has to adopt one general principle, in order to carry researches and draw correct conclusions from premises on this subject. Give full weight and force to every law of God, whether it be a natural law or a law for spiritual guidance, and you will make no mistakes in translations, in science, or in theology. As true as the needle to the pole, you will not only be enabled to point through them to God, but enable others to do the same.

The conclusion arrived at in this matter is, that if the postulates herein laid down will stand the test of the criticisms of Scholars and Scientists, and are in harmony with existing laws of God, they are a constellation of the brightest stars that have ever arisen over the horizon of the Christian faith. It will open the Genesis to a plain and consistent reading, with no confusion of terms in English and Hebrew dotted into the account. It will strengthen belief in the whole Scripture, where belief is now wanted, for the reason alone that the Genesis cannot be understood. It will also enable each enquirer to solve the all-absorbing question propounded: "AM I JEW OR GENTILE?" For, by inspection, each one can determine to which type of the human races they belong, and can run back by the Divine Law of reproduction to their origin in the creation, either in ADAM or THE ADAM.

ADDENDA.
February, 1891.

GENESIS NOT UNDERSTOOD.

A Bishop of the Episcopal Church in high standing, in a conversation about the Genesis quite lately said: "As to the Genesis, we take it as a whole and do not go into particulars." This was a timely and true observation, from which may be deduced the well-known fact that the English Genesis has not been and is not understood, and the Bishop's remark is a call upon all for information on that subject, and from any one who can throw light upon this abstruse portion of Scripture. He could have added one more sentence to his remark, that the English Versions in the absence of Adam and The Adam from their proper places in the account, *can never be understood*. No Hebrew scholar or Divine will deny that these names appear in the original, as we have stated in the forepart of this Book.

The pertinent question then would seem to be, why were they left out of the English Versions, as they are the pure words of God, and the English terms substituted for them are not?

There are three conditions of knowledge; ignorance, belief, and actual knowledge. Ignorance is the absence of belief and of actual knowledge. Exact knowledge is derived from our senses of mind or body, or from those of others applied to the developed immutable laws of God in Nature, and is the only exact knowledge man can possess. Belief is founded on information or conclusions not drawn from the operation of those laws of Nature, and while on many subjects may have the same effect, is not exact knowledge.

When the translation of the Bible was made in about the year 1540, there was but little actual knowledge on the subjects here treated of, and the people were enveloped in a haze of traditions and superstitions. Among these were, that the earth was flat and rested on a turtle's back, while the sun revolved around the earth. Coincident with these was the prevalent tradition that all of humanity sprang from one pair. Time and the development of exact knowledge have wiped out many of the then existing traditions, while that of the unity of the race, based upon the same violations of God's Natural Laws, still remains in our English Versions; but true science has long since consigned it to the same fate as the others.

The following out of this tradition of the unity of the races of mankind, however honestly intended to make the Genesis what it should be, according to the convictions of the translators, not what it was, involves the following principles and conditions. The English reader is misled from the true meaning of Gen. 26, 27, in the Hebrew, by the use of the same term "Man" in both Verses, for Adam and The Adam. See pages 14 and 15:

That Adam and not The Adam was the Husband of Eve. See page 18, Gen. II., 7, and page 22, Gen. II., 22.

That the object of God, in making The Adam and Eve, was to propagate from them a race of people. See Gen. I., 28.

That Adam being the *name* of a number or class of male and female created, could not propagate from Eve—see page 21, Gen. V., 2—it being a universally known fact that reproduction in the human family, can only take place by the mysterious operation of the Natural Law of God between a male and female, and the issue in type is the same as the parents, sometimes a hybrid, and sometimes a pure type, and sometimes a monstrosity in type, but never another and distinct type.

That the declaration of the unity in origin of the races of mankind is in direct conflict with the law of reproduction established in Gen. I., 28, and the indicated diversity in Gen. I., 26, 27, 29, and the teachings in Leviticus.

That there is no correct genealogy of Jesus Christ in the English Versions, because there is no reproductive head named in the creative account. For no reader could tell from the English Genesis that Adam had any connection with that account, and he would be justified in assuming that the name was an interpolation, as it does not appear in the King James Bible till we reach Gen. II., 19, nor in the Oxford Revision, till we reach Gen. III., 17. See page 20, Gen. II., 19, and page 26, Gen. III., 17.

That the unity of the races is fixed in the English Versions in Noah by the translators doing violence to the Hebrew by eliminating words and substituting others not found in the original, thereby making the flood universal in the human family, except Noah and those who entered the Ark with him, while in the Hebrew only The Adam's descendants were destroyed except Noah and his family. See page 36, Gen. VI., 7, and the remainder of that account.

The omission of Adam and The Adam from their places in the King James Bible and the error of translation respecting the flood, led the early Churches and Divines to accept the tradition that Adam and Eve, not The Adam and Eve, were the created heads of the races of mankind. This education continued for a long period without any opposition. Those ignorant of the Laws of Nature, and especially the Laws of reproduction accepted, and still accept, blindly these teachings, believing in the analogy that the sun still revolves around the earth.

As knowledge spread wider and wider, and as God's Natural Laws became better and better known, the conflict between these Laws and the English Genesis became more bitter. The concrete of exact knowledge, which is the developed action of these laws, gradually extended throughout civilization. Among those who were instrumental in this work were the scientists, who acknowledged and obeyed these laws. For this reason they have been denounced by the teachers of the unity of the races as unbelievers and opponents of the Bible, till the matter has assumed the startling proportions of a conflict between religion and science.

The Scientist disputes the universality of the flood claimed in the Genesis.

The Ethnologist smiles when the unity of the race is proclaimed from the pulpit.

The Philosopher sees all reproduced forms in nature following implicitly the Laws of reproduction, and properly asks why the races of mankind are excepted from these Laws.

The Geologist attacks the foundation and superstructure of the Genesis fiat creation in six days for similar reasons, and makes evolution the main prop of his theories.

The Agnostic wants more proof than the English Versions give him.

The Infidel sneeringly asks, " Did Cain marry his sister ?"

All these are more or less pounding away at the Genesis, and some of them scoff at the Christian religion because of these errors of translation. But restore Adam and The Adam in the English Versions and correct the translation in regard to the flood, and this vast multitude will flock to the support of the Genesis, and believe in it as the Foundation Stone of the Christian Religion and incidentally to a belief in the whole Bible. We will now proceed to show the reasons for these conclusions.

GENEALOGY OF JESUS CHRIST, PROVING HIS DIVINITY.

It would be truly gratifying to the Christian to be able to read in his Bible the correct genealogy of the Saviour. We now have his genealogy in Luke III., running from Joseph to Adam. This we claim is incorrect, as it should be The Adam, the created head of the Jewish line, which evolved Christ. To understand this fully, the reader should not be satisfied with the simple reading of Gen. I., 26, 27, where he is informed in the Hebrew that Adam defined in Gen. V., 2, as the *name* of a class of male and female, the number not being limited or indicated, and has no individuality connected with the name. The Gen. I., 27, records in the Hebrew the creation of The Adam the husband of Eve as subsequently shown, and also a like class as above of male and female. In these two Verses we claim were two separate and distinct classes of human beings created.

The question arises, who were the human beings thus created, and were they created in single pairs of each class, or in numbers over the face of the whole earth, or was the entire Creations in the two Verses confined as claimed by the advocates of the unity of the races to a single pair?

In discussing these questions we rely upon no speculations or theories, but entirely upon biblical proofs. The first class under the name Adam were to have dominion over the Fish of the Sea, and over the Fowl of the Air, and over the Cattle, and over all the Earth, and over every creeping thing that creepeth upon the Earth. Gen. I., 26. This is clear and definite, and about which there can be no controversy.

The second class created under The Adam, and male and female, had no such power conferred upon them. Gen. I., 27. This is also clear and definite, and about which there can be no controversy. History confirms this position of Holy Writ. By the Laws of reproduction we find upon the earth six distinct types of the human family, namely : the Caucasian, Mongolian, Malay, Indian, Negro and the Hebrew, all persistently reproduced in type. All except the Hebrews have held the dominion referred to through all history, and now hold that dominion, while the Hebrews have twice attempted to make themselves a Nation for dominion and failed, and are now a scattered race throughout the world. This would seem to show us clearly who were created under the name of the class Adam, and who were created under the class The Adam, and male and female.

About this there should be no controversy it seems to us.

As to numbers created we must look to Gen. I., 29, which is fully discussed in the next article, "Biblical and Scientific Proof of the Genesis Creation, as from the Hebrew," but will remark in passing, that food was provided for animals and created beings "over all the earth." God said to those created beings, "Behold," (which means to see,) "I have given you every herb yielding seed which is upon the face of *all the earth*, and every tree in which is the fruit of a tree yielding seed, to you it shall be for food." We assume that God did not create things in vain, and when He called upon his created beings to see the food provided for them over all the earth, the conclusion must be that those beings were co-existent with the food "over all the earth." This would seem to dispose of any assumption of a single pair of each type or of a single pair created.

The correct Genealogy of Jesus Christ would seem to follow as a matter of course. He having been a Hebrew and a Jew, his blood line to the Creation, by the Law of reproduction, was both Hebrew and Jew.

The name of Jew is particularly applied to His genealogy, and is a specific line of Hebrews within the Hebrew race. Under the class male and female created in Gen. I., 27, the Hebrews proper were made in numbers, so that Cain had no difficulty in finding a Hebrew wife in the land of Nod.

The Genealogy of Christ starts in the Creation of The Adam and Eve, runs through Noah and his descendants to Joseph. Luke III.

The inevitable conclusion from all this is, that it is our duty as being far safer for us to rely upon God's translation of His word through His immutable Laws of reproduction, than accept that of men ignorant of those Laws, and acting under traditions and superstitions.

In what way is the English reader who may be ignorant of the Hebrew and the Laws of reproduction to derive any true benefit from the reading of this portion of Scriptures? If the Bishops of the Church, who are educated men in Hebrew, are compelled to skip this portion of God's word as not understandable, what can be expected from the uneducated who desire to read their Bible, and find out all about their Saviour, especially his genealogy?

At present we know of no way except to follow the same course that we pursued over thirty years ago, being then unacquainted with the Hebrew, but had a full knowledge and understanding of the Laws of reproduction in the various races of mankind. Such was our confidence in the inspiration of the Genesis that we were satisfied there was something wrong in the English translation.

We procured a Hebrew Student's Manual, which contained the word for word translation by the best Hebrew Scholars. We found that Adam and Ha-Adam, or The Adam, were persistently used in the Hebrew, as we have given in the forepart of this work.

We then took all of our family Bibles and erased the translations, and restored Adam and The Adam wherever they occurred in the Hebrew, and of necessity corrected the translation of the flood.

Light then beamed over the whole subject, and with a knowledge of the Natural Laws of God and their application to the Genesis account of Creation, there was no difficulty of understanding it, which in this development is clear and lucid.

The reader, by making these restorations, while he may not understand the Creation account, which depends upon a knowledge of the Laws of Nature, will clearly see the creative origin of The Adam, the husband of Eve, and that they were the created heads of the line of humanity that evolved Jesus Christ.

As we understand it, these errors of translation are not in conflict with any article of the Christian faith, but are obstacles to its ready reception by a very large class of intelligent people. From our experience, we fear that these corrections will be very slow in accomplishment, as the present clergy have all been educated otherwise, and they have little time to investigate anything new, and the orthodox press will not go athwart the teachings of the churches. It is to be hoped that the effort to this end may be made by those having special charge of this matter, but if not, the only hope the reader has to get what he is entitled to, is from the secular press, which, when it has investigated this matter fully, and finds that the positions taken are correct (for they are matters of plain common sense and history), they will turn in and help the Bible as contained in the Hebrew.

The main point in the whole matter is, that the Christian should be enabled to read in his Bible the correct genealogy of the Saviour, in order that he may judge of his Divinity. The pulpits of the land ring with able and apparently conclusive arguments to prove this position. But at best, all such proofs are inferential. What will the reader find on the return of Adam and The Adam to their places as in the Hebrew?

He will find in Gen. I., 26, 27, the Creation of two distinct classes of people.

He will find in Gen. I., 27, the Creation of The Adam, and male and female, which is the Creation of the Hebrew race, and that The Adam was the husband of Eve, and tracing their descendants through (after making the correction in the translation of the flood) he will find a distinct line of people called Jews, that evolved the Saviour of mankind.

He will find too, other Hebrews reproduced persistently and parallel with the Jewish line, and that they have been a distinct and separate people throughout all history.

The Adam, the male head of the Jewish line, was selected by God to undergo the test of obedience to His Laws, and the Hebrews as a race to make, publish and ventilate those Laws by writing in the Hebrew the Books of the Old Testament, and in the Greek those of the New Testament, and finally making Jesus Christ crucified the index of those Laws · That race has been the chosen people of God for those purposes.

All the design, plan and forethought of this Creation had its origin with the Great Creator for an end, and human thought must centre upon something as the object to be attained.

Is there any human being, even in the plenitude of his ingenuity, who can assign a reason for the Creation of anything, as being simply a Creation?

The reasoning mind must rest right here in oblivion, if it cannot reach forth and find some ground adequate for the great conception.

The scheme of salvation, it seems to us, is the only one which satisfies the equation of design. The Creation of The Adam and Eve to evolve in due time Jesus Christ, His crucifixion, His rising from the dead, His ascension back to Heaven, the preeminent success of His teachings and doctrines, are things in harmony with the plan. No other event or train of events, can be found in all history which compare in importance with these. In fact, there is nothing in the whole Creation that the mind can fasten upon that shows design, execution and fulfillment that can be compared in importance with them.

We, therefore, say that the Divinity of Christ is beyond all cavil, and that His genealogy from The Adam and Eve to Joseph is correct.

BIBLICAL AND SCIENTIFIC PROOF OF THE GENESIS CREATION, AS FROM THE HEBREW.

There have been so many attempted explanations of the Genesis Creation, and so many attempts to reconcile the English Versions of it with nature and with theories, that the reading world is tired out with their considerations. Theories innumerable have been advanced, based partly within and partly without the account in the English Versions, but never one as we have had the good fortune to see, based solely upon the Hebrew, and written entirely within the account.

It is our purpose to do this, to keep strictly within the Hebrew record, to advance no theories or explanations not found therein or deducible therefrom, and conclude and prove it by the record, what will undoubtedly be considered a bold assertion, that the Universe was created by fiat in six days substantially as it now exists. That this planet earth was finished on the sixth day replete with the vegetable and animal kingdoms, substantially as they now are all over the earth in quantities, and that the various races of men now persistently reproduced in type, were created in numbers of each race in the various portions of the earth where they now exist. In other words, that this planet in all its parts, and all things upon it which are continued by reproduction, were created in quantities within the six days.

This proposition is so inconsistent with generally received opinions, that the reader may be inclined to stop just here, and pronounce it a vision. But have a little patience with us, and read this article to the end, if not for edification, to satisfy your curiosity, you may come to a different conclusion.

Having written previous articles, containing many points cited here, we shall be compelled to repeat many things said therein. We only excuse that necessity by saying that truth cannot be too often repeated.

There are several causes which have conspired to make the reading of the Genesis Creation difficult, if not almost impossible of understanding. The mind of the reader, if intelligent, is crammed full of theories and theologies on the whole or parts of the account. He cannot, and does not, read the account as it was written to be read, and hence he slides from point to point till he arrives at the end with scarce a period or a comma, and then declares that it is a jargon of terms which are not understandable. This is all natural, and as a rule is believed to be true. There is but one such account, and one such production in the known world, and there is but one way of reading it to understand it.

The reader must, if possible, strip his mind of every theory and every theology, of every tradition and of all knowledge intervening, except what he reads about. He should read no faster than the account is given, and no faster than he can understand, for if he does not understand one part he will fail to understand the remainder, as every subsequent part is dependent upon the preceding part. When he has read the first day's work, he should stop, as the account stops, over night, and consider just what has been done and no more. He must then look into the terms used, determine their meaning and import, and he will then see how far the Creation has progressed and know the condition of things then, and no more.

There are certain general principles, however, which the reader must have the education and mental ability to grasp and comprehend, before he will be prepared to read the Genesis Creation with benefit. He must know the difference between creating and making. Creating is bringing into existence a new element by fiat, while making is the combination of these elements into new forms.

Gen. II., 1. And the heaven (not heavens) were finished and all the host of them.

Gen. II., 2. And on the seventh day God ended His work that He had made; and He rested on the seventh day from all His work which He had made.

Gen. II., 3. And God blessed the seventh day and sanctified it, because that in it He had rested from all His work which God *created to make*. (Hebrew.)

From this last clause we learn that God created certain things out of which He was to make *all His works*. We must then look into the account to find the created elements, and then look for those things made or combined from them. This calls for a high education, called in these days, Science or the tracing of God's unwritten Laws in Nature.

That no one may be misled by the term science, we say that there are true sciences, and many so-called sciences that are false, as there are true religions and false religions. True science is the developing and tracing in action God's Natural Laws ; true religion is based on God's revealed word.

So that true science is the handmaid of true religion, the one dealing with the unwritten Natural Laws of God, making our existences on earth possible, while the other deals in written Spiritual Laws, and hence easier of comprehension by all.

The account of the Genesis Creation is a concatenation of Natural Laws of the most intricate and abstruse nature, requiring all the elements of the highest order of intellect and education to do ample justice to the great subject. We have spent many years of devoted study and writing upon it, going little beyond, and still feel that we have not reached its boundaries. While we may be able to explain the leading features of created elements and their combinations to make existing forms, and repeat the discoveries of the laws of gravity, attraction of cohesion, law of reproduction, evaporation of water, of electricity, magnetism and the like, we can go no further than point out their effects.

The controlling law which governs the Universe of the heavenly bodies is the attraction of gravity, while the controlling law that governs all reproduced forms on this earth, is the law of continuance, commonly called the Law of reproduction "after its kind." There are innumerable other subsidiary laws, while not so controlling, are equally important in the grand chain.

By giving these two controlling laws and their dependencies full force and vitality, for the one is just as binding upon us as the other, or any other law of God, the creative account can then be understood by the ordinary reader for all practical purposes.

The Law of gravity is now well known to be the curb which holds the Heavenly bodies to their duties, gives us day and night and seasons, brings us rain, holds the seas to their bounds and all things upon earth to their places. We know of no Natural Law so universal in its action and so useful in its effects. So far as this earth is concerned, the Law of reproduction and the Law of evaporation of water are of the next importance, but would be useless and inoperative without the Law of gravity. Of what practical use would the Creation of perishable forms on this planet be, without some provision for their continuance. That provision has been made and the Law of reproduction established, and each and all of us owe our existence to it. That debt some have paid by utter neglect, others by positive denial of its provisions. This Natural Law is as binding upon us for acknowledgment as any one of the Ten Commandments, or any other Divine Law, and still it is denied or ignored in some theologies and so-called scientific theories.

The law in its operation can be compared to the tracks of an animal upon the snow, where each track represents a new reproduction. You trace the tracks back and you find the beginning or creation, and forward and you find the living thing—the tracks are all alike. All history and our own experience show the persistency of these reproductions in type—no type has ever been known to reproduce another type—so that existing types give us the means of tracing back all lines of existences to the beginning or into the creative account, thereby proving what was created or made.

We then have the right to demand of the Genesis account that the six races of humanity persistently reproduced in type should be provided a place in that account, with some indication of their status on earth. Gen. I., 26, provides for five of these races under the name Adam.

The other race, the Hebrews, are a persistently reproduced people over all the earth. This gives them place in Gen. I., 27, as well as their subsequent genealogy.

In ordinary Holy Writ the rules of grammar made by experts on language should be invoked where God's Natural Laws are not involved; but when they are, it is safer to let those laws define such portions, rather than trust to rules of grammar, translations or constructions made by men.

The Law of evaporation of water is the handmaid of the Law of reproduction, and makes the successful operation of that law possible. The feeding processes of the earth are accomplished by these evaporated waters. They rise in the atmosphere, and when they become too heavy by collective affinities, fall in rain upon the mountains, hills, valleys and plains of the earth. But pure rain water alone will not supply the vast quantities of carbonate of lime, and other things required for the bones of animals and man, and for the scales and bones of fishes, and the shells of the large class of crustacea. The amount is enormous, but the provision in nature is made equal to the demand. The mountains and upper levels of the earth contain vast supplies of lime stone, and the rains descending upon them percolate their fissures, and each particle of water bears its tiny load to the waiting plants, animals, and man on the lower levels. When these store-houses become exhausted by attrition, provision is made for new upheavals to expose to the rains new store-houses. Hence the earth was made with mountains and hills, that the feeding process should be from the beginning continuous.

The same Law of reproduction extends to every reproduced crystaline form, to reforming rocks with all their elements, the same as in the vegetable or animal kingdom and in man, with all their elements.

Another important point to aid in the reading of the Genesis account is to determine the distribution of created things upon the earth. No theories, however plausible, can determine this question; it must be arrived at solely from the record in the account itself. To this end we quote from Gen. I., 26, to Gen. I., 30, inclusive:

Gen., 26. And God said, let us make Adam in our image after our likeness, and let them have *dominion* over the fish of the sea, and over the fowl of the air, and over the earth, and over every creeping thing that creepeth upon the earth.

Gen., 27. And God created The Adam in His own image; in the image of God created He him; male and female created He them.

Gen., 28. And God blessed them ; and God said unto them be fruitful and multiply and replenish the earth, and subdue it, and have *dominion* over the fish of the sea, and over the fowl of the air, and over every living thing that creepeth upon the earth.

Gen., 29. And God said, behold, I have given you every herb bearing seed which is upon the face of all the earth, and every tree in which is the fruit of a tree yielding seed, to you it shall be for food.

Gen., 30. And to every beast of the earth, and to every fowl of the air, and to everything that creepeth upon the earth wherein there is life, I have given every green herb for food, *and it was so.*

This quotation should be read by the intelligent reader as though he had never heard of the Bible, except what he has read of the account, or of any theories, theologies or traditions on the subject, for if the account be a true one, which we claim it is, it should stand upon its own foundation without any extraneous support.

Gen. I., 26, 27, have been fully considered in a previous article, except as to numbers created or made. Gen. I., 28, is the establishment of the Law of reproduction in the human family, and also the extent of the dominion which Adam (male and female), were empowered to have over the fish of the sea, and over the fowl of the air, and over every living thing that creepeth upon the earth. This power of dominion is broader and more extensive in Gen. I., 26, than it is in Gen. I., 28. The two Verses together make the dominion over all the earth.

As God has never revoked a Natural Law or changed one, the same law which He established then exists now upon the earth, and we know what types of the human family are now persistently reproduced. Not only does this Law of reproduction bear upon numbers created, but the food question in Gen. I., 29, would seem to conclusively settle it: "And behold, I have given you every herb bearing seed which is *upon the face of all the earth*, and every tree in which is the fruit of a tree yielding seed, to you it shall be for food."

This is converse held directly between God and His created people. "Behold, I have given you this food, which is upon the face of all the earth." God says, behold! that is, see the food

I have given you "upon the face of all the earth." To see a thing is to have it within the range of vision, so that the created humanity addressed must have been in the immediate vicinity of the food given them.

It is a well known fact that the same kind of food does not grow "upon the face of all the earth," and that every section of the earth has food peculiar to itself. Most of the leading articles of food used on this Continent have been brought from foreign countries, while the native Indians and the Negroes of Africa subsisted well on the created foods of these lands, and have done so to the present day.

The same argument applies to the food given to the animals in Gen. I., 30. It may be said that this whole subject of food was intended to apply to the future of mankind, and not particularly to those created. This is met by the last four words of Gen. I., 30. It was not only a future, but a present gift then and there, for the closing words of this subject are, "and it was so," clenching the gift to the then present time, as well as to the future. The intelligent reader of this food gift, if his mind was free from bias, could come to no other conclusion than this. That an all wise Creator would not have created animals and food for them, and for created beings "upon the face of all the earth," and then call upon those created beings "in all the earth" to see the food and enjoy the blessing, when there were no created beings there.

From these considerations and others which will be noted hereafter, we deduce that the Universe was created and made by combination of elements, and finished by fiat of God in six days in true equilibrium, and that that equilibrium has continued to the present time and now exists. That this equilibrium extended not only to the Universe, but to each and every portion of it, and to this earth and all its parts.

Considering then this equilibrium, the Law of reproduction in the mineral, vegetable and animal kingdoms and in mankind, the food question, and Gen. I., 26, 27, in the Hebrew, we are constrained to the following conclusions: That the surface of this earth, and all upon it, was created and made substantially as it now exists. That the vegetable kingdom covered the whole earth, and was made to feed the animal kingdom and mankind alike covering the whole earth. As we have said before, we reason that the Caucasian race was created on the Continent of Europe, the Mongolian and Malay in Asia, the Indian in America, the Negro in Africa, and the Hebrew in the Holy Land. We find nothing in the inspired Hebrew writings inconsistent with these conclusions, but there are constructions in various forms not found in the Hebrew, that are inconsistent with them. These conclusions satisfy every equation in nature, and every equation of existence named and not named in the Hebrew account of the Creation.

We will now point out definitions given by the Hebrew writer of the creative account, of a few terms used therein, which make the account somewhat confused if the reader overlooks them, or does not comprehend their meanings in place.

These terms are "heaven," "earth," "day," "Adam" and "The Adam." "Heaven" is defined in Gen. I., 8, as expanse, which means in this connection space or vacuum.

"Earth" has three meanings in the account, each dependent upon its use in place and definition for the place. In Gen. I., 1, earth is declared as being without form and voidness. This definition would not aid the reader if there was not a second definition of it in Gen. I., 10, "and God called the *dry land* earth." The first was earth without form, and the second, earth with form or "dry land." True science comes in here to explain these definitions. The first earth was created elements, the second earth, these in combination in solid tangible forms, science having established the fact that "dry land" contains every primordial element in combination.

It will be seen that dry land is not the ponderable mass of this planet, and hence not the third definition of earth. That mass is composed of dry land, seas, rivers, lakes, and other waters and the atmosphere, and is the combined mass of this planet complete revolving around the sun.

The Scriptural "day" is defined in Gen. I., 5, as the light portion of what we call day, which includes the four divisions of light, evening, night and morning. This day is of different lengths in different planetary bodies. In those revolving quicker on their axis than the earth, the day or light is shorter, while on those revolving slower, the day or light is longer.

Adam of Gen. I., 26, is a group of human beings made of the dust of the earth, or dry land, or in other words, of elements of created matter, and is defined in Gen. V., 2.

> "Male and female created He them and blessed them, and called their name Adam in the day when they were created."

It will be noticed that there is no limit fixed to the numbers thus created. In order that the language should conform to the ordinary construction, that one male and one female were created under the name Adam, the definition should read, "a male and a female" created He them, etc. The language is broad and capacious, indicating numbers created.

The Adam of Gen. I., 27, is an individual male created, and the material from which he was made was also the dust of the earth. Gen. II., 7.

With these principles, explanations, and definition of terms, which are in exact accordance with the Hebrew, the general reader can readily understand the creative account of the Universe and of this earth, whether that account be read in the Hebrew, in the English Versions, or any other language. We will now proceed to give the account accordingly.

In beginning, or commencing, God created the heaven (space or vacuum) and the earth (primordial elements in the places of the Universe where required, for combinations) and these elements were without form. And God created light and established the four divisions of our day, namely: morning, light, evening and night, and gave the Scriptural name of day as the light. And there was evening, and there was morning, the day one.

The question has been asked, why if God had the power to make the Universe in six days, why did He not make it in one day or less? The answer is, that He could not do so without violating His own laws, and using unperfected materials to accomplish His work. Very many things in nature, and we do not know but it applies to all things, have different qualities in the four divisions of our day, and hence every creation and combination required to go through these cycles to become perfected creations or combinations. This law is not violated in any instance in the account.

The work of the second day was the combination of the perfected elements of hydrogen and oxygen, and completing the waters of the Universe wherever required, both fresh and salt, prepared for use with all that we call impurities, but are really essentials, and giving the definition of "heaven." And there was evening, and there was morning, day the second.

As there has been no gravity or motion established yet, these waters remained quiescent in the places where they were combined, until they were required for use on the next day in the crystaline and vegetable kingdoms, and to make seas, lakes, rivers and the like.

The work of the third day was the combining of elements of matter to make the "dry land" called earth, throughout the Universe, and complete the surface of our earth in all its parts of rocks, earth, and soils, and prepare it to receive the vegetable kingdom. To gather together and wrap the earth with seas, and dot it with lakes, and thread it with rivers—then to plant "over all the earth" the vegetable kingdom with its fruits and seeds for food for the animals and created human beings to be made thereafter. And there was evening, and there was morning, day the third.

It is difficult for our minds to step back to this point of the Creation, isolate them from all education and worldly surroundings and contemplate the state of things at that moment. Such we must do if we wish to get a clear conception of the situation. The heavenly bodies were all completed in space and in place. Not a leaf had stirred, nor a planet rolled on its axis or swung in its orbit. The silence of God and the Universe were the ruling elements of the hour. Every thing was now in readiness for the grand start of the heavenly bodies through space on the coming day.

The work of the fourth day was the grand climax of the Creation. The Great Creator had viewed His works and pronounced them very good, and action for the grand purposes were now in order. The heavenly bodies, at God's command, quickly started on their long journeys from an initial force applied to each, simultaneously with the establishment of the force and law of gravity to curb them in their united action through space. The reader, in order to grasp this portion of God's work, must know the scientific principles that a body started in space or a vacuum by an initial force will travel in that vacuum at the same speed forever, without increase or diminution of that force, and if a smaller heavenly body is attracted by the force of gravity by a larger one, the smaller will revolve around the larger in an orbit. These scientific principles will enable the ordinary reader to comprehend not only the magnitude of God's works, but the natural Laws which regulate the action of these whirling worlds.

These heavenly bodies were then endowed, some of them with the ability to emit light, and some to reflect light. Light for the previous three days was made to come—to make morning and day, and to go—to make evening and night without the intervention of planetary machinery

As the engineer starts his machine, first working it by hand, and then clamps its automatic parts, so with light for three days made to come and go, till clamped to the heavenly bodies which were thereafter to emit it automatically, to make the greater and the lesser light, the one to rule the day, the other to rule the night, and to be for signs, and for seasons, and for days, and for years. And there was evening, and there was morning, day the fourth.

The work of the fifth day was exclusively devoted to making the moving creatures that have life in the waters, in abundance, and all fowls that fly in the air, and establishing the Laws of their reproduction, " after their kind." Gen. I., 22. And there was evening, and there was morning, the day fifth.

The work of the sixth day began by making the beasts of the earth "after their kind," and establishing the Laws of their reproduction; and finally came the crowning act of the Creation in making Adam, (male and female), to have dominion over all the earth, and also creating The Adam and Eve, and male and female, who were not gifted with the power of dominion. The Adam and Eve were the Created Ancestors of Jesus Christ, and were the head of the Jewish line that evolved the Saviour. The Law of their reproduction was established in Gen. I., 28. In **Gen. I., 29**, is the gift of the food for the human family "over all the earth," and for the animals, in Gen. I., 30.

There are very many things not specially named in the creative account as having been made, but that deficiency, if it be one, is covered by the closing clause, Gen. II., 1. "Thus the Heaven and the Earth were finished, and all the host of them."

The account is plain, simple and consistent as set forth in the Hebrew which we have followed. Who then believes it, though it be a record of the word of God? It is not for us to answer this question; we simply ask it, and let each one answer for himself.

If there be any who believes the account in part and not the whole, or that the Creation of all things was not accomplished in six days, or that part was made in one length of day and part in another length of day, or that God took millions of years to make the surface of the earth which the account says was made in one day, or that some existences have evolved in a long lapse of time from an insignificant point to something greater and nobler, or many other antagonistic points unnecessary to name, these would undoubtedly confess in their hearts, that they are unbelievers in the account.

It is just as easy and easier for anyone to believe it as it stands in the Hebrew, as it is to believe anything else, for the account is supported by the evidence of our senses, by true Science, and by other Divine records; while theories differing from it, are the vaporings of men's minds, with no support except what they receive from those unsettled intellects who are ever looking about to catch at anything.

To the believer in the Christian faith, the account is his polar star. The first clause in the Apostles' Creed is: "I believe in God, the Father Almighty, maker of heaven and earth and of all things visible and invisible." If he believes in his God, he believes in His recorded word. All men, it seems to us, should accept the account as true, follow it, and believe in it, or reject it entirely as unworthy of their notice, which would clearly draw the dividing line between believers and unbelievers.

This brings us to a personal explanation. We believe in the word of God as written in the Old Testament by Hebrews, and of the New Testament as written by them in the Greek. We do not believe the English Versions of the Bible on those points antagonistic to God's Natural Laws, or that are not faithful transcripts of these languages, of which there are many, and some very vital. No translator should assume to be the conservator of the word of God. He may imagine that there are inconsistencies or even contradictions which he may not understand, but he need not be alarmed ; time will explain them all, and if not explained, will not in the least affect those parts that are explained and can be understood.

Truth has leaden heels, while error has the wings of the wind.

SECOND ADDENDA.
January, 1892.

ALLEGED ERRORS IN THE BIBLE.

Dr. Briggs, of the Union Theological Seminary, Dr. Hyde, of Bowdoin College, and Dr. Harper, of Yale, have each made public announcement of "Errors in the Bible," but as far as the public has seen, neither of them has stated what one of the many Bibles extant they find in error, nor have they charged any specific error in any of them. This has confused rather than enlightened the Christian mind.

This position naturally suggests the enquiry, which Bible is in error or are they all in error, including the Hebrew and Greek INSPIRATIONS. It is assumed by Christians that a Bible means, in its general sense, the INSPIRED record of the Word and laws of God. It matters not whether it be in English, in Hebrew, in Greek, or in any other language, if it be assumed as the true INSPIRATION, all Christians accept it as such, and on these terms. For our Christianity is based on the fundamental principle, that the Hebrew of the Old Testament and the Greek of the New are the languages in which INSPIRATION has been given to mankind.

So that these distinguished scholars, when they speak of "Errors in the Bible," are supposed to mean errors in the King James' Bible, and that those errors are errors of translation only, and not errors in the Hebrew and Greek INSPIRATIONS. This we take for granted.

Considering the time and circumstances under which the Great Bible was translated, in 1540, and which was generally followed by the translations of the King James' Bible, in 1611—except that they were restrained by Royal authority and acted under the fear of the King's displeasure—and that all of these translators laid no claim to INSPIRATION or a knowledge of God's Natural Laws, and that they acted throughout under the instincts, traditions and convictions of humanity then prevalent, the surprise is not that we have errors in the English Bibles, but that we have so few comparatively. It is hardly supposable that translators, acting under such influences, could give to the World the niceties of the INSPIRATION complete. There is no sound reason, however, why the history, the natural facts, based on God's natural laws, and the Science of INSPIRATION should not be accurately rendered, and if not so rendered by reason of the circumstances surrounding the translators, the errors, when discovered, should be speedily rectified ; for to continue to teach them as Such, or to remain Silent about them, is simply administering poison to the Sources of all Christian effort.

A Booklet styled AM I JEW OR GENTILE? OR THE GENEALOGY OF JESUS CHRIST, PROVING HIS DIVINITY, was published by E. H. Coffin, 49 John St., New York, price 25cts., by mail, to accomplish this object in respect to the Creation and origin of the human races, founded solely upon the Hebrew INSPIRATION, and the conclusions arrived at are considered as settled, for the following reasons : The author of this work commenced his publications on this subject some forty years ago, and in all of them he kindly asked all Hebrew Scholars and Divines to criticise his postulates severely, and set him right on any point if he was in error. Although the gratuitous distribution of the publications have been widespread, no Divine or Hebrew Scholar during that time has criticised, denied, or found a word of fault with his postulates, some of which are as follows :

Gen. I : 26. Records in the Hebrew INSPIRATION, the creation of a class of human beings under the *name* of ADAM, and that name is defined in Gen. V: 2, as "male and female," created —not born of woman. This class was to have

DOMINION over all the earth, and as no such power was conferred upon any other human beings created, it points directly to the creation of the Caucasian, Mongolian, Malay, Indian and Negro races, which have exercised dominion over all the earth, through all history, and now hold that dominion. Pages 14, 58.

Gen. I: 27. Records in like manner the creation of THE ADAM, and a class of male and female. These were the Hebrew Race, which included the Jewish Race, which was also Hebrew. These created people had no power of dominion given them, and although they have attempted twice to make themselves a Nation for dominion, have twice failed, and are now a scattered race throughout the world. THE ADAM and EVE were the created heads of the Jewish blood line that evolved Jesus Christ.

Gen. II: 21, 22. Recorded in like manner the special making of EVE, the wife of THE ADAM. Page 22.

The name ADAM occurs five times as the name of a class in the first eleven chapters of Genesis in the Hebrew, while the name THE ADAM, the husband of EVE, occurs Thirty Six times in the same Chapters, and its equivalent ADAM, with the article dropped, occurs eleven times, making forty-seven times in all that THE

ADAM or its equivalent is used in these eleven Chapters.

The account in the Hebrew has been somewhat confused by the use of ADAM so many times for THE ADAM. But the INSPIRED writer had the right as well as the power to use any term or name for THE ADAM which carried his identity; that is, either as the husband of EVE or as the individual. These identities are the INSPIRATION. Those who are not satisfied with this explanation can take the more charitable view of the matter, that the articles have been dropped by clerical error in copying the manuscripts, which was undoubtedly done by persons having no claim to INSPIRATION. ADAM proper being a plural noun, while THE ADAM is a singular noun, we must either accept these equivalents for THE ADAM, or credit EVE with two husbands.

Although the name of THE ADAM occurs so frequently in the Hebrew INSPIRATION, that name has never appeared in any English Version of the Bible. Gen. I : 26. These created beings were made in numbers "over all the earth." Pages 59, 75 and 80. The Caucasians were created on the Continent of Europe; the Mongolians and Malays in Asia; the Indians in America; the Negroes in Africa, and the Hebrews in the Holy Land.

While the English Versions destroy all of humanity except Noah and his family by flood, the Hebrew INSPIRATION only destroys the descendants of THE ADAM and EVE, except Noah and his family, leaving the remainder of mankind unharmed by that catastrophe. Page 38.

The English Versions have no correct genealogy of Jesus Christ. The Hebrew has, however, a correct one, running from THE ADAM and EVE to Joseph. Page 57.

The theology of the unity of the race, derived from the English Versions, made so by the erroneous use of the name ADAM as the husband of EVE; the suppression of her real husband's name, THE ADAM, and the garbled translations of the extent of the flood, are the controlling errors in the King James' Bible.

These errors have worked incalculable mischief in the would-be Christian World. They have led vast multitudes to disbelief, not only in the truth of the errors themselves, but incidentally to a disbelief in the whole Bible. They have gone further and permeated the relations between independent races, to the great detriment, socially and politically, of the weaker.

We refer of course to the purely white Caucasian race and the purely black Negro race. The more the common origin of these two races has been pressed in religious teachings, the more set has the Caucasian race become in its antipathy, until present results are here, which every one knows and most every one regrets.

The Negro race is an independently created race of God's people, and is entitled to that rank with all its equal rights, privileges and immunities.

Our experiences many years ago in the far West, where White men were scarce, Indians plenty and Negroes rare, was the adoration of the Indian for the Negro. The pale faces held no such position in the Indian's estimation. His principal amusement was to take hold of the curly locks of the Negro's hair, straighten them out and then let them spring back, whereupon his laughter would be more than immoderate. We do not know whether this worship continues universal under a more extended contact of the two races.

It is a glorious discovery to have found out that the INSPIRATION is confirmed by every existing law of God in nature in respect to reproduction in the human family, and of their political distribution and destinies as separate races, and that the hands that inscribed it have written superior to, and more accurately than, all the combined education and knowledge of nearly nineteen centuries of the Christian Era. Is not this a complete and satisfactory proof of the INSPIRATION itself, and of its Godly origin as tracing our creation, our duties and our destinies? Who can ask for anything more, or who wants anything less?

We quote: "No translator should assume to be the conservator of the Word of God. He may imagine that there are inconsistencies or even contradictions which he may not understand, but he need not be alarmed. Time will explain them all, and if not explained will not in the least affect those parts that are explained and can be understood." Page 87.

God speed the noble efforts of those able, distinguished, and learned men, who have set this ball of "Errors in the Bible" in motion, and for the good of mankind and the advancement of the Christian religion it is to be hoped that they will stop at nothing until a solid foundation for creeds and doctrines shall be presented to the world in a Bible containing the *pure* INSPIRATION, where there are no errors. And the quicker the better; for who will assume to say that there are errors in the INSPIRATION excepting God himself?

ERRORS OF TRANSLATION IN KING JAMES' BIBLE.

The controlling errors of translation in the King James' Bible, from the Hebrew Inspiration, are due to the misuse and want of use in places of FOUR words, namely: First, the interpolation of the word "the" as the second word of Gen. I., 1, thereby opening a space of time. "In *the* beginning," for speculations and theories before the Genesis account of creation proper, absolutely began. That space in the Hebrew inspiration is closed up by "In beginning," &c. Second, the misuse and want of use in places of two names, Adam and The Adam; and third, the unwarrantable use of the word "So" at the head of Gen. I., 27, in place of the rightful word "And," as in the Hebrew.

We give below the English terms used in the King James' Bible and the corresponding terms in the Hebrew inspiration in the first eleven chapters of Genesis, or until the dispersion of the Jews, the descendants of The Adam and Eve, among the Isles of the Gentiles and Nations of the earth:

Errors of Translation

Chapter and Verse.	King James' Bible.	Hebrew Inspiration.
Gen I., 1	In *the* beginning.	In beginning.
Gen. I., 26.	Man.	Adam.
Gen., I, 27.	Man.	The Adam.
Gen. I., 27.	So.	And.
Gen. II., 5.	Man.	Adam.
Gen. II., 7.	Man.	The Adam.
Gen. II., 7.	Man.	The Adam.
Gen. II., 8.	The Man.	The Adam.
Gen. II., 15.	The Man.	The Adam.
Gen. II., 16.	The Man.	The Adam.
Gen. II., 18.	The Man.	The Adam.
Gen. II., 19.	Adam.	The Adam.
Gen. II., 19,	Adam.	The Adam.
Gen. II., 20.	Adam.	The Adam.
Gen. II., 20.	Adam.	Adam.

Here Adam in the Hebrew, is the equivalent of The Adam as indicating the husband of Eve, and is a singular noun governed by "him" in the same sentence, while Adam proper is a plural noun. Gen. V., 2.

Gen. II., 21.	Adam.	The Adam.
Gen. II., 22.	Man.	The Adam.
Gen. II., 22.	The Man.	The Adam.
Gen. II., 23.	Adam.	The Adam.
Gen. II., 25.	The Man.	The Adam.
Gen. III., 8.	Adam.	The Adam.
Gen. III., 9.	Adam.	The Adam.
Gen. III., 12.	The Man.	The Adam.
Gen. III., 17.	Adam.	Adam.

Here in the Hebrew, Adam is identical with The Adam who was the husband of Eve.

Gen. III., 20.	Adam.	The Adam.
Gen. III., 21.	Adam.	Adam.

Here in the Hebrew, Adam is identical with The Adam the husband of Eve.

Gen. III., 22.	The Man.	The Adam.
Gen. III., 24.	The Man.	The Adam.
Gen. IV., 1.	Adam.	The Adam.
Gen. IV., 25.	Adam.	Adam.

Here in the Hebrew, Adam is identical with The Adam the husband of Eve.

Gen. V., 1.	Adam.	Adam.
Gen. V., 1.	Man.	Adam.

In this verse, Adam is used twice in the Hebrew, and is a singular noun governed by "he, him" in the same sentence, and hence is the equivalent of The Adam.

Gen. V., 2.	Adam.	Adam.

This Adam is the plural noun—"Male and Female people created."

Gen. V., 3.	Adam.	Adam.

The Identical The Adam, the husband of Eve, and father of Seth.

Gen. V., 4.	Adam.	Adam.

The identical The Adam, the father of Setn.
Gen. V., 5.   Adam.   Adam.

The identical The Adam, the singular noun governed by "he" in the same sentence.
Gen. VI., 1.   Men.   The Adam.
Gen. VI., 2.   Men.   The Adam.
Gen. VI., 3.   Man.   Adam.

The identical The Adam, a singular noun governed by "he" in the same sentence.
Gen. VI., 4.   Men.   The Adam.
Gen. VI., 5,   Man.   The Adam.
Gen. VI., 6.   Man.   The Adam.
Gen. VI., 7.   Man.   The Adam.
Gen. VII., 21.   Man.   The Adam.
Gen. VII., 23.   Man.   Adam.

See explanation on pages 38 and 39. This Adam in the Hebrew is identical with The Adam.

Gen. VIII., 21.   Man's.   The Adam.
Gen. VIII., 21.   Man's.   The Adam.
Gen. IX., 5.   Man.   The Adam.
Gen. IX., 5.   Man.   The Adam.
Gen. IX., 6.   Man's.   The Adam.
Gen. IX., 6.   Man.   Adam.
Gen. IX., 6   Man.   The Adam.
Gen. XI., 5.   Men.   The Adam.

POSTULATES IN THE GENESIS CONSIDERED AS SETTLED ON THE BASIS OF THE HEBREW INSPIRATION.

Postulate First.

That the Universe including our Solar System was created in Six days in the order laid down in the Genesis account.

Postulate Second.

That nothing material existed before the time to which that account refers. That "In beginning" refers to the first act of Creation and the first act of the first day's work.

Postulate Third.

That the first day's work consisted of creating the heaven, the earth without form and light throughout the Universe. Heaven, meaning in Hebrew expanse, and in this connection Space or Vacuum, while earth without form means primordeal elements uncombined, and those elements in combination is dry land, and still called earth. Earth, in its general sense, is the ponderable mass of this planet revolving around the Sun.

Postulate Fourth.

That the Second day's work was the combining elements to make the waters of the Universe.

Postulate Fifth.

That the third day's work consisted in combining elements to make dry land or earth throughout the Universe and gather together the Waters combined on the previous day to make seas, lakes, rivers, etc. Then to plant on the dry land or earth the Vegetable Kingdom with its fruits and seeds.

Postulate Sixth.

That the fourth day's work consisted in giving motion to the Heavenly bodies which were completed on the third day in space and in place, and at the same instant establishing the law of gravity and giving some bodies the power to emit the light already made, while others were given the power to reflect light to be for signs and for seasons, and for days and for years.

Postulate Seventh.

That the fifth day's work consisted in creating the moving creatures that have life in the waters and all fowls that fly in the air.

Postulate Eighth.

That the sixth day's work consisted in making the beasts of the field and making all of mankind required to start the races in reproduction.

Postulate Ninth.

That the two verses Gen. I: 22, 26, records solely the creation of two distinct classes of people. The first were peoples, male and female, called Adam, and were made by the plural Godhead. "And God said let US make Adam in OUR image after OUR likeness and let THEM have DOMINION over the fish of the sea, etc." These peoples were to have dominion over all the earth. The second class created in Gen. I: 27, where Jesus Christ was to be subsequently involved, was done by God alone. No power of DOMINION was given to this class. "And God created The Adam in HIS OWN image; in the image of God created He him; male and female created He them."

Postulate Tenth.

That the first class created under the name Adam were the Caucasians, the Mongolians, the Malays, the Indians and the Negroes, who have held Dominion over all the earth through all history, and still hold that Dominion; while the second class was the Hebrew race (including the Jewish race), which has never held dominion, and have been a scattered race throughout the world from the time of the dispersion among the Isles of the Gentiles and the Nations of the earth after the building of the Tower of Babel to the present time.

Postulate Eleventh.

That The Adam, the husband of Eve, was a representative Hebrew, and was created to be the head of the Jewish line to evolve the Saviour Jesus Christ. The Adam and Eve were the only created beings specifically named in the Creative account.

Postulate Twelfth.

That the genealogy of Jesus Christ begins in The Adam and Eve, runs through Noah to Joseph and Mary.

Postulate Thirteenth.

That as the Hebrews were created in numbers throughout the Holy land and to be co-existant with the food created for their use, Cain had no difficulty in getting a Hebrew wife in the Land of Nod.

Postulate Fourteenth.

That the flood destroyed the descendants of The Adam and Eve except Noah and his family, leaving the remainder of humanity unharmed by that catastrophe.

Main Postulate.

That the Hebrew race has been the chosen people of God for the following purposes: To write, publish and ventilate His will and laws to the world and establish the Christian religion. As the result, that race has written all the Books of the Old and the New Testaments, and given the every-day history, both good and bad, of this people, and have evolved Jesus Christ who, by His Divine character, was to be an exact pattern in living to all exemplary Christians.

Concluding Postulate.

That Christian religion is conduct, spiritual or otherwise, guided by the laws of God, and following the example and teachings of Jesus Christ, or their equivalents.

SONG OF CREATION.

Written in 1856, but not Published.

INVOCATION.

I.

Whisper to me, O gentle Muse of heaven,
And be thy holiest inspiration given!
Infuse my soul with courage to explore
The depths profound on Time's remotest shore!

II.

Bring forth to light from that unfathomed deep
The pearls of truth that there in darkness sleep;
Tell how from naught the Universe could rise,
With worlds on worlds in new-created skies!

III.

Beyond the birth of matter or of man
Stretch forth thy ken, if that thy power can span
The nothingness of nothing made or known—
The spaceless void around the Eternal Throne!

IV.

Tell when the worlds were not that now revolve,
And aid Creation's mysteries to solve:
Tell of Almighty God, and where His home
Before the starry orbs illumed His boundless dome

NOTHINGNESS.

I.

CAN mind, howe'er gigantic, comprehend
GOD's truths untold, and with a void contend?
Can it on Nothing fix, or blank complete,
Or Nothing's attributes to man repeat?

II.

If so it were, the ever-searching mind,
Could here concentrate, and solution find;
Illume with mental rays what was not known
Of aught before Creation's work begun.

III.

Rise, ye profoundest powers of human mind,
And say what embryo then your strength confined!
Where spread your fields of action proud and bold,
Of strifes victorious, in the realms untold!

CREATION'S DAWN.

I.

VAIN were the search, for e'en the mightiest mind,
Howe'er intent the birth of GOD to find—
Creation's dawn, though plainly shown to man,
His previous being Time can never span:
No trace, no mark, no measure, hint, or line,
Of holiest Writ, could fathom the Divine.

II.

Creation's birth and e'en the birth of Time
Are finite things within the Great SUBLIME—
Are dots imperfect on the age-worn world
' Compared with cycles in the past unfurled.

III.

GOD was alone, all perfect and unseen :
Thus to that era had He ever been.
But mental vision shows to man his GOD ,
Reflects His image in the moulded sod ;
Opes the wide door for man to trace his way
Through ages backward past the first-born day
And stand, where Revelation doth not tell
Of heaven, as yet unfashioned, or of hell !

IV.

There was GOD, great, majestic, and sublime !
No days, no years, no marks of unmade Time
Disturbed His empire of repose profound ;
Nor did His angels' praises there resound.

V.

Here sprang the God-thought of Creation bold,
From nothing, mighty worlds on worlds t' unfold ;
To stretch the azure curtain of the skies ;
To deck it with its million shining eyes ;
To ope Creation from His hand a scroll,
And poise the whirling worlds from pole to pole

THRONE OF GOD.

I.

WHAT is the Throne of GOD, or what its mould ?
Does Inspiration sure this truth unfold ?
Or, if unfold, can mortal comprehend
Its vast beginning or its vaster end ?

II.

Where rests its base—where do its columns rise ?
And where its domes that swell within the skies ?
What bounds its circuit, what its viewless height,
Except the glorious omnipresent light ?

III.

Where meet its arches, hung with festooned rays,
And studded round with bright and parted days ?
Where the entablature so high, so bold,
That, could a mortal's vision once behold,
Height, depth, and distance, all would fade and die,
As sight extended on the boundless sky !

IV.

Yes, with our powers of vision search to trace
The arching piles in labyrinthine space ;
And wander ever through the doming skies,
As tower on tower doth toward GOD arise.

V.

Turn then the eye upon yon crowning height,
Not made of earth, but ever glorious light ;
Piled up in massive beauty far and high,
Rolling in fleecy brightness in the sky !

VI.

Turn then, again, upon the snow-white Throne,
Such as to mortal sight was never shown—
With clouds of radiance circling high and low,
Like blushing Morning on ethereal snow.

MYSTERIOUS FORM OF GOD.

I.

Lo! the effulgence of Mysterious Form!
Mightier and stranger than the wheeling storm;
Calm as the placid sunlight on the lea,
Yet infinitely brighter than the day.

II.

What does my closer vision here behold,
Which clouds of volumed God-light now unfold?
Dare mortal man a visioned outline trace,
And dot his folly through a world of space?

III.

Dare he uplift the cloudy drapery bright
That gathers round the Great Eternal Might,
And face to face th' immortal GOD behold,
And peer into the realms of heaven untold

ANGELIC HOSTS.

I.

THERE rests, beyond the ken of mortal eye,
The Great SUPREME within the light-crowned sky ;
There circle round His unseen, mystic place,
Bright angels, beaming with seraphic grace.

II.

Around His throne the ever-swelling strains
Far echo on the rolling, cloudy plains ;
While cherubs float in liquid, glowing day,
And gild their wings in heaven's resplendent ray.

III.

There angels waft their brightness through the glow,
Decked with pure robes that shame ethereal snow ·
While from their eyes a quiet peace doth shine,
Rivalling all, but living light Divine.

LIGHT OF HEAVEN.

I.

AND what is this which blinds my vision now,
As clouds of vapor take their outward flow?
Reveals to me what staggers reason quite,
And shows all yet has been perpetual night!

II.

Sudden, if from the dark to light we turn,
To fires that in the empyrean burn,
From far and wide we bring the focal ray—
Show years of light within a fleeting day,
And then concentrate all this burning light.:
'Twould but feebly tell what dawned upon the sight.

III.

The light of heaven, and brighter light divine,
That in no humbler realm could live or shine,
Pours forth the stream that gilds the road to heaven,
And lights the light that has to man been given

IV.

Great GOD Omnipotent! do we now behold
Thine eye supreme that these bright clouds unfold:
From which flows on the never-ceasing stream,
And constant with the never-varying gleam—
From centre ranges through its verging way,
And lights in outward worlds the living day!

GOD'S ATTRIBUTES.

I.

With mental vision scale this lofty height,
And hope to tell what dawned upon the sight !
Approach His glowing seat on high once more,
And in these hallowed realms devoutly soar.

II.

Sweep round His brow, O mental vision bold—
Truth, Mercy, Justice, Patience, there behold :
Guide on, nor cease the love divine to trace
That shines resplendent in a FATHER's face.

III.

Behold the crown that rests upon His brow,
Where angels and archangels meekly bow ;
Behold the FATHER's eye with love serene
Flashing majestic o'er Creation's scene
Range through bounds that hold the glowing sky,
We yet find there, His ever-present eye.

SEAL OF HEAVEN.

I.

When, mighty mandate, mystery sublime,
Wilt thou be blotted from the book of Time?
When shall the seal, set here by God's command—
This mystic seal be broke—and by what hand—
That mortal may behold Him face to face,
And roam at will His sacred fields of space?

II.

Presumptuous mortal, 'tis not to thee given
To soar in space's height in upper heaven;
To wrest the secret and bring down to man
And blazon to the day His wondrous plan—
Roll back the mighty curtain of the sky,
And God's repose profane with curious eye!

III.

Yet, Muse supernal, solve to us this cause
Why should not worlds or universes pause,
Open to mortal eye this vision bright,
And blind him with a flood of heavenly light—
Blot out in 'whelming wonder soul and sense,
And quench his spirit in Omnipotence?

IV.

No; still will roll His mighty wonders on;
Unbroke the seal till Time's career be run,
Nor angels nor archangels shall reveal
The awful mysteries of this holy seal.

GOD.

I.

Then what is God, and why His heaven-born name,
And why His glorious presence earthward came?
Where his first rest before the Triune One,
And when the birth of God, the only Son?
Whence came the Holy Ghost from the Divine,
Before He taught the clustered stars to shine?

II.

Bear up, O God! the feeble human thought
To where Thou hast Thy mighty wonders wrought,
To show Thy rest within the nothing world
Existent ere the darkness was unfurled.

III.

Almighty God, and Cause supremely great,
In harmony with Thy eternal state
With Thy great love, Thou mad'st a world for man,
And based in wisdom Thy omniscient plan.

IV.

Then, creature vain, of God-descended mind,
Plume thy bright pinions, and go forth to find,
Through Nature's network and through Nature's laws,
The first Beginning and sufficient Cause.

V.

God is great God with attributes replete—
He still were God, no attribute complete,
When Time was not, nor yet Creation's thought ;
When Space was not, nor yet with darkness fraught,
He had a Will, although not yet made known—
A power complete confined within His throne.

VI.

This Will Supreme—all perfect in its Will—
For infinite ends was powerful to fulfil
Designs stupendous in the mystic world
Conceived, and in the lapse of time unfurled.

CREATION.

I.

Now sprang the all of moving worlds or heaven
As from His hand the sacred scroll was given,
In order, destiny, and place combined,
From Time, the first create, to man's immortal mind !

II.

Whatever thing there be, in earth or heaven,
To which a color, form, or name, is given,
All came of GOD, and Godward is its end :
Though heavenward bound, we can not comprehend
The paths that stretch o'er this mysterious plane,
Through labyrinthine space, Creation's boundless main.

III.

Ambitious man, with ever-erring mind,
With this great subject fired, thou seek'st to find
The Cause stupendous that could move this will—
Could make all space with whirling worlds to fill—
Could fill these worlds with wonders multiplied,
And infinite mystery through Creation wide :
This all a wondrous problem, never solved,
That a transcendent truth with naught but faith involved.

IV.

Faith is the all of truth that's known to man
Of GOD or GOD's in all Creation's plan—
Of planets, suns, and myriad-systemed spheres,
All Godward bound through chiliads of years.
These wonders wrought within this infinite will—
Their ends to compass, and their fate fulfil—
Through Time and Space in harmony to meet,
And close when Time Eternity shall greet.

V.

Conception staggers at the 'wildering thought
Of GOD Supreme conceiving all from naught :
Evolving instant, with creative power,
The worlds like rain-drops from impending shower !
These are as nothing in their mystic number,
Compared with voids in mighty space that slumber :
All undisturbed in wide Creation's bound,
Where e'en the swift-winged Light no resting-place hath
    found !

TIME.

I.

The first creation, then, not told to man,
But which is gathered from the mighty plan,
Is Time, which though not matter strangely wrought,
Is equally of Godly make and thought.

II.

In utter space, with naught for space to span,
Where God reposed the life of Time began ;
He sprang to being by God's will divine,
The laws of age to mark and to define.

III.

A tyrant in his everlasting sway ;
The same for countless ages or a day,
He rolls the years in cycles still the same,
Nor shows inquiring man from whence he came.

IV.

Time then was plumed with pinions bright and rare,
And on his brow God stamped the frown of care ;
His wide-spread wings were tipped with living day,
And he with hope was girt to urge his way.

V.

God willed His course and gave his first command,
" Thy wing, thy glass, and ever-running sand,
Shall note the cycles of eternal day,
And stamp thy footprints on the trackless way !"

VI.

Thus moved creation—then to Time GOD said,
" Go forth, and with eternity be wed !
Until my mighty works have all been done,
Cease not, nor weary in thy course begun."

VII.

Through darkened naught and chaos mingling wild,
Through howling tempest's whirl and zephyrs mild,
Through sunlight blaze and dreary blackened night,
Through mighty worlds of dark and worlds of light,
'Mid whirling planets, stars, and suns unseen,
Beyond where mortal thought hath ever been,
Time onward flies, and in the lapse of years
Bends proudly on his course through countless spheres.
Soon with his promised nuptials he'll be blest,
Then pause and sink to his eternal rest.

VIII.

Time notes the age of childhood or of man,
And all the phases of th' infinite plan ;
The age of races and the age of states ;
The age, from birth, of all that GOD creates ;
The age of planet, satellite, or sun,
Or systems that in mystic circles run ;
He marks the footprints of the mighty world,
In orbit true which GOD himself unfurled ;
He tells the age of sunbeam or of shade,
Or sparrow struck by GOD upon the glade.

IX.

He marks when empires fall or empires rise ;
When suns are blotted from the starry skies ;
When rolling planets from their orbs are hurled,
Or when created matter makes a world.
When systems vast are formed, or when the end ;
When nascent suns their youthful radiance send ;
When lofty turrets rise, or crush and fall,
Or when to ruin sinks the mighty wall ;
When but a child be born, or monarch die ;
When human souls are lost, or sent on high ;
Whene'er a rose may bud, or lily droop,
Or fresh youth spring, or age in tremor stoop :
Time, ever faithful, marks each fleeting hour,
Though falls a universe, or springs a flower !

X.

In ever-hopeful youth, or crippled age ;
In pleasure's whirling dance, or musings sage ;
While welcome death draws nigh, or feasts prepare,
Or victim pleads his awful doom to spare ;
While vilest sinner draws his parting breath,
And helpless suffering prays for speedy death ;
When but a moment would a world command;
Rolls ever onward the unceasing sand !

XI.

Slow flaps the tireless wing of mighty Time
Along his path amid the orbs sublime !
While mortal man runs round from birth to death;
And millions struggle with expiring breath ;

While new-born babes are wrapped in heavenly light,
Or, borne by angels, mount to regions bright ;
While Life and Death are joining hand in hand,
And choosing victims from the millioned band ;
While countless worlds the laws of GOD obey ;
Still flaps Time's tireless wing in his directed way.

XII.

Far backward stretch the death of Time-born years ;
Each marked and mourned by his prolific tears :
See now the line, behold the funeral train,
The eye looks out, the thought peers up in vain.

XIII.

Now outward, onward, run our eager course,
And find by these Time's unknown secret source ;
Onward and upward trace through earth the line,
Till lost in GOD, or quenched in light divine.
Here, then, the source, can we the distance tell?
Easier the height of heaven, or depth of hell !

XIV.

Infinity ! O, whence, without a bound,
Mysterious regions of the depths profound !
That forms complete the never-ending chain,
That circling backward circles but in vain,
To tell the certain mystic source of Time,
Or onward stretching reach the Great SUBLIME.

INSTALLATION OF TIME.

I.

In heaven's vast concave, but beneath no sky,
And seated on His radiant throne on high,
Beyond the bounds of mortal thought, and bright
With the pure effluence of ethereal light,
Was the ETERNAL, robed in power sublime,
Marking the course of new-created Time.

II.

There in His realm, ere yet had sprung a ray,
To wake in living light, the slumbering day,
He saw young Time within the vast unknown,
Forth steady winging from the eternal throne.

III.

Now to His servant, first create of heaven,
Was the ETERNAL's great commandment given :—

IV.

"On, mighty Time, I clothe thy tireless wing
With strength o'er worlds and boundless space to swing;
Bear, then, thy glass, and shed thy running sand;
Thy conquering scythe hold strongly in thy hand,
Till thou the great creation's dawn prepare,
Then humble all to thee and nothing spare !

V.

"I'll make thee worlds and wondrous systems too,
And when destroyed by thee, will not renew.
I'll give thee suns whose golden light shall shine
Till quenched eternally by hands of thine !
I'll make thee Godlike man with form erect,
And in his mortal mould, thou shalt detect
The secret germ of death, not being now,
Then bend his form and mark his furrowed brow.

VI.

"Cities I'll build for thee, with towers and spires,
That thou shalt burn with yet unkindled fires ;
I'll spread the flowing river and the main :
I'll make the monarch mountain, and the plain ;
I'll bid for thee the stormy tempests blow.
To make the fires in maddening fury glow,
While suns and planets from their orbits turn,
And then be lighted by thy torch to burn."

TIME RETURNING THE UNIVERSE TO GOD.

I.

Where wheel God's armies on their march sublime,
Curbed by His will along the course of Time,
Still circling on their steady tramp around
His throne—where peans jubilant resound,
Worlds wheel with worlds in systems broad-cast sown,
Cycling harmonious in the effulgent zone ;
Stars look at stars o'er planet-studded skies,
Where God's proud banners of the nebulæ arise !

II.

Here, in their way-worn paths obedient, bend
The orbs wherever spaces bounds extend ;
And Time shall hover o'er these weary spheres,
Till end their cycles in the end of years.

III.

Time's course fulfilled, the Almighty bids him halt !
Then deep within the empyrean vault,
He, by some sun the brightest in its sky,
Lights his great torch to fire the worlds on high.

IV.

Then round shall wheel the burning balls of fire,
And flames climb upward in a living spire,
And in their widely-sweeping folds embrace
The suns and systems of the fields of space.

V.

Fanned by the wings of Time, these flames shall glow
O'er the wide worlds that wheel and shine below ;
And all the orbs that on their axes roll,
In dire concussion shake from pole to pole.

VI.

Loud crash the worlds as from their paths they wheel !
And systems tremble as GOD's thunders peal !
The tempest thickens, and with rage they burn
As maddened planets from their courses turn.

VII.

Worlds, in their fury, dash at worlds amain,
And scatter terror o'er heaven's boundless plain !
Flames circle flames, and in their eddies hold
Orbs still on orbs the raging fires unfold !
Till the vast vaults of heaven, one living blaze,
To GOD above their burning incense raise !

VIII.

Then all with one convulsive struggle yield
The tie that bound them to their native field ;
And now the yielding, tottering arch of heaven
Is from its blazing station hurled and driven,
And downward with a universal crash,
The suns and systems to destruction dash !

RETURN OF TIME.

I.

God's universe of worlds sublimely wrought,
Fashioned in mystery, passes out through naught,
In primal atoms from dissolving earth,
Convening instant where it had its birth.

II.

God speaks! and space is folded like a scroll,
And back to nothing all the systems roll.
Time's faltering wing flaps slowly in his course,
As he approaches the Eternal Source.

III.

Now in high heaven, before the eternal throne,
Comes Time, all weary with the ages flown,
Sad with his almost infinite career,
He pauses now in God's sublimest sphere.

IV.

Backward he turns, and shudders to survey,
The dreary waste along his trackless way,
Where suns and planets filled the vast profound,
And cycling systems ran their mighty round,
Now sunk to waste, and in destruction all,
And shrouded in annihilation's pall.

V.

Now he approaches with a weary flight,
And stands before the Infinite Fount of Light ;
Faint from the conflict with the worlds borne down,
He yields to GOD his trust, and takes the promised crown.

VI.

Then spake Jehovah !—and throughout the dome,
Where all his children now were gathered home,
His voice in tones of majesty sublime,
Was heard to give his last commands to Time.

VII.

" Behold, a mighty ruin crowns thy day,
And dying Death has sung his requiem lay !
Lo ! the vast suns that blazed with living light,
Are quenched and lost in never-ending night ! "

VIII.

" Now naught in space but thee doth live and move,
Or know that I am all supreme above ;
And now, Great Time, behold thy new-born bride,
And fold thy weary wing upon thy side."

GODHEAD.

I.

PRIMEVAL Time was fashioned by GOD's will,
His end to answer, and his course fulfil—
Onward the same through all Creation's bound,
Nor yet a resting-place his wing hath found.

II.

Now Godward turn our all-inquiring thought,
And ask of Time what mighty work was wrought,
For systems, worlds, or uncreated man,
To move GOD's will, and found His mighty plan.

III.

O Great Eternal GOD, and Great SUPREME !—
Himself a GOD, the GODHEAD now his theme !

IV.

Can man conceive the wonders here displayed,
To show to him the new CREATOR made ?
For love of man, though GOD was perfect now,
He twined a triple glory round His brow :
Out from Himself He called His only SON ;
Thence came the HOLY GHOST—and it was done !
The empire of Creation all His own,
He shared with them His Universal Throne.

V.

Man was unborn—all uncreated still—
Nor loathsome Sin had come, his heart to fill:
But God's omniscience in the distance saw
Man perfect made, but treacherous to His law.

VI.

Man was not made for humble man, but God,
And on this mystery vainly may he plod—
Drive Reason frantic in the fruitless race
This truth to fathom or this mystery trace.

VII.

Though for an end unknown to mortal man,
He made complete this temporary plan
Of worlds, of systems, mountains, depths, and plain,
For Time to lose—Eternity to gain.
He based the GODHEAD on His mighty Throne
For ends omnipotent—to man unknown.

NEW-BORN LIGHT.

I.

Now flashed upon the Great CREATOR'S sight,
At His omnipotent command, the Light!

II.

Like the first radiance from the morning sun,
Forth from His throne the course of Light begun;
And terror-stricken Darkness, in its flight,
Struggled and yielded to the conquering Light.

III.

Forth it careers on its triumphant way,
Through realms abysmal, now illumed by Day;
And wide o'er heaven pursued his wondrous race,
And claimed his empire over boundless space.

IV.

Brightest of the creations, Light divine—
Ordained throughout the universe to shine—
Sublime he enters through the gates of Day,
And passes forth at Evening's latest ray.

V.

He cheers and warms whate'er has life or breath,
Sustains all Nature till it sinks in death;
He tints the rose's petals, or the skies,
And paints the arching rainbows as they rise!

VI.

He sheds to waste his unemployed rays,
And in his pleasure like an infant plays;
And, touching gently with his finger bright,
Silvers the robes of far-retreating Night.

SPACE.

I.

Thus, as Creation rounded on its way,
Space spread her fields to welcome infant Day:
The scroll of darkness opened from God's hand,
And heights and depths unfurled at His command.

II.

Space bounded space in Darkness' silent deep,
Which God's infinity alone can sweep;
It swept throughout Creation's boundless dome,
Nor yet enclosed the circuit of His home!

III.

When man looks upward through the vaulted skies,
Infinite worlds on infinite worlds arise!
Vainly he hopes the outer bound to gain,
He struggles with Almighty Power in vain;
And humbly now to God the palm he yields,
And sings his praises through these space-bound fields.

IV.

Far out beyond the circuit of the skies,
Where over-wearied Thought no more can rise—
Where in these realms the clustering systems shine,
Resplendent in their native light divine—
Yet upward are they spread in depths profound,
Till limits fail, and God alone is found!
Yet onward, through the realms of endless space,
Shines ever bright His Omnipresent face:
Though there our failing fancies trace his way,
'Tis but the morning of eternal day!

DAY AND NIGHT.

I.

Now met in strife the rivals Day and Night,
And Darkness quailed before puissant Light;
Before high Heaven these mighty warriors stand,
Like chieftains, blade to blade and hand to hand!

II.

Light now advances, now retreats again—
Yet night essays his vantage to maintain:
On still the sullen and impetuous Night
Presses his pall upon retreating Light;
But as the conquering Light drives Night in turn,
His radiant smile of triumph makes the morn!

III.

GOD saw victorious Light upon his way,
And placed a crown immortal on the Day!
And when the vanquished made his weary flight,
GOD gave, in love, a sweet repose to Night.

EVENING AND MORNING.

I.
Now up resplendent rose all-conquering Day,
Passing the zenith hours upon his way;
Then on to gentle Eve and blushing Morn—
Now to the new-made World in beauty born.

II.
As lessening Light grew down the tranquil sky,
Smiling he wooed the mantling Darkness nigh;
And Twilight's fold with gentle hand he drew,
And matched it with the blushing Morning's hue.

III.
Now the CREATOR, blending Night with Day,
And then to form their union, quenched for aye
All enmity which was 'twixt Day and Night,
And made both Morning and the Evening bright.

IV.
These true harmonious brothers, hand in hand,
Have journeyed far o'er every sea and land;
A mantling verdure widely they've unfurled,
And twined a belt of beauty round the world!

V.
On they have travelled ages, side by side,
Sweeping o'er many a mighty ocean's tide;
Have chronicled the Days as on they sped,
And Days have chronicled the Cycles fled:
Thus have these brothers trod their way sublime,
Like sentries stationed on the wings of Time!

NIGHT OF THE FOURTH DAY.

I.

APPROACHING Night stoops down her sable wing,
While Evening to the cradled Day doth sing;
And now the lengthening, marching shadows long
Tread lightly to the music of the song.

II.

When the o'er-wearied Day is lulled in sleep,
And sombre Night her watchful vigils keep,
She seems to whisper to the World, "Be still!"—
She seems to ask the little, flowing Rill,
To murmur softly on its pebbly way,
Nor break the slumbers of reposing Day.

III.

She seems to ask the Breezes from the hill
To join in happy music with the Rill;
That they together sing Day's lullaby,
Nor breathe the requiem louder than a sigh.

IV.

Up to the shadowy sky, with eye serene,
She turns and beckons to the Stars unseen,
Wooing from them a glow of softened light
To guide in lonely space her dreary flight,
As o'er the waste of Nature's desert wild
She bears the Day as if a sleeping child!

V.

Now ripples softly on the flowing stream,
Which seems to list the murmurs of Day's dream,
The balmy Breezes through the valleys sing
And Stars to her their twilight offerings bring ;
And thus Night moves along her silent way,
Waiting and hoping for the coming Day.

VI.

TOLLING THE NEW-BORN HOURS.

Loud now is sounded, from Night's lofty towers
The startled tolling of the World's first Hours
And down with gentle step the dew of heaven
Upon the calm, quiescent world is given ;
And while all slumbers 'neath Night's shadowy wings
Earth on her axis rolls, and in her orbit swings !

THIRD ADDENDA.

SUBJECTS:

INEVITABLE CONCLUSIONS.

THE BIBLE OF NATURE.

THE TWO BIBLE SYSTEMS.

THE BIBLE OF INSPIRATION.

THE TRANSLATORS BIBLES.

CAUSE AND EFFECT.

CREATION MAKERS.

THIRD ADDENDA.
January, 1893.

INEVITABLE CONCLUSIONS.

The reader of this book has undoubtedly seen that each individual subject has been discussed upon its own merits, without any attempt being made to combine them or dovetail them together with the adhesiveness of truth, in order to present to the reader's mind a unit idea. While each position may be admitted, standing alone, the combination of them, it is believed, will produce a far higher and grander conception of their scope and importance. In other words, by so doing, the Christian World could be furnished with a Bible, based on the revealed word of God, instead of one based upon the conceptions of translators, if so it be.

To meet this position squarely and understandingly, we must be certain of two things. First, that we have the revealed word of God (which will follow, as proved hereafter, if any proof is needed); and Second, that the underlying principle or foundation of that word is not to be found in any translations of the Bible now in use throughout the Christian World, on the subject of the created origin of the races.

This is a bold proposition, but for the good of mankind, the advancement of the Christian religion, the honor of God and of His word, we hope to be able to prove it to the entire satisfaction of the most bigoted or sceptical.

We will all admit that the total acts and laws of God, from the dawn of creation to the present moment, constitute the GREAT BOOK OF REVELATION to mankind. This book is made up of two parts; The Bible of Nature, and the Spiritual Inspiration. The latter is made up of two parts also; namely, the purely spiritual, and the miracles, neither of which should be questioned. The miracles cannot be classed as belonging to the Bible of Nature, for they do not follow the established laws of Nature, but are special acts of God.

THE BIBLE OF NATURE.

The first sentence of the Genesis is the first sentence of the Bible of Nature. Every act of God from that date to the present moment towards entities, "visible or invisible," make up its contents. It is a wonderful, complex and accurate history. This Bible is read, and has been read, by every human being on the face of the whole earth, from the cradle to the grave, and understandingly by each one, according to the knowledge they possessed.

The whole of this Bible, of course, does not appear in what is known as the Bible of Inspiration, since a very small portion of it is contained therein; small, however, as it is, it is all important, as giving the manner of creation of the universe, and especially of mankind, and the subsequent history of a portion of them.

We call it the Bible of Nature, as it is well entitled to that name, because the laws of God are uniform, consistent, instructive and dependable, whether natural or spiritual, and are equally entitled to our obedience and consideration, whether they govern the atom, the universe, or the salvation of the soul.

The more minutely we investigate forms in nature, such as the bone and sinew in man or animal, the leaf on the tree, the blade of grass in the field, the flower in the garden, the stone on the mountain top, or the crystal in the bowels of the earth, the more closely is the enquirer brought in touch with God and his attributes.

The Bible of Nature and the Bible of True Inspiration, of necessity, cannot conflict the one with the other; they should, and do coincide and agree. There can be no conflict between the Laws of God, Natural or Spiritual.

The Bible of Nature requires no translator; it only contains facts which we all see, know and feel, as exact knowledge. If there appears in any translation of the Inspiration a conflict between the Laws of God, we may at once conclude that something is wrong with the translation, either in its correct understanding or in the rendering from the original.

There may be attempts made, as has been the case, to show that the Laws of Nature have changed, in order to prop up the flimsy theory of the unity of the race by asserting, without the possibility of proof, that the Negro's ancestors were white Caucasians, and that change to a Southern climate has changed him to a Negro. If there was any ground for such an assertion, the reverse should be true, that by returning him North, he would again become a white Caucasian, which we all know could not be possible. The Bible of Nature must be taken as the standard of exact knowledge, and all other questionable constructions or theories must yield conformity to it. This subject will be continued under a subsequent head of "Cause and Effect."

THE TWO BIBLE SYSTEMS.

There are two Bible Systems; the Bible of Inspiration and the Translators Bibles. These two systems are based upon entirely adverse principles. The Inspiration, from the Hebrew, gives a diversity in created origin of mankind, while the Translators Bibles, as far as our knowledge extends, are grounded upon the unity in a single race, of which ADAM and EVE were the created heads. No two peoples were ever more antipodes than these two systems, to give information to mankind of the design of the great Creator for their benefit.

The Inspiration sets forth that God created the types of mankind substantially as they now exist, in numbers, and for an object, while the Translators Bibles stultify this broad creation and design by declaring that God did not do what He did do, and so said through Inspiration, but contracts this grand act, to the creating of ADAM and EVE to be the heads of reproduction of all types of humanity on earth. This announcement is its own refutation, as ADAM is defined in the Inspiration, Gen. V., 2, as the *name of a class*, and hence could not reproduce a human being from EVE.

The Hebrew Inspiration unfolds, on the other hand, a magnificent and consistent design in the creation of mankind. A Saviour was to be evolved in due time, who was to take on the human form, in the manner stated. Is it not reasonable to suppose that God would make some special provision for the accomplishment of this stupendous act, and not leave to chance, the birth of His only Son among the new-born of the earth?

The Inspiration tells us that He did make this special provision. That He created the heads of the Gentile and Hebrew races, and to make His act more clear, He gave the names of the Created Heads of this Hebrew-Jewish line, THE ADAM and EVE, the only individuals created under a name, whose blood line was to evolve the Redeemer and Saviour of mankind. This special act of creation is all wiped out in the Translators Bibles, the name of THE ADAM, the husband of EVE, has never appeared in any one of them. We make this assertion with sincere regret, and nothing but a high sense of duty in the past has induced us to do so; nor would we do it now, but for the plain proof of its correctness, which we give in the next article.

THE BIBLE OF INSPIRATION.

Nothing is more vital to the Christian than the true Inspiration of the Bible, and, therefore, to determine that point, it should be the first duty of every enquirer. It is not our intention to go further in this direction than the Created origin of mankind, and incidentally to the history which follows, as far as completing the genealogy of those created heads. Mankind being the subject which forms the whole theory of the Bible, every item of the Inspiration regarding it should be scrutinized with the utmost severity.

Two points are necessary to be arrived at in order to compass a correct conclusion, namely, to find out what the Inspiration is in the Hebrew, and then determine whether that coincides and agrees with the Bible of Nature, where we have exact knowledge of the types of humanity, commencing with the Creation, and continued to the present time, and carried on in reproduction before our eyes daily.

There are three verses in the Genesis that give all the account we have of the Creation of mankind, namely, Gen. I., 26, which gives the

Creation of ADAM; Gen. I., 27, which gives the Creation of THE ADAM, and male and female; and Gen. II., 22, gives the making of EVE, the wife of THE ADAM. These three verses correctly translated from the Hebrew, are as follows:

Gen. I., 26. And God said, Let US make ADAM in OUR image after our likeness, and let THEM have dominion over the fish of the sea, and over the fowl of the air, and over the cattle, and over all the earth, and over every creeping thing that creepeth upon the earth.

Gen. I., 27. And God created THE ADAM in HIS own image; in the image of God created HE him; male and female created *He* them.

Gen. II., 22. And the rib which the Lord God had taken from THE ADAM, made HE a woman, and brought her unto THE ADAM.

On page 58 will be found who were created under the name ADAM, and who under the name THE ADAM, and male and female. Under the name ADAM were created the five Gentile races, who have held "dominion" over all the earth during all history, and the definition of the name is given in Gen. V., 2, as follows:

"Male and female created he THEM, and blessed THEM, and called their NAME ADAM, on the day when they were created," namely, in Gen. I., 26. Thus it will be seen that ADAM is a plural noun, and is the name of a class created.

The second division of the Creation of mankind was the Creation of THE ADAM, and male and female, which, with the making of EVE, was the establishment of the Created heads of the Hebrew race. THE ADAM and EVE being representative Hebrews, and the heads of the Jewish blood line, which evolved the Saviour, and the male and female, the Created heads of the Hebrews.

If the flood had been universal, as has been claimed in the translations, all of humanity would have been destroyed except Noah and his family, and Noah and his wife would have become the heads of the human races; but, the universality of the flood is not borne out by the Hebrew Inspiration. The daughters of THE ADAM committed the heinous offence of marrying into the Gentile races, and having children by them, as a punishment for which offence, God brought on a flood.

Gen. VI., 7. And the Lord said, I will destroy THE ADAM, whom I have created, from the face of the ground, from ADAM unto beast, and the creeping thing, and the fowl of the air, for it repenteth me that I have made them.

It will be seen from this, and further examination of Gen. VI, and Gen. VII, and Gen. VIII, that every THE ADAM except Noah and his family were destroyed for cause, "from ADAM unto beast."—ADAM the Gentiles being the boundary on the one side, and beast on the other, so that even the Hebrew people were not destroyed, and no others except the Jewish line, which committed the sin. In fact, all of humanity except the descendants of THE ADAM and EVE, remained unharmed.

The reader will naturally ask—How do I know that these renderings of Gen. I., 26, Gen. I., 27, Gen. II., 22, and Gen. VI., 7, are correct, when they differ from all the translated Bibles in common use that I have ever seen? We answer, that this subject substantially has been presented in pamphlet or book form to at least two thousand Divines or Hebrew scholars, with the request that if we had made any errors or mistakes, that we would be truly thankful to have them pointed out that corrections might be made.

Although this request has been run through a period of many years, not a single adverse criticism has been received, but, on the contrary, many have coincided and admitted that the positions taken are correct. Even this statement may not satisfy some readers, and in order that they may satisfy themselves, if they do not read the Hebrew, we would suggest that they ask any Divine, acquainted with the Hebrew, or any Hebrew scholar, the following questions :

Q. Is ADAM found in Gen. I., 26, in the Hebrew Inspiration, and is its meaning defined in Gen. V., 2 ?

Q. Is THE ADAM found in like manner in Gen. I., 27 ?

Q. Was EVE made from the rib of THE ADAM ?

Q. Hence, was THE ADAM the husband of EVE ?

Q. Was any more of humanity to be destroyed than THE ADAM, as stated in Gen. VI., 7 ?

If these questions be answered in the affirmative, the reader will require no further aid in rightly understanding this portion of the Genesis, and by reading the remainder connected with it, he can form his own conclusion as to its accuracy and importance. Will these conclusions coincide and agree with the Bible of Nature, of which they are a part?

The Science of Ethnology has established six original types of the human family, namely: the Caucasian, the Mongolian, the Malay, the Indian, the Negro, and the Hebrew. These have also varieties in type. We see with our own eyes, these types persistently reproduced, and all history confirms our present knowledge. Then where is their place in the Genesis Creation, in order that they may have been continued to the present time by reproduction in type?

The heads of the Gentile races are found in Gen. I., 26, in ADAM, while the heads of the Hebrew race are found in Gen. I., 27, and Gen. II., 22, in THE ADAM and EVE, and male and female, so that the Bible of Nature on these points exactly coincides and agrees with the Hebrew Inspiration. Here, then, we have exact knowledge proving thus far the Hebrew Inspiration, and as the result, the following genealogies:

The five Gentile races, trace back their genealogies to ADAM, in Gen. I., 26.

The Hebrew, proper, trace back their genealogies to male and female, Gen. I., 27.

The Jewish line, which is also Hebrew, is plainly laid down in Scripture, and can be distinctly traced back to THE ADAM and EVE, giving a clear and unmistakable genealogy of Jesus Christ, from them to Joseph and Mary.

From this it will be seen that there is a solid foundation in Natural facts for the Spiritual Inspiration of a Bible.

THE TRANSLATORS BIBLES.

There seems to be no doubt that the Septuagint was the first compilation and translation into Greek of the inspired Hebrew manuscript, made 290 years B. C. This was the first Bible put in circulation among the Jews, for their information of what was contained in the Inspired manuscripts, and, of course, only contained the books of the old Testament. Considering the state of knowledge at that time of the intricacies of the Laws of God in Nature, or in other words, the reading of the Bible of Nature, it is not surprising, that when the translators undertook to write of these laws, they were liable to make gross errors.

The Septuagint seems to be responsible for the first establishment of a unity of the race in ADAM and EVE, and from this has followed two sets of translations, the Protestant and the Roman Catholic versions, each of which follow the mistake of the unity of the race as in the Septuagint in substance, but accomplish it by different processes in Gen. I., 26, 27, while both arrive at the same result by the flood.

As there are but two general Divisions of translations distinguished by the mode of making a unity of the race, we shall take the King James' Bible as the representative of the Protestant Division, and the Douay Bible as the representative of the Roman Catholic Division. We shall also give by name simply the various translations of any importance in the two Divisions, that the reader may see the diversity of views and conclusions of Christians upon the teachings of the Bible. Our investigations must be considered as applying alone to statements of Natural facts, and not to constructions of any spiritual portions of Scripture. We claim that that belongs exclusively to the Theologians.

As the Roman Catholic Bibles are the oldest translations, they must, of necessity, be first considered. The only authorized version of a Bible in the Roman Catholic Church is the Latin Vulgate, and it was in use as the old Latin Vulgate Bible about two hundred years before St. Jerome completed the translation of the present Latin Vulgate from the Hebrew and Greek manuscripts, in about 400 years A. D.

Although there have been any number of translations from the Vulgate into different languages, as the necessity of the case arose, their publication has only been approved by Bishops when they agreed with the Vulgate. No authority has ever been given by the Holy See for their publication as authorized versions, so that the Douay Bible now in use throughout the English World is not the authorized version of the Roman Church, its publication and circulation is only permissive by Bishops. Their New Testament was translated at Rheims, in 1532, and the Old Testament at Douay, in 1509–1510.

After the reformation in 1521, the necessity arose for a Protestant Bible, and numbers by different translators appeared; Tyndal's being the first attempt at Cologne, in English. Although what he did was not a complete Bible, he has been acknowledged a correct translator as far as he went. He took much from Martin Luther's German Bible, which was begun before the reformation, and finished in 1532.

Miles Coverdale, in 1535, printed the first entire English Bible.

Mathew's Bible, published in 1537, was a revision of Tyndal, and was finished by John Rogers.

Travner's Bible, published in 1539, was the Mathew's Bible corrected.

Cranmer's Bible, published in 1539, was called the Great Bible.

The Geneva Bible was published at Geneva in 1560, and was a revision of the Great Bible.

The Bishop's Bible, published in 1568, was also a revision of the Great Bible.

The King James' Bible, published in 1611, is the authorized version for the Protestant Churches.

The Westminster or Oxford Revision, published in 1886, is a revision of the King James' Bible.

We now give the extracts from the Douay and King James' Bibles, that establish the unity of the race.

DOUAY BIBLE.

Gen. I., 26. And God said, let us make man (Hebrew ADAM) to our image and likeness, and let *him* (Hebrew them) have dominion over the fishes of the sea, and the fowls of the air, and the beasts, and the whole earth, and every creeping creature that moveth upon the earth.

Gen. I., 27. And God created man (Hebrew THE ADAM) to His own image; to the image of God He created him; male and female, created He them.

Gen. V., 2.   He created them male and female and blessed them, and called their name ADAM in the day when they were created.

Gen. VI., 7.   He said, I will destroy man (Hebrew THE ADAM), whom I have created, from the face of the earth, from man (Hebrew ADAM) even to beast, from the creeping things unto the fowls of the air, for it repenteth me that I had made them.

KING JAMES' AUTHORIZED VERSION.

Gen. I., 26.   And God said, let us make man (Hebrew ADAM) in our image after our likeness, and let them have dominion over the fish of the sea, and over the fowl of the air, and over the cattle, and over all the earth, and over every creeping thing that creepeth upon the earth.

Gen. I., 27.   So (Hebrew And for So) God created man (Hebrew THE ADAM for man) in His own image; in the image of God created He him; male and female, created He them.

Gen. V., 2.   Male and female, created He them, and blessed them, and called their name ADAM in the day when they were created.

Gen. VI., 7.   And the Lord said, I will destroy man (Hebrew THE ADAM for man) whom I have created, from the face of the earth, both man and beast (Hebrew from ADAM unto beast, for both man and beast), and creeping thing, and fowl of the air, for it repenteth me that I have made them.

The Westminster or Oxford Revision follows the King James' version in these verses, with but two exceptions. The translators returned the Hebrew word "And" for "So" at the head of Gen. I., 27, a material and very important correction, fully referred to heretofore. The other variation is quite immaterial in using the word "ground" for "earth" in Gen. VI., 7.

In the King James' version the unity of the race is accomplished by leaving out of the Creative account in Gen. I., 26, the name ADAM, found in the Hebrew, and substituting "man," and the same term for THE ADAM in Gen. I., 27. As the word "So" has to be dropped by ecclesiastic authority, and the Hebrew word "And" substituted, we make no account of this. In addition to this, the destruction by flood of all humanity except Noah and his family. Noah, by this translation, which is not correct, became the head, in reproduction, of the race of mankind. This, if correct, would complete the unity.

As the account now stands in the authorized version, with the restoration of the word "And," we cannot imagine how any one could make sense out of the two verses. "Man" is made plural by "them" in the same sentence in 26 v., while in the second, "Man" is made singular by the use of the word "him" in the same sentence. Can any one give a reason why ADAM and THE ADAM were left out of these verses by translators, without they had an object in doing so, especially as only twenty-four verses ahead ADAM is dropped down into the account for no apparent reason, and certainly with no explanation of the meaning of the term.

It is claimed in the authorized version that all of humanity had their created origin in ADAM and EVE, and as we have seen, ADAM is the created head of the Gentile races, therefore Jesus Christ had his created head in these races according to this account. But, if the translation in this version be taken as correct, Noah became the reproductive head of humanity subsequent to that date, and he becomes responsible for the production of the race-types now found upon the earth.

The Douay Bible makes the unity of the race by making "man," in Gen. I., 26, a singular noun, and the same in Gen. I., 27, thereby showing but one man created. It, in like manner with the King James Bible, by an incorrect translation, makes the flood universal, and Noah becomes the head of the reproduced races.

It will be seen that in neither of the translations has the Saviour a defined created head, and it is left for conjecture which of the five Gentile races Jesus Christ had descended from.

The reader will observe that the names ADAM and THE ADAM were given by God himself, and take a far higher rank than other Scriptural names given by peoples. It is a grave responsibility for translators to drop THE ADAM entirely out of sight, and to drop ADAM in places and retain it in others, whereby the reader is misled in his conception of the account, which engenders disbelief.

It would be just as scriptural, if not less so, for the translators to drop the names of Eve, Noah,

Abraham, David, Daniel, Solomon, and Joseph and Mary, and translate them according to his will.

The names ADAM and THE ADAM are the rightful property of the reader, and they should appear in every Bible in places where they occur in the Hebrew. God will take care of a Bible in His own words, but the unrest, the non-communions, the bickerings, open quarrels and general contentions in the Christian Churches, require some oil to be thrown upon the troubled waters.

CAUSE AND EFFECT.

That the same cause, operating under the same circumstances, produces the same effect, is a universally admitted law of Nature, and about this there can be no controversy or misunderstanding. It is a law in use in our every day life, and in all our varied occupations and operations—without it we should not be able to foretell any result from Natural causes. We would sow our fields with grain, with a void conception whether they would produce any return or not. Man would strike his fellow man with an axe, without knowing whether it would hurt him or not. The father might cut off the head of his child, without knowing that it would produce death; and so we might go through with a catalogue of every act, and form of act, in which matter forms an element, with the same uncertainty or ignorance of the effect or result, was it not for our knowledge of this universal and well-understood law.

It must be distinctly understood, however, that the law of cause and effect applies only to things and acts of things already created, and not to the mode and manner of their creation, as that can only be arrived at by analogical reasoning ; and while the latter may be facts established by this process, they are not facts within our actual knowledge.

It then becomes of the first importance to find out, of what cause is made up, how controlled, and how operated. If we sow, or strike, or kill intentionally, we know that the mind conceives and designs the act, and the body executes with a certainty of the effect. It is then evident that cause to produce an effect is the operation of a mind to conceive and design the result in accordance with knowledge and previous experience, and this is applicable to all animate Nature.

The same law applies to all inanimate things, the only difference being the kind of mind operating in the causes in the vegetable and mineral kingdoms, if we may be permitted to use mind in this connection. To arrive at some conclusion on this point, we ask the following questions :

What guides the grain of wheat in its growth, and where springs the design ?

What guides the flower in its charming varied colors, and what conceived the beautiful design?

What guides the crystal in its variety of uniform forms in type, and whence springs the varied designs ?

What guides the shooting needle of ice in freezing water, and whence the design?

We might continue these questions throughout the range of Nature, and the answer might be, it is the plan and acts of the Creator. Admit that this would be the first answer to the questions, and we would be compelled to ask another. Are these momentary acts of supervision, or are they the result of law, made inherent in the matter operating them?

No one can answer this question, and it is not material to us to have it answered, as we are certain that the cause produces the uniform effect, whatever may be the elements composing the causes.

We incline to the belief that cause is governed in the animal, vegetable and mineral kingdoms, by what may be termed volition, as a quality endowed upon matter, and that the supervision of God of all things is to see that these laws, established in the Creation, are continued in reproduction in uniformity.

Whether this be so or not, all mankind have settled down, and recognize the law, that like causes produce uniformly like results, and this law is the polar star of our existence. Its proper application will solve many doctrines, theories, and speculations that have confused and mystified the Christian mind, and engendered chaos and doubt where order should have reigned.

The Bible of Nature, of which this law is the basis, as we have said before, has been and now is read by every human being, from the cradle to the grave, according to the knowledge each possesses.

The infant has the mind to execute the design of obtaining food, and seeks the bottle or the breast as the effect of the cause. As the child grows in knowledge, he performs every act of life according to this same law. He gains information as he grows, and that knowledge and experience enables him to cope with life in any department of industry or thrift. He then concludes, and rightly, that he has acquired absolute knowledge, which will serve him at all times and under all circumstances. He will, however, soon learn that the consequences of effects are not the law. For however wisely the effects may be designed for good, he will meet with disappointments, reverses, and heart-rending scenes.

He goes on with his designs to produce effects almost thoughtlessly, it having become a habit, till one day he was pouring water out of a vessel onto the ground, and the thought occurred to him, why the water went down instead of up. He knew no reason himself, because his education had not reached that point, though he knew the facts. He betook himself to a learned neighbor, who informed him that a distinguished scientist named Newton had demonstrated that a law of God, called gravity, existed, which made the water go down instead of up.

He then pursued further his studies through all the scientific discoveries of the chemists, the philosophers, the ethnologists, the botanists, mathematicians, the mineralogists, the astronomers, and all other sciences which have aided in developing the Natural Laws of God. When he had acquired all this great store-house of exact knowledge, he was prepared to read all of the Bible of Nature as far as discoveries have gone, and, of course, was prepared to read the Genesis account of Creation in the Hebrew, which contains every scientific principle in its equilibrium now known. It is doubtful whether any scientist of the present day unaided, could write that account without an error in some of its finer points.

The intelligent reader can thus judge for himself whether the Genesis account of Creation was the product of Inspiration or a literary hit, considering that the principles developed there are supposed to have been unknown to the writer. The salient point to be determined in this connection is, whether the Created origin of mankind in the Hebrew coincides with the Bible of Nature on this subject, or do the translations, or any one of them, coincide and agree with it.

We bring forward this law of Cause and Effect to prove mathematically, as we believe, that the Hebrew Inspiration agrees and coincides exactly with the Bible of Nature.

We will first take up the types of mankind as they now exist on earth, and by application of the law of cause and effect, trace them back through all time to the account of their Creation in the Genesis. During all history, these types have existed, and no type has ever been known to produce another and distinct type. We will consider first the Caucasian or white race, the most important and controlling one of them all. Then what is the cause of the birth of a Caucasian child? The child is the effect, and as every effect is due to a cause, what is the cause? Education and experience on this point are so perfect and universal, that the cause need not be stated in terms. Now, if we found that this child was the only one ever known to have been born from the law of cause and effect, we should have no other fact to rely upon. But this is not so; some other children were born before, and others born after, of the same type, so that the law of cause and effect operated just the same before as it did after the first effect, a Caucasian child always being the same, and consequently the cause was always the same.

Parenthetically, we would say that we do not believe that the most earnest supporters of the unity of the race, or any one else of that race, who was married, would be willing to have the law of cause and effect in reproduction of types repealed or abrogated, and run the chances of having their issue a Mongolian, a Malay, an Indian, a Negro, or a Hebrew. It is a fundamental law of the Genesis Creation that all continued or reproduced forms in Nature shall be "after its kind," and the example of the punishment by flood for its violation by the daughters of THE ADAM, should be a warning to all who disregard or stultify this foundation law.

The Caucasian white race, as we see and know by absolute knowledge, is persistently reproduced in pure type throughout the world where they exist, and we can trace back by the unerring law of cause and effect, from the Caucasian child to its cause, the father and mother, and thence back to their fathers and mothers, and so on till we reach the first of the type in the Genesis Creation. Nothing but a change of the law of reproduction which extends through all Nature, could alter this line of Caucasian reproduction in type. This chain of the law of cause and effect is made up of links welded by the laws of God in Nature, and cannot be broken by the sophistries of speculation or construction, or by the ignorance of Natural Laws by translators.

The same chain is found in every type of humanity, and in every type of the animal, vegetable or mineral kingdoms, and therefore we have the right to expect to find their Created heads in the Genesis account, which we do, and clearly find them there. This proves mathematically thus far, as we believe, the Genesis Inspiration, and that being the foundation of Natural facts of the Bible of Inspiration, it shows conclusively that this is a solid and true foundation for the spiritual revelation.

Every act in Nature, from the Creation to the present moment, has been the output of this law of cause and effect, and is absolute knowledge. The concrete of these acts and results cannot be numbered by any permutations and combinations of our arithmetical figures, so that it is bewildering to consider this vast store-house of knowledge.

There is but one great cause and effect not as yet referred to, and which has no preceding act in type, and none that follows it. It is, however, governed by this universal law, as no effect can exist without a cause. We see a world and a universe as the effect, and by the Nature of the laws, there must have been a cause. That cause, like all other cases of cause, must have had a mind to design, to be executed in accordance with the Laws of Nature as the effect. This demands a Creator or a God as much as any other effect in Nature must alike have a cause. We therefore say, that the law of cause and effect proves the necessity for and existence of a God as a cause, when we see and know by actual knowledge the existence of the effect.

This can be made more clear from analogical reasoning. The number of separate causes and effects in Nature, since the Creation, may be stated as nearly infinite, every one of which is acknowledged as true and exact knowledge. Are not these almost infinite proofs of a law sufficient for our acknowledgment of the one single case of cause and effect in the creation of the universe? On any other subject, even of like importance and magnitude, we should call it a mathematical demonstration.

CREATION MAKERS.

The most numerous class of Creation makers have been the Translators of the Scriptures, in making the unity instead of the diversity of races in the human family, that being the most important element of creation. We believe, however, that they are not wholly responsible for this error—Education is a tyrant, especially upon the subject of Holy Writ. The machinery of the churches has confined education to given lines, and the Clergy have been educated to those lines and are expected to teach within them, or be charged with and expelled for heresy.

It is, therefore, dangerous for a clergyman belonging to any denomination to teach any doctrine not laid down as his guide, whatever he may think or conclude to the contrary. This would seem to be a stern necessity, in order to maintain a system and uniformity of instruction. These facts are apparent from what we see daily of the charges and counter-charges of heresy in some denominations of Christians, who seem to be dealing in differentials as the rule.

While all Christian churches have the same creed, the man-machineries of many of them have amplified it to such an extent that it would seem to an outside observer, that these denominations were striving to have their own Bible and their own creed.

This state of things will continue and grow worse as long as individual ideas are substituted for the pure creed ; and, until we obtain a Bible which will inspire belief in its accuracy of Inspiration, instead of disbelief—or, in other words, until the Bible of Inspiration coincides and agrees with the Bible of Nature, which we know is exact knowledge. When and how this can be brought about is a vexed problem.

There have been various speculations and theories as to the mode and manner of Creation, and various methods concocted to harmonize them with the Genesis account. If the Genesis account be correct, there is no sound reason for any effort to harmonize some other account with it, for the simple announcement to endeavor to harmonize indicates a conflict. Among the most important of these theories are those of the Geologic and Evolution theories. The Geologic theory is rather on the wane, and the Evolution theory is coming forward to take its place.

It is very difficult to state in terms the exact principles claimed by each. The Geologic theory requires so many suppositions and assumptions in order to make even a plausible connection possible, that a settled and scientific mode of Creation, without the violation of Natural Law, cannot be arrived at.

The whole theory from beginning to end is based on appearances of created forms, and the science so called is simply mineralogy, with these appearances added to show the mode and manner of creating minerals and metals, and from these to reason as to the mode and manner of creating all other existences.

The Geologist first assumes a state of fusion, and then cooling of the mass of the earth, and this supposition is made from certain appearances in the primary rocks. We need not ask what became of the water gases and the easily-used metals and minerals, all of which have a different point of fusibility.

The next supposition is, that rocks called sedimentary, were deposited by degrees by water rubbing against something, and the debris settled into layers, and from these appearances they draw this conclusion. In order to gain time for these operations, which required millions of years, they have to make the Scriptural day referred to everywhere in Scripture, and especially in the Ten Commandments, an elastic rubber string of no defined length or elasticity. Then to apply the acknowledged law of cause and effect, how can they account for the almost infinite variety of existing rocks from the same cause? But, they say, the various fossils found in these rock formations, determine their precedence and age. Can any Geologist determine from appearances a created fossil from one which followed the laws of cause and effect? If two men were presented to him, the one created and the other reproduced by the law of cause and effect, could he tell from appearances which was which?

The assumption that God did not make the fossil as He made all other things which are reproduced, is the vital and controlling assumption of the so-called **science of Geology**, and until it can be shown otherwise, Geology has no standing as a science further than simple mineralogy.

In discussing the Geologic theory, we are aware that we run counter to the teachings in many institutions of learning and the opinions of many learned and scientific men; and on the other hand, there is probably an equal number who do not accept the theory. Nothing but the necessity of a full discussion of the subject in hand, has led to a reference to the theory at all. The opinion, however, of one man, will probably not produce a ripple on men's convictions in the premises.

EVOLUTION.

A theory that claims as its salient point that God did not make the created man in full and perfect form as he is now on earth, but experimented by first creating what had no semblance to a man, and by degrees and thousands of years trying, brought forth something resembling a man, and then jumping the chasm of the "missing link," seize on to other forms still more resembling man, till the real man is finally reached and made in the image of God, is at least not a concluded theory, as the missing link is still wanting.

The theory is degrading to the wisdom of God's design and power to execute that design, and lowers Him to that of an experimentalist, placing Him in the same rank with the student sculptor, who at first moulds his clay into fancied forms, and after years of labor and trials is finally enabled to arrive at his original design of exactness in beauty of the human being, after the image of God.

Evolution is an attractive word, and it is attractive because it is a true term, if no other meaning is attached to it, which it does not deserve. All things are evolved from the hand of God, or by reproduction in type. But the deduction from this theory is, that types have been evolved from other and distinct types, till a perfect type in the present complete form of man was obtained. Thus God's design to make man, started, as is claimed, in a type of the Molusk, and by successive jumps to other types till the monkey type was reached, and then again, by successive jumps in the monkey types to the highest type of the monkey races.

Unable to go further and show that man is a monkey or a monkey a man, the theorists acknowledge that the link-type to do this is wanting, and here they are compelled to acknowledge Scripture teachings and the law of cause and effect, that God did make man, and did do so in the manner therein set forth. It may be a matter of pride for those favoring the theory of evolution, to boast of their aristocratic ancestors having been evolved from this monkey and snail business, but to those who regard this theory as humiliating to the power of God, and as violating all His Natural Laws upon the subject, it is regarded as a criminal libel against

Him. Those Christians who love the Saviour, are overcome with disgust at the bare announcement, that He, the purest, and most exalted conception by God of the human form, should have sprung from the lowest animal type of His creation.

The theory of evolution as developed, is in exact coincidence with the reasoning of the wag, who claimed that Fox was derived by development from Fog by the following direct process. Fog — mist — rain — rain-fast — rain-hard — Reynard — Fox.

That there have been improvements in types will be acknowledged by all, and that these improvements have naturally altered the original forms. But there is a material difference between improvement in type, and evolution of one type from another and distinct type. Improvement in type does not make a new type, no more than the cleaning of a rusty stove makes a new stove.

Creation-making is the assumption of the powers of God. We shall never know why He made this or made that, nor determine the reason or manner of making each individual thing, except so far as such thing is a necessary element of the whole. It would be truly gratifying if we could have one uniform Bible for all Christian churches, and until we do, there will be a suspicion resting, that many of them or some of them are wrong, and this suspicion and uncertainty will continue to the detriment of mankind, until all Christendom shall have a Bible bereft of apparent errors, and which shall coincide and agree with the Bible of Nature, the only source of exact knowledge we have. The intelligence and progress of the Nineteenth Century would seem to demand a change.

FOURTH ADDENDA.
January, 1894.

SUBJECTS:

OBEY THE LAWS OF GOD.

CHRISTIAN RELIGION.

BELIEF AND FAITH.

CONSCIENCE, THE RUDDER OF LIFE.

THE HIGHER AND UPPER PLANE OF CHRISTIANITY.

FOURTH ADDENDA.

January, 1894.

OBEY THE LAWS OF GOD.

It was not our intention to continue this subject further than the material laws, connected directly, or indirectly with the creation, and subsequent reproduction of humanity on earth. But from the elucidation follows as a necessity, corollaries of fact, highly interesting and instructive, bearing upon the great design of the Christian religion, and its final accomplishment and workings.

There is nothing in the universe that is not the Creation of God, whether material or immaterial, and nothing which has not its individual law to regulate its action, and perform its allotted part in the great scheme. Every compound form, that is every form made up of elements essential to its perfection, has its group of elementary laws, acting in unison with each other, and with the general law which governs the body, and the group of elementary laws. Simple elements, such as light, heat, air, space, gravity, electricity, magnetism and the like, are each a law unto themselves, so that the number of separate and distinct laws are just equal to the number of distinct elements comprising the universe.

We know nothing of the composition of these laws, any more than we know the composition of God, but we see and know the effects of both, and are justified in our conclusions as to the existence of both. No one, we think, can realize the magnitude and sublime accuracy of the scheme and design of the Christian religion, without they have a knowledge of the laws governing the material and immaterial elements of our bodies. The material elements have no primary connection with our responsibility to God, but as will be seen, are used by the immaterial faculties to assist, when such subjects are presented for action.

The human body contains material and immaterial elements, almost without number. In the course of reproduction of the various types, some one of these elements would be neglected or forgotten if left to human agency; but the laws of God never forget, never change. Millions are born, millions die, and other millions follow, but the elements in each type are always the same, always have been, and always will be, till the end. As has been remarked, every element of the universe has had its law established to regulate its existence, and but for these laws of regulation no mind can conceive the state of chaos that would result. But we are left in no such dilemma, order reigns throughout. The sun rises and sets. The seasons come, loaded with food for man. Flowers decorate the land, the Springs of the earth gush forth their pure, cool waters, and we would all be happier and better if we would study the Bible of Nature deeper, and see what God is doing for us every moment, hour and year.

The interesting problem is to determine what law has been established to regulate our responsibility to God and our conduct towards our fellow-man. No material law of the body will answer to this requirement, because every result of such law is material. There is a group of immaterial laws, which is generally denominated mind, and among these we must look for the one law, which opens the gateway of the immaterial man to the immaterial God. Considering the variety of views entertained on any subject of this nature, our knowledge teaches us that the law must be confined to one faculty of the mind, as in any other event there would be conflict. The way must be open, clear and direct, as on this point rests all man's responsibility to God, and certainly He would not cloud this vital path with any division of power, between conflicting elements.

When this group of laws of the mind is examined, one by one, the wisdom of the single law governing all the others, on this particular subject, is made apparent. This law is conscience, and will be fully treated under that head in a future article. It is enough to say in this connection that it is the monitor of right or wrong, and is constituted with an option to decide to do the one or the other. It must be remembered that the law establishing the conscience is one thing, and the application of the law by man is quite another, so that sin, which is the violation of God's law, is not of God, but the choice of man.

In order to gain a clear conception of the connecting link between man and his God, it will be necessary to go back to the beginning of Creation, and then trace forward the evident design of each step to accomplish this end. It would be the height of folly to suppose that this grand Creation of a universe of worlds, of which this world of ours is one, and then create the noble classes of men to enjoy the blessings which flow from it, without constructing man with qualities that would enable him to appreciate that he was made to fill some important place for some appreciable end.

We have an accurately scientific account of the Creation of the universe given in the Hebrew Genesis, which has been certified to as correct, by the discovery and development of laws, established for its regulation, and which now exist and carry on this stupendous work, and he is neither a scientist, or a wise man, who undertakes to improve upon God's plan of Creation, and continuance of His creations by established laws. Each law, in a compound form, is dependent upon every other law in that form, and also dependent upon every other law of any other form acting in conjunction with it, so that no law can be changed or abrogated without a destruction of equilibrium in the entire structure ; and as equilibrium is essential to the working of the universe, worlds, suns, planets and satelites, we state it as a scientific fact, that no law of God, applicable to matter, has ever been changed one iota since the Creation. What we see and know of these laws to-day, was the same yesterday, last year, and a thousand years ago.

Immaterial laws being from the same fountain as material laws, have the same binding force, and are in all respects as unchanging.

Conscience, Reason and Will, as immaterial laws were the foundation stones implanted in man, for the purpose of erecting upon them the scheme of the Christian religion for his protection and guidance in the world. When Christ had finished His work on earth, and completed His platform of the Christian religion, every word of that platform, and every sentence of it was the fixed, unchanging and everlasting Word of God, and was a law as a whole and a group of subordinate laws, all acting in harmony. He gave no authority to any one, to add to or deduct from these laws one iota in word or sense.

What means have we of verifying this position, and what authority can we cite to satisfy the intelligent mind on this subject? We answer, first, the laws of God in operation, which we see and know; second, the Old and New Testament in the Hebrew and Greek respectively. We think the commonly used terms, Natural and Spiritual laws are misleading, and should be called material and immaterial laws. The material laws being those applying to matter alone, and the immaterial when matter is incidentally concerned. It is, however, of little consequence what these laws are called, so long as people can understand their existence and use.

If we had no Bible record, the existing laws of God compiled would show the Creation, and the working of all its elements the same as it now exists, has existed, and will exist for all time. This is a part of God's Bible, the Bible of Nature. If this Bible had been printed and circulated as the Word of God, with clear explanations of all His material laws, it would astound the larger portion of mankind, and there would not be a voice raised against it, for it would be just what they see and know daily. They now read every Bible, printed in various languages throughout the world, which overrides and violates God's law in the most vital point, namely, man's existence and relation to his Maker being committed to the theology of the unity of the race in ADAM and EVE ; that is, that all types of humanity that have existed on earth have been reproduced from one man and one woman. It would have been a little more satisfactory, but none the less true, if the theologians had informed us whether ADAM and EVE were Caucasian, Mongolian, Malay, Indian, Negro, or Hebrew.

This theology of the unity of the race, has done more to engender and spread disbelief in the Bible as a whole, than all the preachings on this point have done good ; for now as knowledge and education have extended, this disbelief has become universal, for all men have eyes, and are enquiring why God and the present Bibles are in conflict. There is so much good and instruction in the remainder of our Bibles, though handicapped as they are by this glaring error, that true Christians still cling to the hope of salvation, which they contain, condone the error, and ask why such teachings go on in our churches, and why Bibles are still put forth, copying this error made by men, no one knows who, 290 years B.C., and blindly copied ever since.

This subject has been fully discussed in this work, and no adverse answer given to the position taken, either as to the Creation or the flood, by any Divine or Hebrew Scholar; but as some do not seem to understand it fully, we will again call attention to the Creation portion of it. On pages 150 and 151 will be found a correct translation from the Hebrew of Gen. I., 26, 27, and Gen. II., 22, and Gen. V., 2, from which any reader of English will see that Gen. I., 26, 27, records the Creation of three classes of people, namely:

Gen. I., 26.   ADAM, male and female, *created*.
Gen. V., 2.
Gen. I., 27.   HA-ADAM, or THE ADAM, *created*.
Gen. I., 27.   Male and female *created* He them.

It has been claimed by the advocates of the unity of the race, that these two verses give the account of the Creation of ADAM and EVE, from whom have come all of humanity. The first error is—that EVE never was *created* at all, but was *made* from the rib of HA-ADAM or THE ADAM, some time after he was put into the Garden of Eden to dress it and keep it, and after all the created things were in full working order.

The second error is—the assertion by the advocates of the unity of the race, that no other females were created except EVE. God's word declares that there were females created on the day of Creation, and as EVE did not exist on that day, and was never *created*, a direct and complete denial of the truth of God's word results. This is not all: for these advocates deny the truth of God's laws of reproduction in the human family; and as we know these laws by experience and knowledge, to ignore and deny them is a more flagrant sin than to deny what we believe to be His Word written by men. As the created heads of mankind were the foundation of God's work in establishing the Christian religion, a correct understanding of that work is of primary importance to Christians, and any conflict between God and man on this subject, throws a cloud over the whole scheme of salvation, and laws regulating man's conduct on this earth.

It is then of paramount interest to review the Scriptures, and examine each act of God, step by step, tending to this end, throughout the extent of this magnetic line, from the Creation to the finishing of Christ's work; and that all events were drawn to, and aided in its accomplishment.

All collateral circumstances of history, which the superficial reader would regard as isolated and independent facts, had some direct bearing to bring about the accomplishment of the great design. The Creation of the universe presents nothing more grand and conclusive than the means used to send Christ on earth, after a series of years of preparation, to finish God's purpose.

> Here sprang the God thought of Creation bold,
> From nothing, mighty worlds on worlds t' unfold;
> To stretch the azure curtain of the skies;
> To deck it, with its million shining eyes;
> To ope Creation from His hand a scroll,
> And poise the whirling worlds from pole to pole.
> Page 109.

Here was the stupendous design, and at once followed its immediate consummation, and mankind on this earth was furnished with a beautiful home, stored with all conceivable varieties of delicious food, with the glorious sun light by day, and the spangled draping of the skies by night. Volumes could be written, describing the beauties and uses of our home ; but every one knows just what we would say, if they will but stop and think.

Our home being thus prepared and finished in all its parts, and in complete running and working order, mankind was created, all over the face of the earth, with the command to increase and multiply. The Genesis account informs us of two classes of people created; those in Gen. I., 26, were to have dominion over all the earth, while those created in Gen. I., 27, had no such power given them. This word "dominion," gives the careful reader the power to determine what people were created, and endowed with that quality, and what people were not endowed with that quality. Another evidence of the distinctive Creations is, that the first class was created by the Triune God. "Let *us* make ADAM in our image, after *our* likeness, and let them have dominion, etc." The second class, when Jesus Christ was to be involved as a lineal descendant of HA-ADAM, or THE ADAM, and EVE was created by God alone, without the assistance of Jesus Christ and the Holy Ghost. " And God created HA-ADAM, or THE ADAM, in His *own* image; in the image of God created He him; male and female created He them."

As history tells us, who and what races have held dominion on the earth for all time, and now hold dominion, and also the race which has not held dominion, and is now a scattered people over the face of the whole earth, it follows that the first class comprised the Caucasians, Mongolians, Malays, Indians and Negroes, and the second class the Hebrews. THE ADAM and EVE and their descendants were Hebrews; but being selected by God as the heads of the Jewish line, that was to evolve Jesus Christ, the Bible History is mainly made up of the acts of this particular line of people, who were in later times called Jews. The question may now be asked, what has this Creation, and this distribution of humanity to do with the establishment of the Christian religion? We think they have everything to do with it, and we will give our views about it for what they are worth. They principally relate to the Hebrew race. This race is admitted to be the chosen people of God, and we think the admission is well founded. The selection by God of THE ADAM and EVE out of this race, to produce a line of descendants, that should evolve Jesus Christ, the Saviour of mankind, is conclusive evidence that God directed this particular mode of bringing Christ on earth, that he might make for the world, by his sayings, doings and example, the platform of the Christian religion.

The mode of making EVE out of the body of THE ADAM, has its peculiar significance. We all know what a strain of blood is, in animals, as well as in mankind. Peculiarities of character in families, run sometimes for generations, then disappear, and reappear again in after generations. This is a law of blood strains, not an accidental trait of the parents, and results from a mixture of the different strains in the issue. By making EVE out of the rib of THE ADAM, there would be but one, pure strain of blood, without adulteration. Hence Christ would be born in a pure strain, direct from the hand of the Creator. This may be considered by some, far-fetched; but it must be remembered, that THE ADAM and EVE were the only pair linked together for reproduction in this peculiar way, all others of humanity created, were to be married and given in marriage. The case of THE ADAM and EVE is the only one known, where God chose the wife for the man, and performed the ceremony of marriage Himself.

We have said that the Hebrew race was the chosen people of God. Why chosen, and for what purpose? The Bible history clearly shows this by the direct supervision of God over, and His acts towards them, and when we come to consider the part they played in the crucifixion of Christ, and what resulted, we are constrained to say, that we are indebted for the consummation of the Christian religion to this race, which we think, can be clearly shown. The first evidence we have of a religion was God's command to THE ADAM, not to eat of the tree of life, and his violation of that command. This presents the governing principle of the Christian religion, namely, man's responsibility to God, and his punishment for disobedience of His laws. Here then was the first step in the establishment of the Christian religion, as this simple principle is its foundation stone; and as responsibility to God was equally applicable to all men, reason teaches us, that all created beings were subject to this responsibility. We have no Scriptural account in the Genesis of this applicability, except to the Hebrew race, and particularly to the Jewish line that was to evolve Christ, the Redeemer, and Finisher of the Christian religion.

The second evidence we have of these principles was the disobedience of God's laws of reproduction "after its kind," by the daughters of THE ADAM, marrying into the Gentile races, and having children by them, which would be Hybrid Hebrews and Hybrid Gentiles, for which offence, and the offence of THE ADAM, dire and direct punishment was brought upon both, and upon their generations. First by the expulsion of THE ADAM from the Garden of Eden, and the hardships imposed upon him and his descendants. For the offence of the daughters, by which God lost all patience with this Jewish line, He brought on a flood that destroyed all the descendants of THE ADAM and EVE, including his daughters, except Noah and his family, who had committed no offence against God's laws.

The first organized religion of which we have any reliable account, was the Hebrew religion, established upon the laws given to Moses, of which the Ten Commandments contain the leading ideas, and these are embodied in Christ's platform of the Christian religion, and form the largest part of His teachings. The coming of the Messiah was taught in all the Hebrew Temples and was a leading idea in that religion, and so continued, up to the coming of Christ, and it still exists as part of their present religion. Their prophets frequently prophesied His coming, and appointed times and seasons for that event. So that the Messiah and His coming, were held up to this people, as an event as certain to take place as the rising of the sun ; and this education, undoubtedly, excited their imaginations to conceive the Messiah a doubtful form of grotesque man, or angel.

When Christ's Birth was announced, as having been born in a stable, and that the child outwardly was like any other child, they were all greatly disappointed.

The history of Christ's life need not be referred to for our purposes, except to say that He continued in the Hebrew religion, was circumcised, and preached in their synagogues. His wonderful success in making converts to His principles, excited the envy of the Hebrews. This was the culminating point of the establishment of the Christian religion, the greatest and grandest event of the world, brought about by a long and continued struggle between God, the Hebrews and the Jews, to prepare them to join the Messiah on His advent. A few on hearing the logic of Christ's teachings were His converts and followers ; the masses, however, did not believe that Christ was their Messiah, and there arose two parties and a division in the Hebrew religion, and without that division, the crucifixion of Jesus Christ, under the then existing state of things, could never have taken place and the prophecies and Scriptures been fulfilled.

As we are informed, the Romans would not voluntarily have crucified Him, since Pilate the Governor said He had committed no offence against the law, and washed his hands of the affair; and his followers, certainly, would not have done this painful thing to a friend, so that there was no one to consummate His death except the envious Jews, whereby they unwittingly established the Christian religion, and raised an everlasting monument to Jesus Christ, reaching from the land of Judea to the very throne of God in Heaven. It is well here to refer to our previous remark, that under the circumstances then existing, we are indebted to the Jewish line of the Hebrew race, for the completion of God's design of establishing the Christian religion, and this could not have been done without a division in the followers of the Hebrew religion, one party acknowledging and accepting Christ as the True Messiah, the other rejecting Him and holding that the Messiah was yet to come.

The Hebrew race, the chosen people of God, were relieved of all the labors and responsibilities of temporal government, or "dominion," as called in the Genesis, and were scattered throughout the world, among the nations of the earth, to teach man's responsibility to God, and pave the way for the coming of the Redeemer by their writings in the Old Testament; and when, and after He came and proclaimed His religion, they wrote the Books of the New Testament, which contain the entire platform of the Christian religion. That platform was complete in every word, sentence and idea, and was the finished, unchangeable, and everlasting law of God.

There are two important divisions of this platform; the first is *conduct* in this world, this side of the grave, to be in accordance with its requirement; the second is faith in the promises held out to man, of a future state, beyond the grave, and both are explicit and clearly defined.

This platform, in all its parts, is a stereotyped law of God, fixed, unchanging and unchangeable as any other law, and takes equal rank with all others, for acknowledgment and obedience. For what is a law of God? It is His mode of regulating everything material or immaterial in the universe, and the law to regulate men's conduct in this world, to bear seed for the life to come, differs in no respect or character from His law, governing the growth of the plant, which we see every day of our lives, which consummates into the seed, to be sunk into the earth to bring forth a new existence and a new life. The promise to man is just the same as the promise to the plant, and the quicker man will come to this conclusion the quicker he will realize his full relation to God, and his real condition on this earth.

There is a class of Christians who claim that the translated Bibles now in use throughout the world, by the various denominations, are the Word of God. If this be so, what have they to say about the Bible written in the original language, and by men authorized by God to do so. The one is the Word of God by His authority, the other the work of man. Which shall we recognize, obey and teach, when the one plainly contradicts the other, and the one coincides and agrees with the active and daily recurrence of His laws which we see and know, and the other is not a transcript of the original language, nor an agreement in this respect. The one was written by God for the information of man, and the other to make out theologies.

We now come to one of the great principles of **advanced** Christianity. Shall the teachings of the Bible and of Christ be in accordance with God's laws, or in violation of them? If in accordance with them, we should examine carefully, closely and accurately what these laws are, and then examine with equal care what is the translated Bibles record of them. If on such examination it is found that the Bibles and teachings are in violation of them, both should be corrected, and the quicker the better for the Christian religion; for if the principle be admitted and taught that God has changed any law at any time, what security have we that He may not change His laws, in respect to the Christian religion, and the promises there held out to man for a future life of happiness, if he comply with all its requirements.

Another principle, which must be admitted as a corollary to the above proposition and examination is, that every completed step in a law of God is identical in all its governing features with every other step, from the Creation to the end of its existence. We now come to our closing remark on this portion of our subject. Christians must either admit these two propositions, or abandon the Christian religion as a certainty.

THE CHRISTIAN RELIGION.

The Christian Religion is CONDUCT, spiritual or otherwise, guided by the laws of God, and following the example and teachings of Jesus Christ, or their equivalents.

This is an active, not a passive definition, and places the Christian Religion and its object upon the basis of a natural fact, where it should be, and not upon belief, which we will show hereafter, under the head of belief and faith. There are two divisions of the Christian Religion : one made up of facts or history relating to conduct this side of the grave, and the second, faith in rewards or punishments promised beyond the grave, in a life to come, as the result of that conduct. This is plain, simple, and within easy comprehension of the most common intellect. The main point is for the Christian to find out what the conduct is that is required, and where and how he is able to reach that information.

The disciples of Christ who were intrusted by Him to teach all nations by preaching His Gospel, were mostly fishermen, illiterate and uneducated. Hence, they were not entrusted with their mission under any authority to add to, or deduct from, what they were authorized to teach, namely: the teachings, sayings, and to portray the exemplary every day conduct of Christ Himself. This is all of the platform of the Christian Religion. When Christ had finished His work on earth, that platform was completed in all its parts, simple, plain and conclusive, without mystery or cloudy evasiveness. The simplest mind could comprehend all of its requirements, and this is a standing proof that it was not made for high intelligence and the educated alone, but alike for all grades of intellect. It has, therefore, every element for a universal Religion for mankind, which no other religion now in existence on the earth possesses. It clearly points out man's responsibility to God, and shows the way that that responsibility is to be met and satisfied. The first thought then presented to the mind, is why there are so many different denominations, with different creeds and beliefs. This brings us to a more serious question, to ascertain which is right, or which is wrong, and still another, which is nearest right, and which is nearest wrong; and still another of graver importance, who is to be the judge and give the true answers to the questions? It is evident that no result could be obtained that would bring any two denominations to a coincidence of agreement, and still more, that no coincidence of agreement could possibly be obtained for all of them.

To the inquiring mind, these are momentous questions, and have engendered doubt in the minds of many, whether any persuasion of Christians has a solid foundation, and why? Because, as beliefs and faiths differ in every Christian Denomination from every other, who can, with certainty, declare that any one of them is the true and only true faith and belief? To arrive at any definite conclusion on this subject, we must first ascertain what is the Christian Religion, and what are its requirements, and then closely investigate our belief and faith and determine what they are, and how founded. The Christian Religion to have any standing, must be a unit as a whole—a law of God—finished, complete, everlasting, and unchangeable. It must be recognized as a general law, acting in conjunction and in harmony with a group of subordinate laws, composing the platform of the Christian Religion, which was completed when Christ's work on earth was finished, and consisted of His teachings, sayings, and exemplary conduct. Every word of Christ was a law of God; every sentence uttered by Him was a law of God; and every idea that He gave to the World was a law of God.

It is interesting to examine and see how the so-called Christian sects have originated, grown up, and extended into large proportions. The Bible, as a whole, and in every verse, is almost universally taken in all Christian Churches, as the words of Jesus Christ, and as a part of the Christian Religion. All of the Old Testament was written many years before Christ appeared on earth, and by authors who knew nothing of His Religion under the teachings of the Mosaic religion of which they wrote. When Christ did come on earth, they spurned Him and His religion, and crucified Him because they did not believe He was the true Messiah. They taught in their Temples and Synagogues the coming of a Messiah, and their Prophets so prophesied, so that collaterally, they believed in a Messiah. Their writings throughout the Old Testament were not of the Christian Religion, but of a religion adverse to it in many respects, though they struck some of the key-notes of that religion at times.

The Old Testament is the Word of God, giving the history of the Creation and the Hebrew race, a people whom He used to bring about and establish the Christian Religion.

While it is an invaluable part of the Bible to give us an insight into His work of creating the universe, and to show us how He worked and worried with this race of Hebrews, to evolve Jesus Christ, and prepare the way for His coming, it is not to be read as Christ's sayings or doings, or as the platform of His religion. The New Testament, on the other hand, contains all of Christ's teachings and the entire platform of the Christian Religion, and it also contains much new ground outside of that platform.

We shall content ourselves by giving one or two examples. According to our investigation, St. Paul was the author of the theology of original sin in Adam, by which all men after him were born sinners, and it required a Saviour to redeem mankind from such sin. We do not find this in the teachings of Jesus Christ. He taught that a Saviour was to redeem those who had committed sins, and repented of them, and that those who died in their sins unrepented of, were to be punished in Hell. Nor did He speak of the unity of the race in Adam and Eve, for He knew there was a law of God in existence, plainly given in the Scripture, fully explaining the creation of the origin of mankind. St. Paul was a great and good man, and an over-zealous Christian. Where he obtained his idea of original sin from, we are unable to say or trace. That he was sincere in his convictions on this subject, there can be no doubt; but with all his zeal and piety, he was human and not a Christ.

This theology when referred to the laws of God, will not stand the test of coincidence with them, and no theology should stand that will not meet these requirements. ADAM (for we use the same term that St. Paul used) committed the sin of disobedience to God's command, which was an overt act. If all of his descendants had committed the same or similar act of disobedience, they would have been alike sinners. As there can be no sin without an act in thought or deed, we must, if we wish to gain a clear conception of the subject, find out where these thoughts and deeds culminate to make the sin. Sin by thought or act is a resultant outside the material of the body, for thought is directed in such cases always to external things, while the acts of sin are in like manner plainly external. Some think that the propensity to sin is what is transmitted; but the propensity to sin does no harm, and is not sin till the act of sinning is consummated. Nothing can be transmitted from the parent to the child except an element or a quality, and hence sin cannot be transmitted from body to body, as it is independent of every other body, except incidentally to the one committing the sin; and therefore St. Paul's theology of original sin by ADAM, could not have been transmitted to his descendants.

This Christ term Hell, which he defines as a place of punishment, without giving its nature or condition, has been amplified by theologians, to mean a pit of fire and brimstone, superintended by devils with red-hot irons and other implements of torture. This had become, under such teachings, so unpopular, that they are now endeavoring to do away with the word and substitute another, which they call "sheol," and still claim that they are standing by Christ's words and teachings. Thus translators and revisers of the Scriptures go on making changes in sentences and words, to suit new theologies and new ideas. Under such conventional liberties, need we wonder that we have new denominations, with new creeds and new beliefs continually springing up.

We made an appeal to the translators and revisers of the King James Bible, to have Adam restored in their revised Bible, where it occurred in the Hebrew, and had been dropped by former translators out of the King James Bible, and also to drop the word "So," at the head of Gen. I, 27, and restore the Hebrew word "And." This latter they did; but instead of restoring the word Adam, or The Adam, they struck out Adam eight times, from Gen. II., 18, to Gen. III., 10, and put in "The Man" in its place. The only reason that can be given for this extraordinary performance is, that they wished to clinch their theology of the unity of the race, and judging from these two steps of striking out these Hebrew names, it is fair to conclude, that in the next revision of the Bible, these names will disappear entirely. This will be making a man Bible with a vengeance and a certainty.

The theology of the apostolic succession, is still another theology, involving some very important, if not vital principles. It consists in the requirements in some denominations, that the Gospel of Jesus Christ shall only be preached by men, chosen by men for that purpose, on the ground of succession, by direct authority of Jesus Christ. Christ found it necessary to perform miracles, in order to convince the people that He was the true Messiah, and the Son of God, and the miracles He performed had the desired effect. The same necessity existed, when He gave His apostles directions to preach the gospel to all nations, and, in doing so, to perform miracles, as He had done, to heal the sick, to cast out devils and raise the dead.

While these apostles had such authority from Christ, there is no direct language of His, that gave them the power to confer that power upon others, thereby giving the successors of the apostles, God's power, through all time, to men appointed by men ; and this is the gist of the theology of apostolic succession. What is the logical result? To establish that principle, we must interpolate in the New Testament the fact that Christ did give this power to His Apostles. If He did give that power to His Apostles that power exists to-day, not by reason of their own acts, but by reason of its being a law of God, which can neither be revoked nor changed ; so they can heal the sick, cast out devils, and raise the dead at the present time.

If they have that power from God they can easily prove it to the world ; but until they do these things, we must assume the Scriptures to be correct in its statements, that no such power was given to any one, except Christ's Apostles, to whom He gave such power. We cannot see the benefit or advantage of such a theology, if the successionists preach the pure Gospel of Jesus Christ. It is, however, an excrescence of belief, which prevents many from receiving the benefits of the Church, and is a dead weight upon Christianity.

In order to gain a clear conception of the Apostolic succession, we must have a clear conception of the Scriptures. There are three classes of subjects treated of in the Bible—material laws, immaterial laws and history. Then, who can read all of the Bible understandingly, who do not know all God's laws, material and immaterial? That question can be answered by those who know of the education of the Apostles. Could they not make mistakes in both departments of these laws? We think Christ Himself settled this question of Apostolic succession, when He said, "Where two or three are gathered together in my name, there will I be in the midst of them." In other words, two or three will make my Church, and I will be in the midst of them. So that any one can teach the Gospel of Jesus Christ, if they do it in His name.

The general impression of the inspiration of the Scriptures is, that God inspired men to write what God had communicated to them, and this in a general sense is correct. But inspiration has a closer meaning, and that is, to write under the direction of God, matters in unison and harmony with His laws, and when writing of historical facts to relate them truthfully.

All Christian denominations claim to be teaching Christian religion, in addition to their other creeds and beliefs. So long as they teach the Christian religion they are doing good, by disseminating Christ's Gospel, and the various denominations have spread the Christian religion over a vast territory of the world. Where the harm comes in, by further creeds and beliefs as requirements for salvation, is that these additional requirements confuse, discourage and prevent people accepting the Christian religion. The simple and plain religion of Christ is the easiest to teach, and the easiest of acceptance.

We would invite any one to examine the faith, belief or creed of any Christian denomination, and determine first: whether they are exclusively based upon the teachings of Jesus Christ; and, if so, the denomination is Christian, and purely Christian in their belief. Second: To examine and determine if the denomination has not requirements of belief not found in the sayings and teachings of Christ, even though those beliefs are assumed as being founded upon other texts of Scripture. If the denomination requires a belief in the platform of the Christian religion and has canons and tenets of belief outside that platform and not contained in it, such denomination is teaching a hybrid religion, the religion of Christ and man. There is reason to fear, as time wears on, and man's power becomes more pronounced, that these man parasites and fungi will eat up and overshadow much of Christianity, except the name.

This fear we hope is without foundation, for as God's Word and the Church of Christ are works that will never yield to man's power, darkness may overshadow them for a time, but the clouds will vanish and the sunlight of truth will guild them, and they will remain when all other things will pass away. It must not be assumed from remarks made about denominations, that we regard them in any other light than to disseminate Christian truths and improve the conduct of mankind, and keep them mindful of their obligations to God.

They may have internal defects, which should be rectified; but it is admitted, that notwithstanding those defects, they have spread the seeds of Christ's religion over a vast territory of the earth. All recognize the good they are doing and have done; but the present condition of the Christian world in its unrest and bickerings and quarrelings within and without denominations, leads us to halt and examine the causes and suggest remedies. Every new article of belief insisted upon by Church officials, is an invitation for discussion, sometimes for discord, sometimes for a quarrel, and sometimes for a fight. There would be no discord if all Christian Churches had identically the same belief, and that belief was concentrated upon Christ's platform of the Christian religion; we would then have unity in the Christian belief, which all Christians seem to hope for and are aiming at in their discussions throughout the world. There never will be unity until they all plant themselves on Christ's platform, pure and unalloyed.

In the definition of the "Christian Religion" at the head of this article, we use the terms "or their equivalents." As some may not understand what is meant by equivalents, we will explain. Suppose a man who never heard of God, or of Jesus Christ, but by the action of his normal conscience, which tells him what is right and what is wrong instinctively, he pursues the right and never the wrong—that is, by no external teachings, he leads a pure, Christian life, we simply state it as our opinion, that he will be among the blessed. Then on the other hand, if he had committed some sins and had repented of them, we state it as our opinion, that he would come under the blanket of salvation through Jesus Christ.

It is evident from the fact that Christ commanded His disciples to preach His gospel to all nations, that He did not hold any one responsible for a violation of His teachings until they had heard of Him, His relation to God, of His Christian religion, and of its requirements. So that all others of humanity were under the care and protection of God Himself, who, as we understand it, did not require baptism and the Sacraments of Christ's religion as laws of His to be obeyed. In fact these laws were not in existence until they had been proclaimed and reached the Christian hearers.

BELIEF AND FAITH.

These terms are used interchangeably throughout the Bible, and in all religious writings. We think this an irregularity, which the true meanings of the terms do not deserve. Belief, as used by Christians, is a conclusion from the narratives of men, as history of certain steps, taken by God, in the founding and final establishment of the principles and doctrines of Christianity, as given by Jesus Christ. Every step of that work is recorded, as a natural fact, and each must be, and is received as such, by every Christian. The dictionary definition of Belief, is credit given to something we know not of ourselves.

As the reception of the Christian religion rests entirely on this word BELIEF, it is the most important word of the languages to the Christian, and he should know the length, breadth and depth of its meaning. It is the more important under these circumstances, because it is the field of contention, controversy and dispute, throughout the Christian world. As belief and faith are interchangeably used, it may be inferred, that they have the same meaning, and as far as the general use of the two terms and their dictionary meanings go, that is certainly the case. There are two periods, to which the Christian platform applies; man's temporal period before death, and his condition in the life to come, after death.

In the first period, every point relating to the Christian religion, is related to us by another, hence we must take it all in the common acceptation of belief. But if we had lived at the time these occurrences took place, we could have verified them ourselves, and no belief would have been necessary. This does not apply to the future state, as no one has seen the subjects referred to in that connection, and they are not natural facts, that we could believe on the relation of another. They are all conditional promises of God and Jesus Christ, based on the Christian religion. It seems, therefore, apparent, that belief cannot cover the grounds of faith, nor faith cover the grounds of belief. We then say, that **belief** applies to all facts of the Christian religion, this side of the grave, and faith applies to the conditional promises, given by God and Jesus Christ, relative to the life to come, beyond the grave. We now come to a very important point in this discussion, and that is the analysis of belief, as applied to the facts of Christian religion. What are these facts? We have a Bible History in the original language, that plainly relates them all, from the creation to the ascension of Jesus Christ. Unfortunately for Christianity, mistakes have been made by translators, in carrying the Word of God from one language to another : but if such errors do not touch any vital point, in the establishment or development of the principles of Christianity, they carry no more weight than a typographical error. Our Bible translations in regard to the creation of mankind being the object and foundation of the Christian religion, is a warp of truth, with a filling of error, and is in violation of God's unchanging law of reproduction in the races of mankind.

The vital point in this erroneous translation is, that our Saviour has no defined genealogy, while in the Hebrew, THE ADAM was created and EVE made from his rib, being the only beings who were named specifically, and who, by their issue, was to evolve Jesus Christ, which gives a clear genealogy of Christ from THE ADAM and EVE, instead of no genealogy from Adam and Eve, as resulting from the unity of the race translations. As the reception of the Christian religion depends on belief, let us see where belief stands on this question. As knowledge of the laws of

God has increased and extended, there is not, as far as our information can reach, scarcely an intelligent person who believes that the white Caucasian and the Negro ever had a common parentage, and the reason of this is apparent. They see all things, including the races, reproduced after "their kind," and, as they know, the laws of God have never changed, and never will change, they are more inclined to believe their eyes, and accept what they see, as knowledge, than to believe the works of a translator, or even a theology, for they know that God or Jesus Christ never said that all mankind have descended from the same pair of human beings. Every step in the preparatory plan for the establishment of the Christian religion, and every step in the making up of Christ's platform of that religion is history, and Christians accept all as truth.

Belief, in the ordinary acceptation of the term, does not come up to and fulfill this condition. If the Christian's belief is strong enough to accept these things as true, then they become facts for the Christian; and if facts, they become laws of God; and if laws of God, they must be admitted upon the same plane as any other law of God. The simple question remaining is, whether the Christian world will be willing to advance their belief to its ultimate logical conclusion, which, we think, is its present real position. Belief at present, without any restraint of this kind, is made to cover a vast territory of ground, on which varieties of religions, under the name of Christianity, are established and promulgated. From what we can see and learn from the spiritual discourses between Christian denominations, they will be very ready to place a fence around belief, and confine it to the ultimate logical conclusion of a fixed law of God, where there will be no more discussion about it, than about the result of sowing wheat or the growth of a plant.

The same principle will apply to faith in the promises of Christ, for good or ill, of the future life beyond the grave. If the Christian faith be worth anything, it should be strong enough to accept these promises, as to be fulfilled; and if fulfilled, they are true; and if true, their foundations are facts; if facts, they are laws of God; and if laws of God, they are accepted facts, about which no discussions can possibly be held, except as to the reliability of these promises, which no Christian ought to deny.

As belief and faith are the acknowledged foundations upon which the foundation of the Christian religion rests, and if these foundations be advanced from the elastic and boundless field they have occupied, to the fixed and unvarying laws of God, where there are no grounds for differences of opinion, every Christian denomination can determine its exact status to the requirements of Christ's platform of His religion. If such denomination is teaching the tenets of that platform, in exactness, and no more, it is, unquestionably, a pure Christian denomination.

If, on the other hand, it is teaching all the tenets of that platform, and other requirements not contained therein, and by so doing, prevent some from joining their church and receiving its benefits, or by their additional requirements of belief, put so much labor on the hearers, and confuse uneducated and simple minds by such a mass of requirements as to discourage them to undertake them, or any other impediments of like nature, and such souls are lost from the want of the plain and simple tenets of Christ's religion, who is responsible to God for such lost souls? It is not for us to say; but we have our opinion, and such denomination can determine without help, whether it is a Christian one, pure and simple, or not.

CONSCIENCE, THE RUDDER OF LIFE.

There never was a human being born who did not possess a normal conscience, a monitor of right from wrong and of wrong from right. We do not know where this conscience lies in the body; we suppose, and probably, rightly, that it is one of the faculties of the general mind, a term used to denote the aggregate of all laws of God, implanted in the body, except those governing its material parts. Each faculty of the mind is governed and regulated by its own distinct law, so that there are just as many distinct laws as there are distinct faculties. Hence, no one law governing a faculty, has anything to do with any other faculty. This recognized principle applies to every law of God; therefore the law governing and regulating the conscience does not apply to any other faculty of the mind.

As every law of God, as far as we know, is dependent upon some other law for its execution, so the law of conscience depends upon other laws of the faculties of the mind to execute its decisions. The law regulating the conscience differs from any other known law in this respect, that the execution of all other laws is direct, having but one object, while the law regulating the conscience is, if we may use the term, double-headed, that is, it has the power to call upon the other faculties to do right, or to do wrong. This brings us to the very important conclusion, that conscience governs every other faculty of the mind, directly or indirectly; for every act that we perform, has in it the element of right or wrong. Conscience then becomes the rudder of life, as its decisions enter into every act and every thought, as the base of an act.

If conscience acted normally throughout the world, right would be right throughout the world, and wrong would be wrong; but we know this is not so; what one community claims to be right, another community, acting according to the dictates of their consciences, deny, and claim it to be wrong. This is not owing to a defect in the law, but to education, surroundings and influences to change, not the law, but the conception of the law—that is the outward appearance of the law, by reason of these things. To show this clearly, we will take the instance of the plant; and as there is a similarity of action in all of the laws of God, there is a similarity of action between the action of the plant and the conscience. The plant starts from the seed, and peeps its head above the ground, and if not interfered with in its normal growth, will rise from the earth and increase in all its parts, until it arrives at its ultimate proportions according to the objective law of its existence.

If, on the other hand, its normal growth be interfered with by processes well-known to every one, it can be made to grow, inclined to the right or the left, and finally be made to grow down instead of up. We have here then an exact parallel with the growth and action of the conscience, though the influences to guide its growth are quite different. This brings us to determine the standard of education, which is to guide the conscience in its normal condition. In the various religions throughout the world, what religion educates the conscience, to understand man's responsibility to his God and his fellow-man? We know of none, except the Christian religion.

Let us now examine and ascertain what link joins the platform of the Christian religion with mankind. If God had not implanted something within the bodies of men, that responded to man's obligations to God, of what use would any religion be to him? That platform is an independent group of laws of God, demanding certain duties of man, to be performed as a recognition of His love, goodness, and power, also of conditional promises for good or ill in the life to come. All God's work in founding and establishing the Christian religion, and all of Christ's labor and agonies in perfecting it, would be lost, if some provision had not been made to bring the knowledge of it home to mankind.

That provision has been made, and it only remains for us to investigate all the laws implanted in man, until we find one answering the requirements—this we find in the conscience, and we only know of the law by its effect, and by the same process by which we judge of any other law. The conscience, though it can make its decisions, has no power to carry these decisions into effect without the aid of the will, which is also one of the group of laws of the mind ; and the will itself has no power to carry out the decisions of the conscience into overt acts, without it is aided by the material laws of the body. There is an intermediate law between conscience and will, which we call reason, to which all subjects presented to the conscience are referred, and its finding is presented to the conscience, which has the power of option to direct the will to execute that option of right or wrong in the overt acts which follow.

So that conscience is the judge, reason is the jury, and will, with the aid of the functions of the body, is the executive.

The action of these three laws is instantaneous, by their very nature, as we know; subjects are flashed through them to action, by the body, and conclusions of thought with lightning speed. It is impossible to measure the time that elapses between the thought which presents the subject to the conscience, and the reference back to it by the reason, while the conscience may take a very long time or a very short time to determine what its direction to the will will be, whether to do the right or the wrong act, and this will depend on the power of option given to the conscience. If the decision be to do the right, according to his obligations to God's will, it is righteousness; if to do wrong against His will, it is sin.

These three laws of God—*conscience, reason* and *will*, are the foundations implanted in man of the great temple of Christianity, which reaches from earth to Christ's platform of the Christian religion in heaven.

THE HIGHER AND UPPER PLANE OF CHRISTIANITY.

We do not assume to dictate any condition of Christianity, but knowing that it is the equal right of every one to investigate for himself, and if in such investigation, anything is found that may be of interest to Christians, it is his privilege, alike with all others, to make suggestions that may lead to a more perfect understanding, not only of the Scriptures, but the foundation principles upon which the structure of Christianity is based. As every thing in the universe is from God, and under His control and management, and we see and know that these are continuous and the same always, we therefore call them laws of God. It is then of paramount importance for every one to know what these laws are, in order to gain a clear conception of our position and our relation to them. We then give a compendium of some things *we found on our examination.*

The first step is to find out what God's laws are, then to acknowledge and obey them.

Every completed step in a law of God, is identical with every other completed step, from the Creation to the end of the existence of the subject to which it applies.

The Creation can be proved in all its details, by finding out the law governing each element, then running back each law, step by step, to the beginning, even without a record in Scripture to guide us; but when we find that the Hebrew record exactly coincides with the proof, it proves the record to be correct.

The created origin of the races of mankind is a law of God, clearly stated in the Hebrew Genesis, and proved by the operation of that law, in the persistent reproduction in type of these races; and with them rests the foundation of the Christian religion.

The Creation of THE ADAM, and the making of EVE, was for a special purpose, that of producing a line of people that should eventually evolve the Saviour of mankind.

The theology of the unity of the race in ADAM and EVE is an error on its face, as ADAM was not the name of an individual, but the name of a class of male and female created (Gen. V., 2.) This theology is in violation of God's laws of reproduction in the human family, and in violation of the Hebrew inspiration (Gen. I., 26, 27).

The flood, by the translations, is made universal, destroying all of humanity then existing, except Noah and his family, while the Hebrew inspiration is, that every THE ADAM was destroyed, except Noah and his family, leaving the Gentile races, and the remaining Hebrews not in the Jewish line, unharmed.

We have been thus particular in repeating the laws of God, relating to the Creation of mankind, that an enlarged and correct conception of the magnitude of the man subject of the Christian religion should be arrived at; and this is the first step on to the Higher and Upper Plane of Christianity.

Read the Scriptures by the light of the laws of God. Know the laws first, then read intelligently. These laws are material and immaterial; the remainder of Scripture is history, which is to be received upon the same general principles, except the miracles, which are special acts of God.

Christ's platform of the Christian religion plainly laid down by Him, consists of His sayings, teachings, conduct and requirements to develop man's responsibility to God, and man's responsibility to man, and the consequences to him of such responsibilities.

The theology of original sin, of which St. Paul was the author, assumes the unity of the race in ADAM and EVE, which we have seen is in violation of God's laws. That theology calls for ADAM being created pure, without sin, and then that his generations were sinners. This involves a change in the laws of reproduction, not by God's interference, but by ADAM. Man cannot control his issue, further than to reproduce himself in type. This theology has no standing, when referred to the laws of God, for Christ said nothing of that kind in His Gospel.

Teaching the Gospel is not only commendable but necessary : but the theology of the Apostolic succession, while it accomplishes this object, claims that those teachers have a direct authority from God, derived through Christ and His apostles. We find that Christ gave His apostles certain powers, but we do not find that these apostles were given the authority to confer these powers on any one else. If they did so, the result might have been beneficial ; but they did so without authority of Christ. When their authority ended with their death, the Gospel was completed and was Christ's Church, and was the law of God, and any one could place himself on it and explain its foundation. Order and discipline in denominations requires succession, but not the succession by authority of Christ. He knew His apostles, but He did not know who would or might come after them.

Belief, the foundation upon which we rest the Christian religion, does not go far enough to express what our real belief is. It is in these days an open and elastic field, apparently with no limits or bounds. If belief be carried forward to its ultimate logical conclusion, it will then become fixed, and the field be circumscribed. If our belief be strong enough to result in a conviction that it is true, then to the Christian it becomes a fact, and if a fact, it is a law of God. The same condition applies to faith, and with the same result. About the laws of God there can be no disputes, no differences of opinion, and all quarrelings about beliefs must cease, if denominations place themselves on this Higher and Upper Plane.

Conscience, the Rudder of Life, is the most important immaterial law implanted in us, to determine our obligations to God, and to distinguish right from wrong, and governs all the other faculties, of which we call in the aggregate, mind, in this world, and soul in the life to come. Each faculty has its own particular law to govern it, hence we have three immaterial laws in action in every act, aided by material laws of the body—CONSCIENCE, REASON and WILL. Conscience is the judge, Reason the jury, and Will the executive, the latter aided by material laws of the body to complete the action, and conscience decides by its power of option whether that action shall be in obedience to God's laws, or in violation of them.

Considering the circumstances which surrounded the early translators and compilers of the Scriptures and of their conceptions of laws of God, if they had any beyond the traditions then prevalent, it is not surprising that errors have been made which the search-light of actual knowledge have made apparent and glaring. Every law of God, material or immaterial, stands upon the same level for our acknowledgment and obedience, and this must be admitted as the foundation fact of all Scripture, of all theologies and of all true religion. Then, is Christ's platform of the Christian religion a law of God? Is it sufficient for a saving religion? We think these two propositions will be admitted, and if so, what results? That that platform is a law of God, and is all that is required as the basis of a true religion, without an addition or deduction in one iota of belief or faith requirements.

Christ's platform having been made by an infinite mind with infinite knowledge, no human being can tell the effect upon its provisions by additional requirements of belief, faith, or creed not contained therein. They might be considered as aids by the human mind, while they might be antagonistic to the Divine mind. Since then we have a Divine completed system of Christian religion, it is safer to follow its plain requirements than to undertake any improvement upon it by man theologies. While such intentions may be from the higher order of Christian zeal, we can see nothing gained by such experiments. We therefore conclude that no improvement can be made in Christ's platform, and that it contains all the foundations of beliefs, faiths, and creeds necessary for the Christian religion, and that that platform should be acknowledged and accepted as the **Higher and Upper Plane of Christianity.**

READING THE BIBLES

BY

CO-ORDINATES OF TRUTH.

JANUARY, 1895.

SUBJECTS:

READ THE BIBLES BY CO-ORDINATES.

WHAT IS A CO-ORDINATE?

WHAT IS INSPIRATION?

ESTABLISHING THE CHRISTIAN RELIGION.

THE JEWISH AND CHRISTIAN RELIGIONS CO-ORDINATED.

THE BIRTH OF JESUS CHRIST.

CONCEPTION OF MARY, MOTHER OF JESUS.

REWARDS AND PUNISHMENTS.

READING THE BIBLES BY CO-ORDINATES.

There is no subject so vital to the Christian as the proper reading of the inspiration of our Bibles. In the first place, we should ascertain what inspiration is, and in what Bibles it is to be found, and then read that inspiration in strict accordance with the laws of God, which is true inspiration. It is not our intention to criticise translations from the original Hebrew and Greek further than we have done, except where they violate well-known and established laws, or where they introduce new ground and new principles not found in the platform of the Christian religion framed by Jesus Christ.

It must be regarded as a settled principle that God never inspired any writer of a book of the Old or New Testaments to make a statement by His direction or authority that could be construed as in violation of any of His laws, material or immaterial. How are we to determine these points? It becomes evident that no one can be competent to compass the subject without a thorough knowledge of these laws and of the inspiration, the subject of comparison. These laws are divided into two classes: the material and immaterial, usually called natural and spiritual; we do not consider the natural and spiritual the best classification, as natural laws frequently run into and form part of spiritual laws.

We must then look to find out where these laws originate, and where the record of them can be found. God's work, both material and immaterial, should not be considered as independent subjects, but as parts of a stupendous design, the machinery of which is governed by His never-changing and never-varying laws. By what authority do we claim these laws as unchanging and never varying? The scientist claims it from tangible knowledge and experience, while the theologian claims it for the immaterial laws, because they are laid down and recorded in the inspired Bible, and both are correct and both are scientists, in the true sense of the term.

This brings us to the definition of true science, which is, *the development and tracing in action the laws of God.* These laws as such are all immaterial, but the subjects on which they act are material and immaterial. There can be no distinction between the binding force of one law over another. There is, however, a great difference in importance to man; the material being of less consequence to him than the immaterial. For brevity and convenience, we call these laws material and immaterial, more to designate the subjects on which they act, than to be accurate in nomenclature. There can be no misunderstanding in applying the term scientist to those engaged in developing and tracing in action the material laws of nature; but when applied to theologians and the Christian clergy, the application would seem at first to require some explanation. Without specifying any with which they have to deal, we state, in a general way, that in our Bibles, they are the laws that apply to the Jewish and Christian religions. In these the clergy should be expert scientists. They would, however, be complete masters of the whole subject if they were equally well informed on all of God's material laws, for there is, as has often been said, "a sermon in every blade of grass and in every combination of matter in nature." We have said before in a previous work, and now repeat it here, that Christ's platform of the Christian religion is composed of laws of God. We now go further and say that Christ's platform is made up of plain and explicit laws, and contains also sayings of His, that could not be understood even by His disciples. It seems to us that these plain sayings and teachings should be codified by a convention of Christian churches, and these sayings about which there would be any doubt as to their meaning, should be stated also and left unexplained, thereby following the example of Christ, when His disciples asked Him for an explanation, He remained silent.

This will give us Christ's platform on Basic principles and as Basic laws, which will be captivating to the intelligence of all Christians, as we believe.

This position brings us to explain partially the use of the Base Co-ordinate in reading the Bibles. The Basic principles of the Hebrew or Jewish religion, and also of the Christian religion, will be thus clearly defined, and every repetition of those Base-Co-ordinates will be Co-ordinates if the repetitions be correct. So that the Base Co-ordinate once established, every repetition of it must of necessity be correct, and if not a Co-ordinate, the error can easily be detected. Such a test will do away and exclude all constructions and opinions of learned men and of commentators if they do not conform to the Base Co-ordinates of plainly-expressed principles in the original Hebrew and Greek of the Old and New Testaments.

Our Christian religion cannot be relied upon if it is not acknowledged to be founded upon the laws of God, which we denominate Base Co-ordinates, nor will that religion ever arrive at an approximate unity until the laws establishing it shall be tabulated in a definite form where all can see whether the denominations in which they are worshiping are following the Basic principles of Christ's platform or not. As matters now stand in this respect, it is difficult for the uninformed hearers to know more of the Basic principles of Christianity than they derive from the teachings from the pulpits; we never have had the pleasure of hearing these principles as such referred to from that source as laws of God. On the other hand can be heard from some of them personal quarrels and constant abuse of other Christian denominations, with many other things quite as foreign to the simple and charitable teachings of Jesus Christ. The question naturally follows: "Would not Christianity be promoted if such pulpits did not exist?

Then there is another class of Christians, sincere and devout though they may be, that are not satisfied with the word of God in the original Hebrew and Greek, but by translations and constructions have made some of our Bibles what they thought they ought to be; with them right here rests the responsibility of the various digressions from Christ's Gospel into sectarian denominations. Some of these found their religion upon passages in the Jewish religion of the Old Testament, while others found theirs on passages from the Christian religion in the New Testament. The translator or constructionist who assumes to change, alter, amend or extend the word of God found in the originals, takes upon himself a responsibility entirely untenable as a Christian. He substantially places himself in the footprints of God and Jesus Christ, and assumes to say what They thought, intended or desired.

Is it not well, then, for all of us Christians to candidly examine ourselves and the whole subject, and see whether we are educated in the Basic principles, or, more properly, in the Base Co-ordinates of Christ's Gospel which sets them forth, and taken together as a unit, make His Church? The meaning of the term church to-day is a building, with a congregation and a minister; and we hope all, and we do believe many of them, come within Christ's definition of His Church. We never can be deceived or go wrong if we adhere strictly to the Co-ordinates of these Base Co-ordinates. The Co-ordinate is the living principle of all God's works, as we shall now endeavor to show.

WHAT IS A CO-ORDINATE?

Everyone should know, and many probably do know, what a Co-ordinate is, for every human being on the face of the whole earth uses it every moment of their lives, except when they are sleeping. In general it is the comparison of one thing, idea, principle, or subject with another, to determine its kind or its equality, and is *the foundation of all knowledge.* We shall be compelled to be somewhat prolix in order to explain fully its use and application. In the first place every Co-ordinate has its Base Co-ordinate, and by this we mean that everything we see or know of, and every idea or principle, has had its beginning in the first of its kind. That is, every mineral, metal, rock, stone, soil, plant, vegetable, flower, tree, shrub, animal or man, had its first form at some time, and the only means we have of determining what each of these is, is by comparing the thing we see or idea or subject presented with its predecessor. The first predecessor is the Base Co-ordinate, and all succeeding ones of the kind are Co-ordinates.

In like manner there are Base Co-ordinates of color, taste, smell, quality, form and general appearance, which enable us to determine whether they are Co-ordinates of the Base Co-ordinate or not, and if anything does not Co-ordinate with a known Base Co-ordinate, we are at a loss to know what it is, and if we cannot find a known Base Co-ordinate, we would be compelled to give it a new name, and the knowledge of its existence would make it a new Base Co-ordinate.

To illustrate this more clearly we take the grasses as an example, because they are the most common and well known kinds of existences. Ordinarily, the farmer is well acquainted with these various kinds, and from his knowledge, not of a Base Co-ordinate, but of the kind of grass, he is enabled to place each blade in its proper line of existence, and at once determine whether it is red clover, white clover, timothy, June grass, wheat, oats, rye, barley, etc. The botanist is, however, more scrutinizing in his research, and often comes upon a grass which no one has seen or knew of before. He is at a loss as well as delighted. He has discovered a new grass not before known in botany, and he gives it a name as the discoverer, and henceforward it is a Base Co-ordinate, and his name goes down in history.

As every line of existence—by which we mean every distinct form in nature—whether reproduced or not, has its Base Co-ordinate, and every element of those lines has its Base Co-ordinate also, it is needless to call attention to the universality and numbers of these in the material of this earth alone, without going further into the universe. Even these are only a portion of Base Co-ordinates applying to the material, while the still vaster field of Base Co-ordinates of the immaterial is as yet unconsidered.

We have used the Base Co-ordinate of the material as a stepping-stone to the higher and more glorious Base Co-ordinates of the immaterial, the laws of God; being the forces of the material and immaterial, are the Base Co-ordinates of the Christian religion. The material forces, as far as discovered, are well known, and their Base Co-ordinates established by actual knowledge. There are undoubtedly many yet to be discovered, as all the mysteries of God's creation have not yet been developed; for like reasons, many of the delicate points of Christ's platform have not yet been arrived at by the world, while the salient principles of that platform are well understood and have become settled Basic principles and established as Base Co-ordinates.

The laws of gravity, electricity, magnetism, attraction, cohesion, light, air, reproduction, continuance, and the like, are all well known, and we naturally ask ourselves for what purpose has all this complicated machinery been put in motion and continued? We cannot conceive any reason for it in its mere existence, without a design for an end.

There is implanted in the normal conscience of all, an instinctive veneration and turning of the mind to a Supreme Being, as can be proved by the fact that when dangers threaten, when the storm rages, the lightnings flash near, and the thunders roll and roar, men's hearts turn upward for protection.

We say, then, as a logical sequence that the Christian religion has been established by God as a response to such yearnings, and as a protection from the miseries that might result from annihilation or worse, if we do not follow its warnings and heed the teachings of Jesus Christ. If we admit this proposition, is it of consequence that we should examine carefully Christ's platform, dissect its Basic principles, and determine the length, breath and depth of each one of them? No doubt some will say that this is at present the end of all Christian teachings. If it be, why so many divergent results in creeds, beliefs and faiths?

The reason of this is that there has been no settled concentrated platform of Basic principles to confine speculations to Base Co-ordinates of Christ-born truth. The whole of the Bibles, entire from Genesis to Revelation, has been the open field, to garner truths of equal importance and of equal binding beliefs and faiths, whether taken from the Jewish religion of the Old Testament, or from the Christian religion of the New Testament.

If the Christian world wants unity of belief, unity of faith, unity of church, and unity of love, let them take the steps necessary to accomplish this much-hoped-for result. Let them have and practice the unity of Base Co-ordinates of the Basic principles of Christ's platform. If the theologians ever get there, they cannot prevent unity; it will be a resultant, and not a desire.

The present dissensions, bickerings and quarrels between Christian denominations and among members of these denominations, would seem to result from many desiring to be a Christ, and insisting upon their individual construction of Christ's sayings and teachings. These seem to forget that every Basic principle of Christ's platform is a law of God, as clean cut, and entitled to obedience, as the well known law of gravity. What would we think of a distinguished scientist who would declare that gravity sometimes acted up instead of down, that it was sometimes suspended and again acted normally? We would undoubtedly conclude that he was ignorant of the uniform action of the law, and of the law itself.

The Base Co-ordinate of the law would be the conviction of his error, and he would no longer be entitled to the distinguished name of a scientist. Then what can we say of those distinguished divines who do not adhere in exactness to the Basic principles of Christ's platform? Can we say that they are ignorant? No, they are learned men of the nineteenth century, and should be more competent even than the unlearned disciples of Christ's time, to follow the clear principles of His teachings. Then what follows? Have they investigated the subject down to the Base Co-ordinates of that platform? We leave the question for them to consider. It is not so much the fault of the learned divines of this day as it is their misfortune to be found in the ruts of education from which, by reason of their surroundings, they cannot easily emerge. The scholar of divinity is not the man who has developed any new thought beyond his seminary education, or enlightened us with the dissecting knife of truth; but he is the scholar who has gathered together the most ideas of other men, even to the remotest ages of history, and the further he goes on the deeper becomes this rut of education, so that the divines of this day, as a rule, are not following the advanced developments of the nineteenth century, but are bound to theologies framed on a limited conception of the Basic principles of Christ's platform, as must be concluded from the fact that such theologies did then, and do now, cover a vast field of beliefs and faiths not required in the concentrated and simple teachings of Christ's church—His Gospel.

No one will deny that the Christian religion is a unit made up of Basic principles. The object of introducing the Co-ordinate is to aid the inquirer to ascertain whether any doctrine is in agreement with any one of the Base Co-ordinates of the principles of Christ's Gospel. All can easily determine this fact after once they have informed themselves of these Basic principles, which are clearly laid down in Christ's teachings. They need not go through the whole of the Bible for this purpose, they are contained within narrow limits in the New Testament.

To make a practical application of the Base Co-ordinate to the preaching of some divines ordained to teach the principles of Christianity from pulpits consecrated to Christ's church, what do we hear? Sometimes a stirring discourse of vituperation and spleen against some other Christian denomination. Can this be Co-ordinated with any one Base Co-ordinate of Christ's platform? We need not go through the subjects of multiform sermons, where independent, possibly, of the text, not a reference is made to the subject of Christianity, or to Christ, from the first word to the last. Others will condescend to take a text from Scripture and forget they have done done so, by scintillations of high-flown oratory to please, not instruct, their hearers. We could say more on this subject, but refrain, thanking God that these are not universal practices.

WHAT IS INSPIRATION?

Inspiration as we understand it is the expression of Divine will or mind through human agency. This being assumed as a correct definition, the natural inquiry results: Who have been the agents selected for this purpose; what have been the subjects; are all the writings of these claimed to have been inspired to be read as inspiration, and where are the records of this inspiration to be found?

As inspiration is only claimed to apply to statements in the Scriptures, the field of investigation is narrowed down to our Bibles. As there are various Bibles in various languages, which are as many versions, as a necessity, we must find out what Bible is the one that contains the pure inspiration. Some able divines and distinguished scholars of late years made public announcement that there were errors in *the* Bible without informing the laity or the public as far as our information extends, *which* Bible was in error, or pointed out any error in any particular one, which we considered as simply talking to the wind, and which did produce a whirlwind in the Christian world.

This embarrassed the subject very much, because no one knew from such assertions coming from scholarly authority what they could consider as inspired truth and what they should reject, because it threw a suspicion and a doubt over the contents of every Bible. No doubt these charges were true and would have been instructive if they had been specific. The Old Testament—the Bible of the Hebrews and Jews—was finished about five hundred years before Christ, and the New Testament within one hundred years A.D.; the former being in the Hebrew language and the latter being in the Greek, which was the prevalent language at that time.

Language is the vehicle to convey thought and is the invention of man and not of God. While a thought may originate in the Divine mind, the machinery to express it is purely human. If language had been the direct act of God we never would have had but one language, every word of which would have had but one meaning, and that with other words would be one of His fixed laws. We all know what language is in regard to definiteness of meaning; but few words comparatively have but one meaning, and most of them have several.

The only safe rule, then, in reading inspiration is to see whether the interpretation of the language assumed Co-ordinates with established and acknowledged laws of God. Some theologians and some Christians claim every word of the Bible in the original Hebrew and Greek, and every translation from them into other languages, are all inspired. We cannot see how they can make such claims with any show of correctness. Every change from the original, in the translation—and we all know there are such—brings them to the acknowledgment that the Bible from which they translate is not inspired in the parts changed, and that the translation is inspired in those parts. Such a claim is its own refutation.

If, then, there is inspiration at all—and we claim there is—where is it to be found? We answer: It is to be found in the original Bible in the Hebrew language and in the original New Testament in the Greek. Inspiration is a unit, and if not, how shall we use the fractions? As time rolls on and new translations are made by new human minds, what security have we that in years, inspiration will disappear from our Bibles altogether, or that they will become so changed that the Christian religion will have no standing in them.

It seems to us that the only remedy for these evils is to confine our claim of inspiration to the material and immaterial laws of God and the amplification of them laid down in Scripture for our belief, faith and practice. This requires an explanation as to what the laws of God are in this sense. A law of God is the resultant from a statement of fact, where continuance in kind necessarily follows. For example, in the Genesis we are informed that God created the heaven and the earth, light, the waters, combined the elements into dry land, planted the vegetable kingdom on the earth, set the universe in motion, created the fishes and fowls of the air, the animals, and finally the races of men, male and female, and The Adam, the head of the Jewish line that was to evolve Jesus Christ.

This is true inspiration, because it is in accord with the laws of God, which we know from experience, and which follow the facts stated, being laws of preservation and laws of continuance by reproduction "after its kind" so persistently repeated in the Genesis. Some may consider that there are words in that account that would not support the idea of inspiration, but the facts and knowledge we have of the laws would correct the meaning of any such words, if there be any, and confirm the inspiration. It must be remembered that the writer of this account, although he had language to express his own thoughts, but having no words to express things of which he knew nothing, might readily have used words in his own language that did not exactly convey the meaning of the inspiration, and it is astonishing that he could have found means to express the mind of God so accurately.

The immaterial laws of God are the next subject for consideration. As connected with the inspiration of Scripture, these are the laws that flow from His creation of the universe, and from the establishment of the Jewish and Christian religions and their amplifications. The principles of these religions are Basic principles, and these are Base Co-ordinates, and any correct repetition of them are Co-ordinates and are true inspiration. It must be remembered that all the laws of God are immaterial, but the subjects to which they apply are both material and immaterial.

The assumption that every word of any Bible is inspired is a theology and not a Basic principle or Base Co-ordinate found stated in the Jewish or Christian religion. That theology is founded upon the supposed fact that certain books of the Old and New Testaments were made a canon of the church, then the Roman Catholic Church, by the men of the Council of Carthage in 397 A.D. There is some doubt even whether the members of that Council ever voted upon the question, and the weight of evidence goes to show that the books thus claimed to be inspired were accepted as such by universal consent.

If the members of the Council of Carthage had any right to vote their opinion on this subject, or the people had any right to claim them as inspired, why should not the people of the nineteenth century, with greatly increased knowledge, have the same right to judge of their inspirations? Undoubtedly this is the right of the laity, but the clergy are in a different position; they are bound by their theology and can have no opinion that does not harmonize with it, or suffer temporal punishment. This is neither Christian, Biblical, or, in a secular sense, justice, as it contravenes the very foundation principle of religion in this, that we are all endowed by God with a conscience, that directs our way in doing right or wrong, rewarding us for following the right and punishing us for the wrong. Who will assume to take the place of God and revoke His Basic Law in this respect and say that conscience shall no longer be the rule of action with the clergy; but that they shall follow the conventional opinions of man, be they right or be they wrong?

We shall refer in passing to the claimed inspiration of every word of the Old Testament, but shall not specify the particular parts which we do not consider as inspired, for everyone is acquainted with them because they are often passed by unnoticed in public readings. Of what practical utility is this theology of universal inspiration of the Scriptures as applied to the Old Testament anyhow, without it is in charity to cover by this mantle the awful and monstrous deeds of the chosen people of God? The result of such claim is to reduce to one level the good and the bad, to exalt sin and sink righteousness. Of course, this does not apply to the whole of the Old Testament, but only to the part we have referred to.

This theology that claims universal inspiration of the whole Bible, and especially of the objectional parts referred to in the Old Testament, has been the cause of more disbelief than any other cause with which we are acquainted. It naturally suggests the following questions: Is the Bible so weak that it cannot protect itself without the aid of this man's theology? Is it unsafe to let it stand on its own foundation and merits alone? Is it unsafe to let all men read it alike and each one draw his own conclusions whether it is the word of God or not? Do its plain writings and principles require the endorsement of any theologian or scholarly Christian? We think not, and any man or set of men who assume to sit in judgment to determine what God's will has been or is, or what the workings of His mind have been or is, is simply constructively assuming all the above questions in the affirmative, because there is no Biblical authority for the claim in the Basic principles of the Jewish religion or in Christ's teachings—His Gospel.

The subject of having the word of God in our translations of the original Bible is a very important one to the Christian, and we should all agree that, that Word is contained in the original Hebrew and Greek, without that universal consent, and understanding, we might as well lay our Bibles aside as simple literature, having no claim of inspiration, which we cannot and will not do. The fact is patent, and, we think, cannot be denied after a thorough investigation of the subject, that the Christian world has gone too far and been a little too ready to intrust committees of scholarly men to assume to give to us new Bible translations which they claim, of course, to be identical with the word of God in the originals.

In this discussion we shall not question the sincerity of anyone connected with the subject, nor question their intentions of doing the best they knew how in giving us Bibles such as they thought they ought to be, according to their best and sincerest convictions. We do not pretend to be an expert Hebrew or Greek scholar, nor is a knowledge even of these languages necessary to the comparison of the translations with the original languages in the King James Bible, which we take as an example. In this case the translators have left on every page their convictions of inaccuracies, for these consist of side-notes which give the meaning of Hebrew terms in English, while different language not having the same meaning is used in the body of the work. These are so numerous in the Old and New Testaments that it would be a herculean task to count their number.

We invite anyone interested in this subject to examine these side-notes and their substitutions in the King James Bible. There are twelve of such instances in the first chapter of Genesis, and the same number in the second and so on. There are many other places where Hebrew names occur in the original, and are left out in the translation and no name at all substituted instead ; and Hebrew words wrongly translated according to the best authority, and these facts will not be denied by any Hebrew scholar. These are what we call errors, but no doubt the translators regarded them as making the Bible what it should be. These changes from the Hebrew and Greek terms run through the whole of the Old and New Testaments; but they are not so numerous in the New Testament as in the Old.

Language being the vehicle used to convey thought, if the language is changed, the thought is changed. If these translators had made some slight alterations in the language that did not entirely obliterate the thought, there might be no special cause of complaint; but when Scriptural names are dropped and no name given in their stead, and when thoughts found in the original are lost in the translation in such numberless instances, and the seeker after pure inspiration is misled, he has just cause for complaint.

For reasons best known to the members of the committee on the revision of the King James Bible, they have struck out or left out all the side-notes giving the meaning of Hebrew terms, but have retained, as we believe, all or most of the previous substitutions and errors of translation, besides adding many more. This will prevent anyone from following our suggestion of comparison with the Westminster revision, but will not prevent doing so with any King James Bible having these side-notes. As we have a religion from God displayed in His Scripture inspiration, the intelligent and reflecting mind should seek that inspiration for information, rather than trust the opinions of men found in translations which vary by circumstances from time to time.

To meet this difficulty and to do away with all uncertainties, we have proposed to introduce into the reading of the Scriptures, whether in the original or in translations, the principle of the Co-ordinate by which anyone can easily determine whether a translation is correct or not. The first step in this direction is to assume nothing, but accept what all Jews and Christians have never denied, that the Old and New Testaments in the Hebrew and Greek in respect to their religions, and all instructions about them, were inspired of God. These records being made up of distinct ideas, they are the elements which constitute the two religions. Generally there would be no difficulty in carrying these ideas from the originals to the new languages; but if such cases should occur, the normal expression of them in the original should be transferred bodily, as it would be not only far safer, but it would be the duty of the translator not to translate at all, rather than convey an erroneous idea.

This brings us to the explanation of the application to this subject, of the principles of the Co-ordinate. In the exact sciences no result is considered correct without it Co-ordinates, that is, agrees with its Base Co-ordinate which is an axiom, maxim or settled recognized idea or principle. The same rule should apply to inspiration, which is alike recognized as laws of God, which are axioms and maxims to the Jew and Christian. All the ideas in these two religions set forth in the platforms of Moses and Christ, are Base Co-ordinates, and every repetition of them, either in translations or in teachings, if they be correctly stated, are Co-ordinates of the Base Co-ordinate; and as long as translators and Christians work with these Co-ordinates they will have Bibles and Christianity that will be based on God's inspired truth.

ESTABLISHING THE CHRISTIAN RELIGION.

The first step towards this stupendous work was the creation of its theatre of action, and then to people it. To gain a clear conception of this design and its fulfillment, we must grasp the magnitude of the entire subject and acquaint ourselves with all the steps taken in its accomplishment. Where this has been done, and every step in the inspiration scanned and weighed in the scales of human reason, no one, it seems to us, can come to any other conclusion, than that the object of the Almighty Creator was to build up a system which was to redound to His glory and be for the comfort, use and final happiness of His people.

The Genesis gives the account of the Creation of this grand theatre of action. This account being inspiration and purely scientific, and that, too, of the most intricate kind, it is not strange that it is not more generally understood by the reading public. If, however, those readers would take a more common sense view of its order of arrangement, they would have less difficulty in understanding it as a creation for this theatre of action. To give an illustration to this end : If we undertake to build a house, we would first procure a place or space to build upon ; then obtain all the elementary parts of the building materials, then combine these materials to make the parts from the smallest to the greatest before we put them together ; then put them together in accordance with the architect's design, and finish the structure by putting in the windows to let in the light.

Then the house would be ready to be stored with various kinds of food for sustenance. The owner could then walk into his house to enjoy its contents, and have a screen to ward off the storms, and then do his duty as a good citizen, by obeying the laws of the land.

What is this but comparing on a miniature scale, the account of the Creation in the Genesis? Let us see. The first act was the creating of room to be occupied by the material of the universe, called Heaven, Gen. i. 1, and defined as firmament or expanse, v. 8, or more clearly, space. The next was the creation of earth, Gen. i. 1, and the earth was then without form, v. 2, that is, not made into form, and hence must mean primordial elements of matter uncombined. The next was the creation of light, Gen. i. 3, simply, without any quality of being emitted or reflected. The

Establishing the Christian Religion. 271

next was the combining the elements of waters into fluid waters, Gen. i. 6, 7. The next was combining primordial elements of earth to make the dry land called earth, Gen. i. 9. The next was the gathering together the already made waters to make seas, rivers and lakes, Gen. i. 9. The next was the planting of the vegetable kingdom on the dry land already combined, Gen. i. 11. The next was the grand start of the heavenly bodies in motion, to establish the greater and lesser light to be for signs and seasons and for days and nights, Gen. i. 14. The next was the creating of fishes to inhabit the waters and fowl to fly in the air, Gen. i. 21. The next was the creating beasts of the field and creeping things, Gen. i. 25. The next was the making of Adam, male and female, in the image of God after His likeness, to have dominion over all the earth, Gen. i. 26. The next and last act was creating The Adam in God's own image, and another class of male and female, Gen. i. 27.

If man had the omniscient power of God to create, he would undoubtedly pursue a similar course in building his house that God pursued in building the universe, and especially in building man's home, this earth, and more particularly in considering the design for which this earth was created, so that the account in this view is not so deep and mysterious as is generally supposed, because it was executed upon principles used in our every-day life.

There is no mystery about the creation of the class of mankind created in Gen. i. 26, as that class is clearly defined in Gen. v. 2, but there is some mystery and, we may say, more mystery about the creation of the class in Gen. i. 27. An investigation will show that in this class was started the controlling principles of the Christian religion, namely, obedience to the laws and commands of God, so that we may say without the fear of contradiction, that right there in the Garden of Eden was the initial start of the Christian religion; and although a start in a single principle, subsequent events have developed it into a finished and everlasting system.

Gen. i. 27 is devoted to the account of the creation of The Adam and a class of male and female. It was difficult at first to ascertain who these people were and how to place them, and the difficulty was only overcome by the word "dominion" in Gen. i. 26. As the second class in Gen. i. 27 had no such power conferred upon them, it was easy to separate the two classes, as Adam (the Gentile races) have always held "dominion" over the whole earth, and as the Hebrews and Jews were the only remaining race, and had no such power conferred upon them, and have never held "dominion," but have failed twice in their attempt to do so. We have contended that the Hebrews were the class of male and female in Gen. i. 27, and that The Adam was the representative Hebrew who was selected by God to be the male head of the Jewish line that was to evolve Jesus Christ. Subsequent events and history prove this conclusion to be correct.

From the above statement it will be seen that The Adam was a very important human being in the sight of God, and ranked third in that respect, Christ being the first, and Moses the second. While this was undoubtedly true, the name of The Adam, which appears in the Hebrew thirty-six times in the first eleven chapters of Genesis, has never appeared in any of the various translations of the Bible. We cannot, therefore, see why it would not be as proper, in the sense of a correct translation, to have suppressed the names of Jesus Christ and of Moses, as to have suppressed the name of The Adam. Convinced of the great injustice and wrong done to God's holy word, we have written volume after volume and scattered them broad-cast, containing substantially the above facts, and asked of any Hebrew scholar or divine, that if any of the positions were incorrect to inform us of any such error.

We had hoped that some one or more of our Christian brothers anxious to send missionaries to inquiring people would have answered our appeal in the spirit in which it was made, and though years have elapsed no one has denied our positions taken, but a silence equaled only by the silence of the grave has been their answer. Under these circumstances, and with a clear understanding of our responsibilities to God and man, we shall now endeavor to place the responsibility of this condition directly upon the shoulders of those who deserve to bear it. We shall prefer open and public charges with specifications against the translators of the Bible, and as a part of these translators we include all those who, after knowing the facts of the case, teach, approve or accept those translations as the word of God, as far as regards the Genesis.

I, THOMAS A. DAVIES, of the City of New York, layman, do make and publish the following charges with specifications, against the translators and interpreters of God's word recorded in the Genesis in the Hebrew of the Old Testament.

Charge First. That these translators have given to the Christian world a garbled account of the Genesis by which they have misused a sacred trust.

Specification First. In this, that these translators have suppressed the God name, ADAM, from Gen. i. 26, given in the original Hebrew, and that name does not appear in that verse in any of their translations.

Specification Second. In this, that these translators have suppressed the God name, The ADAM, the first ancestor of Jesus Christ, from Gen. i. 27, given in the original Hebrew, and that name does not appear in this verse or in any Bible of their translations.

Specification Third. In this, that the translators have suppressed the God name, ADAM, in our King James Bible in the following chapters and verses up to the time of the dispersion of the Jews among the isles of the Gentiles and the nations of the earth, namely: Gen. ii. 5; Gen. v. 1; Gen. vi. 3; Gen. vii. 23; Gen. ix. 6;

and this name does not appear in these places in that Bible. And these translators have neglected to place the name of The ADAM, which, by identity of person in the Hebrew account, was the name to be used.

Specification Fourth. In this, that the translators have suppressed the God name, The ADAM, in the King James Bible, which appears in the original Hebrew in the following chapters and verses, namely : Gen. i. 27 ; Gen. ii. 7, 8, 15, 16, 18, 19, 20, 21, 22, 23, 25 ; Gen. iii. 8, 9, 12, 20, 22, 24 ; Gen. iv. 1 ; Gen. vi. 1, 2, 4, 5, 6, 7 ; Gen. vii. 21 ; Gen. viii. 21 ; Gen. ix. 5, 6 ; Gen. xi. 5. And although The ADAM was the first ancestor of Jesus Christ, was the third Biblical name in importance in the original inspiration, was the original focus in establishing the Christian religion, and his seed was to give us a Saviour, his name does not appear in that Bible, nor has it appeared in any translation of the Bible.

Specification Fifth. In this, that these translators of the King James Bible have suppressed

Establishing the Christian Religion. 277

the God name The ADAM, and substituted therefor the God name ADAM in the following chapters and verses, namely: Gen. ii. 19, 20, 21, 23; Gen. iii. 8, 9, 20; Gen. iv. 1.

Specification Sixth. In this, that these translators of the King James Bible suppressed the Hebrew terms meaning "from ADAM to beast," and substituted for them, "both man and beast," in Gen. vi. 7; by which the flood was made universal in that Bible, while the account in the Hebrew calls for the destruction of the descendants of The ADAM and EVE only, leaving the remaining Hebrew and Gentile races unharmed. (See side-note in that Bible.)

Charge Second. That by manipulation the translation of the Bible has completely destroyed the God meaning in the Hebrew in regard to the inspiration in the Genesis relating to mankind.

Specification First. In this, that the translators acknowledge in their translations that The ADAM in the Hebrew was an individual man, Gen. ii. 8, 15, 18, and in other places, and deny it in Gen. ii. 19, 20, 21, 22, 23 ; and in various other places, by translating The ADAM in the Hebrew as ADAM, the name of a class of male and female created, which are not an individual man.

Specification Second. In this, that translators have acknowledged in their translation that The ADAM, an individual man, was the husband of EVE, in Gen. iii. 12, 20 ; Gen. iv. 1, and in other places, and denied it in Gen. ii. 23 ; Gen. iii. 8, 20 ; and in other places, by declaring that ADAM, the name of a class, was the husband of EVE.

Specification Third. In this, that these plain and obvious contradictions bring the translators and their translations to the awkward position of declaring that EVE had two husbands, The ADAM and ADAM, and the translations in this regard fall to the ground by their own inconsistency.

Specification Fourth. In this, that the translators undoubtedly intended to commit the Bibles to the theology of the unity of the race in the creation, which the Hebrew does not do, as is seen in that account where two classes of male and female and one other male were created. This theology was the foundation for St. PAUL'S theology of original sin in ADAM and EVE, of which he was the sole author, neither of which assumed facts are found in the Jewish religion, or in the Old Testament, or in Christ's Gospel in the New.

Respectfully submitted,

THOMAS A. DAVIES,
Layman.

This could all have been avoided and the account have been made consistent and to agree with the laws of God by following the Hebrew, in placing The Adam and Adam in the places in the translations where they occur in the Hebrew, and in other respects following the identities of The Adam and Adam.

This can be done, and ought to be done even at this late day, for the errors and inconsistencies are too costly for the reception of the translations of the Bible as the word of God, and hence for the cause of the Christian religion.

The title or head-line of the Jewish or Christian religion is *obedience to the commands or laws of God*, and was first written and proclaimed in the Garden of Eden to The Adam. Each set of these laws is recorded by inspiration in the Old and New Testaments. The specific laws for the Jewish religion are recorded in the Old Testament, while those for the Christian religion are recorded in the New Testament. All the Jewish laws in this direction were written and proclaimed to God's chosen people, as fast as their ability to receive them was developed.

In accordance with this, the Jewish laws recorded in the Pentateuch were given them until Moses received from God the whole law for the Jewish religion. Taking the whole account together in a general view it must be apparent that the establishment of the Jewish religion was only one step in the direction of the establishment of the Christian religion. As we have said before in this work, we cannot see, if we follow God's mode of action in other matters, any way by which the Christian religion could have been established so readily and firmly without following the recorded necessary steps taken to bring about that result; first, by establishing the Jewish religion, and by means of a division in that religion Christ was crucified, which was the culminating point in establishing the Christian religion, which was a startling and important element to bring His sayings and teachings prominently and permanently before the world.

While the head-line of Christianity, obedience to God's laws, was promulgated in the Garden of Eden to The Adam, there was another boundary line shown to him soon after. He received a command from God, and that command he disobeyed, and the consequences followed—punishment for the disobedience. These are the two great boundary lines of the Christian religion, and all between them are duties to be performed in order to keep within them. They are the two salient Basic principles and Base Co-ordinates of that religion. It, therefore, becomes of primary importance to the Christian first to know them and then to find out what laws are recorded between them to regulate our conduct so as to obey the one and avoid the other. These are found in Christ's sayings and teachings, commonly called His Gospel. It thus becomes our paramount duty as well as interest to find out from the inspiration exactly what these laws of God are, not by guessing, not by construction, not by common consent, but to find out what these laws are as naked and unmistakable facts, that we may obey the laws, and avoid the punishments.

We therefore say that the boundary lines of the Christian religion were laid in the Garden of Eden and first applied to The Adam, the head of the Jewish line that was to, and did evolve Jesus Christ. He was accordingly born of the Virgin Mary, was crucified in consequence of a division in the Jewish religion, and afterwards rose from the dead and ascended to heaven, leaving behind Him for the benefit of mankind, His Gospel, the laws of God.

THE JEWISH AND CHRISTIAN RELIGIONS CO-ORDINATED.

In a previous article we have endeavored to show how necessary it is to confine teachings to the pure platform of Jesus Christ as the goal of the Christian religion is conduct, following His example and teachings, and by believing His Gospel.

It will now be our endeavor to show how to apply the Co-ordinate to each Base Co-ordinate of principle of this platform, and by so doing, point out an easy method for all to detect any derivation from inspired Christian truth.

Religions are the outgrowth of a normal or educated conscience, and often from blindly following examples of surroundings, without knowing anything about the Basic principles of the adopted religion. There is another large class in like condition, although blessed with normal consciences, education and all the other gifts of life, who never turn a thought in the direction of the foundation principles of the religion which they profess to adopt.

From the fact of the various denominations which are called Christian with differing beliefs, faiths and creeds, we must necessarily infer that they are not all following one set of Basic principles. In truth, we might conclude that very many of them have no idea of the settled platform of Jesus Christ. As acts of God, we can see no difference, except in kind, in the laws of the Christian religion, which are for the regulation of mankind, and His established laws regulating the vegetable, mineral and animal kingdoms, all of which have separate laws for each separate and distinct element; so that the Christian religion does not rest on mere belief and faith, but on facts, while from these facts flow our belief and faith.

We shall not speak of the Basic principles of the various religions of the earth, which number over three thousand, but confine our application of the principle of the Co-ordinate to the Jewish and Christian religions. God founded the Basic principles of the Jewish religion for that people, and He also founded the Basic principles through Christ for the Christian religion. Each of these religions is a unit in itself, and the Basic principles of each are controlled and governed by each one's own set. So that each is a solid unit and has no necessary connection, without the entire Basic principles of the one Co-ordinate with the entire Basic principles of the other.

We shall not pretend to recite all the Basic principles of the Jewish religion, for they are numerous ; but we will name one which controls and gives character to all the remainder, and that is the hope of a Messiah whom they rejected on the coming of Jesus Christ. What standing should Christians give such a religion? In the wisdom of God that religion was necessary as a stepping-stone to the establishment of the Christian religion, and the Jews had the option to accept it as such. They, however, crucified Christ, subjecting Him to all conceivable tortures; but they could not and did not kill him in one sense, for he rose again from what they supposed to be death, and by this proof of His Divinity gave them another opportunity to accept Him as the Son of God.

But all this did not change their stubborn hearts, and it is not surprising that God at once withdrew his special care and protection over them and their religion, and transferred it to the followers of Jesus Christ.

Is it strange or inconsistent, after all the trouble God had, according to the account, with this, His chosen people, that the edict should go forth that they were incompetent to teach His will to the world? We now ask the question: Do the unit Basic principles of the Jewish religion Co-ordinate with the unit Basic principles of the Christian religion? We believe this question will be universally answered in the negative.

Then why is the Old Testament taught as part of the Christian religion? We cannot understand such theology. While there may be parallels of principles in the two religions, which undoubtedly there are, and although these parallels are not coincidents, why quote them from the Jewish religion when they are also found in the Christian religion? Why borrow from the Jewish religion to teach and support the Christian religion?

Now the two religions are taught from the same pulpits at the same time. We are inclined to believe that this theology has grown out of the canon of the books of the Old and New Testaments as inspired records, which they are, so far as the two religions are concerned; and when God and Christ dropped the Jewish religion for the new dispensation of the Christian religion, it is natural to suppose that the theologians would have followed their example.

We do not desire to see a word or a line of the Old Testament dropped or the cover of our Bibles changed, but we hope to see the Old Testament pursued as a preface to the New Testament, and as a history and monument of God's goodness in giving us the new dispensation of the Christian religion. We also hope that by the aid of the Co-ordinate the Basic principles of the Christian religion will be united to Christ's platform forever, to make a unit of his church and be a warning to all heretics who unworthily claim the name of Christians. These should float the banners of their various theories not found in Christ's platform, such as monkeyites, crustaciaites, sedementaryites, and all other theories, whose doctrines do not Co-ordinate with the Basic principles of Christianity.

Of these we would ask that they take the Base Co-ordinates of Christ's platform and run them through the New Testament like a comb, and then look at the result. They may find some things left behind, but will they find any one of these theories, which are so plausibly taught and insisted upon, co-ordinating with any Base Co-ordinate of Christ's Gospel? We think not; and we ask those promulgating these theories, whether it is worth their while to assume the garb of the Christian in order to strengthen their pretensions or trust to their theories upon their merits for reception. It will be seen from this and other points, that we are not writing for popularity, but to support the inspiration, and especially that of the Genesis, and illustrate the true principles of Christianity.

THE BIRTH OF JESUS CHRIST.

This was the most astounding event of the world, about which, as a matter of course, much has been said and written. It is the most difficult part of our creed to understand and believe, simply because it appears to be a violation of God's laws of reproduction in the human family. As written, Christ had a mother, and she was delivered of a child. This was an every-day occurrence, and the inquirer naturally asks in what respect did this birth differ from that of any other? We read that Mary the mother was conceived of the Holy Ghost. No other process having been given, our information is confined to narrow limits.

As generally construed by the world the recorded birth of Christ is in violation of God's laws of reproduction. First, that a woman can conceive from no other source than a man, and second, that all mothers bring forth children in the same manner and by conception the same. Our effort will be to show that there was no violation of God's laws in the birth of Jesus Christ, by making another and, we believe, a true interpretation. We contend that any construction of Scripture that necessitates a violation of His established and active laws, is not the true construction, and is not the spirit of the inspiration. If we admit that God has at any time changed a law or violated a law, we strike at the very foundation of all things, Christianity included, as we can then depend on nothing.

It is, therefore, of the gravest importance that the construction of the conception of Mary by the Holy Ghost should be relieved of its construction of violation of God's laws and be explained and construed accordingly. In order to understand this subject thoroughly we must dissect it into elements, then investigate each element by itself and see whether each agrees with the known laws of God, and if they do, then combine them and we have a result that will in like manner agree with them. On the contrary, if they do not agree, the smartest and most learned scholar in the world cannot make them agree by arguments or assumptions. Then what are these elements?

First. The conception of Mary by the Holy Ghost.

Second. That Mary was a virgin.

Third. That the child at birth was to the observer just like any other human child.

Fourth. That the child had a double nature, Divine and human.

We admit these four propositions to be true if the words used bear meanings that involve no violation of God's established laws. We claim they show no violation and hence our effort to show it.

CONCEPTION OF MARY BY THE HOLY GHOST.

As has been stated before, it is generally supposed that the conception of Mary by the Holy Ghost was in violation of God's laws of reproduction in the human family, and this we claim is an error resulting from a want of understanding what a law of God is. A law of God acts continuously and always the same. In this instance there was no previous or subsequent act of the kind, and, therefore, the conception cannot be ranked as a law of God, but a special act, of which there was no previous type or subsequent continuance. We regard the conception as a *creation* where no law was established for a continuance in type, as was the case in all other creations of humanity. Another and controlling trouble in this matter is, that as far as our information extends there is no definite and completed conception in the minds of the masses what the Holy Ghost is. The teachings have been that the Godhead or Trinity was made up of three *persons*, the Father, Son and Holy Ghost. The uncertainty of what the Holy Ghost is, is the real cause of so much disbelief in the Trinity.

We venture to say that the Holy Ghost is not a person, but is the *mind* of God. The Trinity is a unit in mind, acting with three distinct elements of the Godhead. First, the mind of God acting with God's position as the Supreme Being. Second, the mind of God acting in conjunction with Jesus Christ as the Saviour of mankind, and Third, the mind of God acting upon independent subjects as emergencies arise, and is the Holy Ghost. These three elements have been called three persons, but this nomenclature indicates no distinction betwen the three elements comprising the Godhead. This places the Trinity upon a basis that can be understood, and one upon which it seems to us all Christians ought to agree. We find nothing in Christ's platform that declares he was God, but, on the contrary, he said God was His Father and He His Son. He also said, My Father and I are one. This can only be taken in the sense that God and the Son were one in mind, as, when Christ made this statement, he was in the human form with a Divine mind, while we all admit that God was only Divine and not human. This position brings us to the use of the Co-ordinate to prove this construction. All will admit that God has a mind, that Christ had and now has a mind, and that man has a mind also. Here is a Co-ordinate of kind though not a Co-ordinate of equal rank.

God's mind is the Base Co-ordinate for the mind of Christ, a Co-ordinate, and the mind of man is the Co-ordinate in kind of God's and Christ's mind, although the two first are infinitely greater and purer than the latter. While there are many things of the immaterial nature that we cannot fathom and hence do not understand, there are others we can understand if our belief in a God and in Christ is strong enough to bring that belief within the range of facts. Taking this as the starting-point, we will show that the birth of Christ after the conception by the mind of God followed every existing law of reproduction in the human family, except the one referred to; and the child Jesus presented the same form in appearance as any other child, and as he was declared to be human we must accept that declaration as true.

The child Jesus followed every law of reproduction in the human family except the miracle of his conception or creation, and why? The mother was of the Jew type and the child was of the Jew type; God the Father was of Divine type and the child was of Divine type. In every other respect the child followed the laws of reproduction which we see enacted every day of our lives. Then to apply the principle of the Co-ordinate to the subject. The first-born of The Adam and Eve, the head of the Jewish line, was the Base Co-ordinate, and the first-born of Noah, Abraham, Isaac, Jacob and Daniel were Co-ordinates, and so on down to Mary and her first-born. Christ was alike a Co-ordinate, and he was the last of that line of Co-ordinates, all following the Jew type in purity.

Right here, then, at the very fountain head of our Christianity, is the undeniable and unquestionable proof of reproduction in kind or type in the human family. We cannot see how the theology of the unity of the races in Adam and Eve, and the deducted theology of original sin in them, can stand for one moment under such God descended proof to the contrary. Not one scintilla of proof can be shown by the most accurate historian or the ablest divine or scholar that ever lived, that one type of a race has ever been produced from another. The bare supposition involves our Christianity in the quandary that Christ might have been born a Gentile instead of the God-born Jew that he was, and thereby defeat the entire plan of the Christian religion.

The mother of Christ was a virgin in two senses: first, by the only conception in her by the mind of God, and second, in the ordinary course of reproduction of humanity. We do not assume the *role* of a teacher of Christianity, but only the position of a hearer. But the hearer is more competent to judge of the effects of teaching on him than the teacher who teaches. If the hearer does not understand what is intended that he should understand, he derives no benefit therefrom, while the teacher may suppose that he has accomplished his object in this respect. The result of teachings upon us would be most effective, first, to convince us of the facts of Christianity in order that we might believe in their truth, and then our minds would be in a frame to have faith in the promises of rewards and punishments.

REWARDS AND PUNISHMENTS.

One thing is certain in respect to these two conditions of the future life, that if we perform all the duties required by the Christian religion, we shall have a different condition from those who do not perform them, and do not repent of their sins, if they have committed any. This is all we know in general of either state. Theologies have built up theories upon the first condition as simple happiness without being able to define precisely of what that happiness is to consist; while about the second condition, it is to be a state of punishment and misery, but in like manner are unable to define the kind of punishment to be inflicted.

The great unsettled question has been, and still is, the duration of the rewards, and the time and duration of the punishments. Two terms have been used to define these durations, namely, eternal and everlasting. Eternal is a term not generally understood, and, if understood, not rightly applied. There is nothing, in fact or condition, that is eternal, except eternity itself and God. Eternity has no beginning or ending, and is an indivisible unit and God is its only Co-existent. The temporal plan of the universe is within eternity, but forms no part of it, both being independent conditions; that is, eternity did exist alone with the Co-existing God, without the temporal plan of the universe.

The terms eternal and everlasting are interchangeably used by the writers of the New Testament, when applied to rewards and punishments; but everlasting is used more generally than eternal. It is plain that they used the two terms as synonymous. We must, then, apply the Base Co-ordinates of eternal and everlasting to ascertain what is eternal and what is everlasting. It then appears that the true Base Co-ordinates represent two distinct principles, the one having no beginning or no ending, while the other is a limited time principle, beginning with the creation and ending we do not know when, but it will be when time ends.

We all readily understand what punishment is as applied to our present existences, for it may be of a mental or bodily character. The conscience may be worked upon to produce what Christ calls hell fire, or the body may be tortured with pains or anguish to produce the same result. As Christ does not explain the character or condition of the punishment which he calls hell fire, we must judge of its nature and condition by what we know can punish us here. Just the same conditions that punish us here may not be used to punish us hereafter ; but using, in this instance, the Base Co-ordinate of punishment as an acknowledged principle in this world, we see no reason why this Base Co-ordinate shall not hold in like Co-ordinates in the life to come.

There are some theologians who teach that a man failing in one jot or tittle in the discharge of all Christian duties is to be punished with the same vigor and intensity as the most vicious life sinner, who has committed every sin in the catalogue of crime, and died cursing God with his last breath. Such theologians may apply such teachings to themselves if they like it, but we do not draw the same conclusions from the words of Scripture, which says we are to be punished, without repentance, according to the deeds done in the body ; this is consistent with the justice of God, and is followed by all parents in dealing with their children and by all governments in punishing offenders against the laws. From this it would appear that there are gradations of punishment ; that is, some are to be punished more than others, and this may give us the means of determining the mode of punishment.

If all are to be punished with equal intensity during the times of these punishments, then the punishment by hell fire, in the ordinary meaning of the words, may be the process to be adopted, and this would indicate a restorative to happiness after the punishment was completed. If, on the other hand, the punishments were all to be of equal duration or everlasting, but of different intensities, according to the deeds done, we cannot see how this could be accomplished in hell fire under the ordinary signification of the words, but must of necessity be a condition of which we have no account or knowledge, and must be left entirely to the imagination to conceive.

It is not for us to determine the kind or mode of punishment, and we must be satisfied to know that punishment follows the commission of sin unrepented of; but whether it is begun in this life and continued on in the next, or whether the punishment is all to occur after death, are questions that will remain unanswered in this life. We also know that the punishment, whatever it may be, can be avoided by sincere repentance and belief in Jesus Christ and His Gospel. These will insure us a state of happiness after death; but what that state will be no one has been informed nor can it be defined.

Happiness in the life to come should be the goal of all religious teachings, of all writings and all contentions on that subject. It is, therefore not strange that we should endeavor by every possible means to obtain that happiness. We all know that what is happiness in this world to one individual is torture to another, so that we may say each individual has his own Base Co-ordinate of happiness. It follows, then, that if we know anything about happiness in the life to come, it must be to each individual what it is in this life ; but if all are to be happy alike, it must be a state or condition entirely unknown to anyone before death. It is to be hoped that all who are deserving may reach that glorious goal of a happy state, and to this end is needed concentration on Christ's platform of the Christian religion.

HOW TO BE A CHRISTIAN

BY

THE GOSPEL OF JESUS CHRIST.

DECEMBER, 1895.

SUBJECTS:

ROAD TO SALVATION.

PREFACE.

APPEAL FOR CHRISTIAN UNITY.

CHRIST'S CHURCH.

CHRISTIAN ORGANIZATIONS.

COMPOSITION OF CHRISTIAN ORGANIZATIONS.

GOD'S ORGANIC LAWS.

CATHOLIC AND PROTESTANT LAYMEN.

APOSTOLIC ERA.

FAITH — CHRIST'S CHURCH — BAPTISM

ROAD TO SALVATION

PREFACE.

The appeal of Pope Leo XIII. to the Anglican Church for unity of faith, brings up for consideration two very important points as precedents for its accomplishment. The first is, that the Roman Catholic organization claims to be the exclusive and only Christ's Church of the gospel, and the second is that the so-called apostolic succession carries with it the Divine powers which Christ gave to his twelve apostles.

We find nothing in the Apostles Creed or in its elaboration, the Nicene Creed, that settles definitely these two points: In the Apostles Creed we read, "I believe in the Holy Catholic Church" (Christ's Church), and in the subsequently made Nicene Creed, "I believe in One Catholic Apostolic Church" (Roman Catholic Church). Every one must draw his own conclusion as to the reason why the first name given to Christ's Church was subsequently changed to the One Catholic Apostolic Church, as neither of these two points are found in the gospel, nor in the creeds of the Christian denominations which accept them, nor are they essentials for salvation; it is important for all christians to find out by what authority they are accepted, and whether they are accepted as a faith, or as a discipline, or as deductions.

The twelve apostles had the powers given to them by Christ of healing the sick, casting out devils, raising the dead, and forgiving sins, that they might possess the same powers that He used so successfully in His teachings. As the successionists of to-day are unable to perform these miracles, we naturally conclude that they do not possess the power to perform them, and we are therefore compelled to look into the gospel to find out how Christ disposed of those apostolic powers.

We find in Matt. xvi. 19, that Peter had an additional power of loosing and binding in Heaven and on earth. As the power is not explicitly explained, we must look for some act or acts of loosing or binding done under it for an explanation ; we fail to find a single act of Peter's power of loosing or binding in the entire gospel. This was a permissive power to be used at the will of Peter, and was not a mandatory law. The possession of a permissive power does not of necessity demand its execution, and as there is no record in the gospel that Peter exercised that power, it therefore stands just where it was given, without action.so far as the record tells us.

The powers given to the twelve apostles were given to them personally by Christ, and if any other person or persons were to possess those powers they must have been given by Christ or given to some one authorized by Him to confer those powers upon others. If such powers were ever conferred, as they were very important, it should be recorded in as plain language as that used to confer those powers upon the apostles, and should not be assumed by implication. No powers of the kind having been given by Christ except to the twelve apostles, or given to the apostles to confer them upon others can be found in the entire gospel. We therefore say that biblically no such powers were ever given to any one except the twelve apostles. Even though it be claimed that the Holy Ghost was to instruct them, these teachings would be in harmony with Christ's teachings, and if anything different was given, it in like manner should be recorded to make the gospel complete on the subject.

Notwithstanding this, we have never conversed with a catholic layman who did not believe that the apostolic succession carries with it the Divine powers given by Christ to the twelve apostles and that the Roman Catholic Church alone is Christ's Church. These claims, as will be shown hereafter, are infringements upon the social, political and religious rights of all christians outside of that organization. As a necessity this has produced in the past violent disturbances, destruction of property and has cost thousands of lives, and if continued the same results are possible in the future, as history repeats itself.

The claim that Christ's universal Church is confined to this particular organization, if true, would defeat the object of its establishment, and hence, is inconsistent with the spirit of His gospel. We think there has been a wide misconception of what Christ's Church is as founded by Him. We all admit that the gospel contains all the laws of God necessary to salvation. We say that Christ's Church is the embodiment of the gospel, a Divine law, and is neither a material entity or terrestrial organization. We claim that all religious organizations are for religious instruction to induce people to accept the faith in the truths of Christ's gospel, and be baptized into His Church, when they will come under God's promise and law, securing to them happiness hereafter if they continue to follow the other acquirements of the gospel, or punishment for sin.

Our effort in this little work will be directed to show the bearing of these two claims upon the prospect of christian unity, and more directly upon the social, political and religious rights of the citizens of the United States especially, and of christians generally.

THE APPEAL FOR CHRISTIAN UNITY.

This appeal is resounding throughout the length and breadth of the land and it clearly indicates a deep seated unrest. There is undoubtedly a cause for this condition, and in diagnosing the case if we can discover the cause, we may be able also to discover a remedy. The diversity of faith and belief in the various christian denominations is the real cause of the appeal for unity. It is therefore of the first importance that we should understand what belief and faith are and upon what foundation they really rest, and then to ascertain why such a variety of beliefs and faiths exist.

The terms belief and faith are used in the Scripture interchangeably and apparently have the same meaning in places, whatever may be the cause; belief is the reception of the information about Jesus Christ and His Gospel as truth, and faith is the spiritual conviction of that truth as necessary to baptism into Christ's Church. Belief is entirely terrestrial, while faith is entirely celestial when they are applied to christianity. Belief then is a conclusion we arrive at from information we derive from another or from others, while faith is a mental conviction deduced therefrom.

The only means we have of framing a belief in Christ and His gospel is the record we have in print and oral teachings of those who are educated in that print. We read and hear the entire gospel, and as a whole we conclude our belief, that it was the product of Christ's mind. The imprint has gone through many changes, not only by misprints, but by numerous constructions of some passages, and by different and varying translations.

In our belief, which should we follow, the mind of Christ, or any one of the various constructions, typographical errors, or translations from the original? We say most emphatically that our belief in the great truth of Christ's gospel is founded in the fact that Christ's mind conceived, framed and delivered it to the world. That misprints, misconstructions of particular words or passages or differences of translations are mere nothings, when taken in connection with the great truth that Christ's mind was the author of His gospel, and that this we should believe and follow it in our faith.

The great question then is, have we the gospel as it came from the mind of Christ? If we have, or if all would acknowledge that we have, there would be no necessity for any further effort to obtain christian unity, it would follow as a resultant. If we have not the gospel as it came from the mind of Christ, where rests the fault, and on whom rests the responsibility? It must be either on those who recorded Christ's ideas or on those who have translated from the originals, or on those teachers who have construed those translations in the past, and at the present time.

However faithfully the apostles may have performed their duties in writing down Christ's words from memory on an average of fifty years after they were spoken, it would not be strange if they did not get the record exact from the mind of Christ, still there is no doubt that they recorded the main ideas necessary to salvation. No man can tell at this remote period whether a word has been dropped or a word added at vital points by accident, or that the same result or worse has occurred in the translations by design. Here may be one of the causes of the various contentions in the christian world.

The bibles are considered by all christians as the standard of instruction on their obligation and duties. Is it then surprising that there are so many different sects, having different faiths, each of which take their authority from some one of the various bibles, no two of which issues agree? The first step then towards a christian unity, is to have a uniform bible, in every language, that shall agree with the originals in the Hebrew and Greek, and with existing laws of God, otherwise all efforts at a unity will be as futile as is the present condition of the christian faith.

There is a large class of christians who have the same creed of belief and hence are of the same faith on the points that that creed contains, because faith always follows and is deducible from belief. While these denominations have the same belief and faith, they have very differing disciplines, and it is from these that most of the christian confusion and contentions arise. To agree upon belief and faith on particular points of the gospel as cardinal, by no means binds to a belief and faith upon other points of the gospel as construed by some particular organization to support its particular discipline. These are not cardinal but discipline, the cardinal being the faith and the discipline the constitution of the organization.

As the creed is the foundation of belief and faith of all true christians, it is useful to the proper understanding of our effort to give it in full, and if our space allowed we would give the settled discipline or constitution of each of the christian denominations that have accepted and do accept that creed and deduced faith. Faith in a christian point of view is only effective and valuable as a preparatory step to baptism into Christ's Church, where there is but one Lord, one faith and one baptism.

THE APOSTLES CREED.

I believe in God, the Father Almighty, Maker of Heaven and Earth.

And in Jesus Christ His only Son, our Lord; who was conceived by the Holy Ghost, born of the Virgin Mary; suffered under Pontius Pilate, was crucified dead, and buried; He descended into hell, the third day he rose from the dead; He ascended into Heaven, and sitteth at the right hand of God, the Father Almighty; from thence He shall come to judge the quick and the dead.

I believe in the Holy Catholic Church, the communion of Saints, the forgiveness of sins, the resurrection of the body, and the life everlasting. Amen.

This was the first creed adopted by the catholic organization, and there must have been some important and controlling reason for the great change and the adoption of the Nicene Creed; hence we give it, so that any one can make a comparison between the two and determine the cause of the change.

The Nicene Creed.

I believe in one God, the Father Almighty, Maker of Heaven and earth, and of all things visible and invisible.

And in one Lord Jesus Christ, the only begotten Son of God, begotten of His Father before all worlds; God of God, Light of Light, very God of very God; Begotten, not made; being of one substance with the Father; by whom all things were made; who for us men and for our salvation, came down from Heaven, and was incarnate by the Holy Ghost of the Virgin Mary, and was Made Man; and was crucified also for us under Pontius Pilate. He suffered and was buried; and the third day He rose again, according to the scriptures, and ascended into Heaven, and sitteth at the right hand of the Father; and He shall come again with glory to judge both the quick and the dead, whose kingdom shall have no end.

And I believe in the Holy Ghost, the Lord and Giver of Life, who proceedeth from the Father and the Son; who, with the Father and the Son together is worshiped and glorified, who spake by the Prophets; and I believe one catholic apostolic Church. I acknowledge one baptism for the remission of sins; and I look for the resurrection of the dead, and of the life of the world to come. Amen.

It would seem to the ordinary reader that if the catholic organization had wished to have the Holy Catholic Church understood as Christ's Church, why did they not use the name that Christ gave it instead of using a substitute that required construction? We do not desire to attribute motives that cannot be reasonably drawn from recorded acts. Here we find them taking the first name, Holy Catholic Church, as construed Holy Universal Church, and then the changed name to One Catholic Apostolic Church, or one Universal Apostolic Church. Whose church; Christ's Church, or the Apostolic Church? Every one must be their own judge of the motives of the Roman Catholic organization, of which Peter was the head, of ignoring the name Christ's Church, and making the substitution therefor which has been named.

We do not see much difference except in one respect between the Apostles creed and the Nicene creed, the latter being more verbose and explanatory than the former. But there is one very great and vastly important difference in the one respect referred to. In the Apostolic Creed it reads "I believe in the Holy Catholic Church." What does this mean? All christians define it as Christ's Church, because holy means established by Christ, and Catholic means universal, hence that the Holy Catholic Church means Christ's Universal Church. In the Nicene Creed it reads "I believe in *one* catholic apostolic church."

The result of making a new creed was to change the faith of the then christian world from Christ's Universal Church to the "one catholic apostolic church," because according to the theology of the apostolic succession the Pope had the power to do so. The effect of this change in creed was to narrow down Christ's universal church to the one catholic apostolic church. It aimed to shut out all christian effort except it was made in the one catholic apostolic church, which was then and is now the Roman Catholic organization, the name having been changed while the creed substantially remains the same.

Let us now see what Christ's Church means, and what One Catholic Apostolic Church means. Two different things may have so nearly the same name that the one may be taken for the other. The word church was used by Christ in Matt. xvi. 18, for the first time in the scripture, and the declaration to build His Church was caused by Peter's announcement of faith that "Christ was the Son of the ever living God," as this faith was to, be the rock and foundation stone of His Church. This faith for the christian is derived from a belief of the apostolic creed. The word church is applied to various terrestrial organizations, to various buildings and to various sects, but the meaning in these various uses depends upon the identity of the thing it stands for.

Hence we say that Christ's Church is the embodiment of His Gospel and is a Divine law requiring a course of conduct specified in Christ's gospel, and is not a terrestrial entity or thing, while the word church used to denote entities or things differs widely in meaning from the word church used by Christ. To call His Church by its own name and give it its true position, would be to elevate it above the wrangling factions of earth, which carry its name only as a misnomer which is misleading. Let every theology stand on its own bottom and not dress itself in the assumed livery of Heaven for acceptance before God or man.

To recognize Christ's Church as the goal of the christian is the first step to obtain the means of getting there, which means Christ has laid down as simple and explicit. The after conduct is more complex and difficult and is pointed out by Christ in few but far reaching words, "Love God with all your heart, and with all your mind, and with all your soul, and your neighbor as yourself; on these two commandments hang all the law and the prophets."

If all the christian denominations of the world would accept the uniform faith deduced from the apostles creed, that "Jesus Christ was the only Son of the living God and that His gospel was truth and that He was to judge the living and the dead," it seems to us that we would have substantially a christian unity on this basis. As it is now, each denomination claims that they are right and that all the others are wrong.

To prove it, each one dethrones Jesus Christ as judge, assumes His office, pitches into the others with arguments and documents, and dissensions, bickerings, quarrels and contentions fill the land as the result.

The appeal for christian unity is based upon the supposition of a diversity of faith. If this claimed diversity be well founded, to what is the faith to apply? Is it to Christ's Church, or to the terrestrial christian organizations? It certainly cannot apply to Christ's Church, for in His Church there is but "one Lord, one faith, and one baptism." It must therefore be directed to the temporal organizations. Does the terrestrial organization as such have a faith? If any denomination does not teach the apostles creed, the faith resulting, and Christ's gospel, it is not a christian denomination, and the appeal does not apply to it. If then there are any which teach the apostles creed, the faith resulting, and the gospel, they cannot be called in Christ's Church, because the denomination as such cannot have faith and be baptized to enter Christ's Church, while any individual in that organization can accept the true faith and be baptized into His Church.

It therefore is apparent that the appeal for Christian unity must apply solely to individuals, and the logical sequence is, that it is an appeal for more members of Christ's Church and more effort to obtain them. No terrestrial christian organization can be truthfully Christ's Church, or to be in Christ's Church. The various organizations which assemble in Christ's name for teaching, being taught, or for worship, are recognized and approved of by Christ himself, when He said "Where two or three are gathered together in my name, there will I be in their midst." This it seems to us settles the question as to any particular organization or congregation or assemby being Christ's Church.

In order to unravel the confusion that has arisen by using the name church for all such organizations, we must ascertain from Christ's words what His Church is, and what the apostles first organization for teaching His gospel was.

Matt. xvi. 13. When Jesus came into the coast of Cesarea Phillipi, he asked His disciples, saying "Whom do men say that I, the Son of man am?"

14. And they said, some say that thou art John the Baptist: some Elias: and others Jeremias or one of the prophets.

15. He said unto them "But whom say ye that I am?"

16. And Simon-Peter answered and said, Thou art the Christ, the Son of the Living God.

17. And Jesus answered and said unto him: "Blessed art thou Simon Bar-jona; for flesh and blood hath not revealed it unto thee, but my Father which is in heaven."

18. And I say unto thee that thou art Peter, and upon this rock I will build my Church: and the gates of hell shall not prevail against it.

19. And I will give unto thee the keys of the kingdom of heaven: and whatsoever thou shalt bind on earth shall be bound in heaven, and whatsoever thou shalt loose on earth shall be loosed in heaven.

20. Then charged He His disciples that they should tell no man that he was Jesus, the Christ.

21. From that time forth began Jesus to show unto His disciples how that He must go unto Jerusalem and suffer many things of the elders and chief priests and scribes, and be killed, and be raised again the third day.

22. Then Peter took Him and began to rebuke Him, saying, be it far from thee Lord: this shall not be unto thee.

23. But He turned and said unto Peter, get thee behind me Satan, thou art an offence unto me, for thou savorest not of the things that be of God but those that be of man.

In the conversation of Christ with Peter, after asking him who he was, Peter answered "Thou art Christ, the Son of the Living God." Christ returned the salutation "Thou art Peter, and upon this rock I will build my church, and the gates of hell shall not prevail against it." The faith of Peter that Christ was the Son of the Living God was the rock on which He was to build His Church. This declaration settles the whole question as to who built Christ's Church, or whether it was built by others and called by that name we have Christ's word to deny it, for Christ said *He* Himself would build His Church, and this was done before any authority or power was given to His apostles.

This is clear and explicit, that Christ founded and built His own Church without aid from any one, and it was a completed Church with "One Lord, one faith, and one baptism," an everlasting, universal, unchanging home, with "many mansions" for all who would accept the faith and be baptized. A church having the gospel for its constitution and laws to guide its members in conduct. Can any language express more clearly what Christ's Church is and who built it? It is a spiritual home here and hereafter for the christian.

Christ therefore gave no direction to His apostles to build His church or about building it, or about building churches of any name or kind, but the trend of all His directions to them was to *teach* His gospel to the world after He founded and built His Church and proclaimed by His own teaching, his Gospel; He adopted the plan of apostolic teaching after His crucifixion and resurrection. In order that those teachings should be as effective as His own, He conferred upon His apostles the same outward powers that He had found effective in convincing the people that He was the Son of the Living God. He therefore gave them powers to heal the sick, cast out devils, raise the dead and to forgive sins.

Language is used to convey ideas and is limited in its application and construction to the ideas to be conveyed. What then were the ideas to be conveyed when Christ gave those powers to His twelve Apostles? Was it to give those powers to all the men of Judea? No! Was it to give those powers to any other persons than His twelve apostles? No! Could they by reason alone of having those powers from Christ give those powers to the inhabitants of Judea or to any one of the pagan world, or even to any one of Christ's friends? No! They were therefore to use those powers themselves and for themselves, nor did they do otherwise, nor attempt to do so, as far as the record informs us.

The same directions which Christ gave to His apostles He gave His disciples before His crucifixion.

Matt. xxviii. 18. And Jesus came and spake unto them, saying "All power is given unto me in heaven and upon earth.

19. Go ye therefore and teach all nations, baptizing them in the name of the *Father*, and of the Son, and of the Holy Ghost.

20. Teaching them to observe all things whatsoever I have commanded you: and lo, I am with you always, even unto the end of the world." Amen.

It is evident from these explicit directions to Christ's disciples and apostles, that teaching His gospel was the substance of all His commands to them, so in order that their conduct and teachings should agree, they were confined in the execution of their ministry to the gospel alone. If, therefore, we find in claiming or doing what cannot be found in the gospel, we must set it down as discipline, which is action of the human mind without direct authority of Jesus Christ; while discipline may be advantageous or even pleasant, it must be held as distinct from divine commands, and should not interfere with the social, political or religious rights of others.

We therefore say most distinctly that the gospel does not contain the magna charta that the apostles had given to them in direct language the power to confer upon others, the powers conferred upon them by Jesus Christ. That those powers ceased in the death of the apostles, and this is one of the most brilliant facts to show His wisdom. The powers given to the apostles were for a specific object, to make people more readily believe that Jesus Christ was the Son of the Living God, and when that was accomplished, the gospel remained for the universal use and enlightenment of the world.

If Divine authority ever conferred power upon a human being, there is no earthly power that could revoke that power except death, which is a Divine act. Christ knowing human nature, knew its weakness, and the case of Peter, His favorite apostle, was one in point and like cases were possible and probable to occur. If he had confined the teaching of His Gospel to one particular line of men forever, humanity would assert itself and error creep into the teachings, as it did in various cases of heresy, and if those heretics had asserted their Divine authority, no earthly power could have dethroned them.

As we read the Apostolic and Nicene Creeds, under the Apostolic Creed the Divine apostolic succession was a discipline, while under the Nicene Creed it was made by the approval of the Pope as part of their belief, and hence a faith. Under the Apostles Creed it is "I believe in the Holy Catholic Church," or in other words, I believe in Christ's universal church. In the Nicene Creed the same sentence reads "I believe in One Catholic Apostolic Church, that is, they believe in the Roman Catholic organization made by the apostles, which they call Church after the name of Christ's Church. As the apostles founded the Roman Catholic organization, and if that organization is Christ's Church, then the apostles founded Christ's Church, so that Christ had nothing to do with founding His Church.

The vital question then can easily be answered. Did Christ found and build his Church, or did the apostles? We are compelled to take Christ's words in the matter as binding, and while the apostles did a great and good work worthy of their appointment, they cannot claim the high honor of founding and building Christ's Church. We have said that under the apostles creed, the claimed Divine apostolic succession was a discipline. The succession consists of selection and then of ordaining by the laying on of hands, as a discipline which, in our judgment, is a good one, as it throws responsibility upon the ordainer for the selection of the fittest.

Divine authority must always be derived from examples of Christ or from declarations found in His gospel. As there are no declarations in His gospel that ordination by laying on of hands shall convey Divine authority, or that ordinations shall be done by the laying on of hands, or any particular form shall be used in ordination, it follows that the form of ordination adopted by the apostles by the laying on of hands was a discipline. If Christ had ordained anyone in order to set an example to be followed, it should be found in His gospel; but no such ordination can be found there, much less the ordination by the laying on of hands. Christ selected His apostles simply, without any exterior form.

It is claimed by the Catholic clergy that the Apostles creed, the Nicene creed, and the creed of Pope Pius IV. are the same, and we admit that they are, except as to the name of the organization to which they are applied. Then why did it become necessary to change the name in the Apostles creed to the name in the Nicene creed, and then again change it to the name in the creed of Pope Pius IV.? The reason is well known that the first change was made because the Holy Catholic Church, being Christ's universal Church, covered more ground than the Nicene name, "One Catholic Apostolic Church," while this name left out the word holy, which when restored made the name, One, Holy, Catholic Apostolic Church. This made Christ's universal Church by name The Apostolic Roman Catholic Organization.

As to the faith of the Roman Catholic organization, founded on the Apostles Creed, we have nothing to say except in commendation, but to the name of the organization to which that faith is to be applied, we have something to say, for that is a social, political and religious question affecting the rights of individuals, which under certain circumstances can and may become a serious one, menacing the peace and good order of society. Not satisfied with using the name of Christ's Universal Church, the Church that

Christ founded and built, they changed it to One Catholic Apostolic Church, the terrestrial organization founded and built by Peter, Christ's apostle, which made Peter the head of Christ's Church, instead of Christ Himself, and confirms the apostolic succession from a discipline into a faith.

Not satisfied still with the name One Catholic Apostolic Church, they changed it again to One, Holy, Catholic Apostolic Church, by the creed of Pope Pius the IV. about the year 1563 A. D., and still another addition was made to this creed by Pope Pius the IX., referring to the supremacy and infallibility of the Pope. The new creed of Pope Pius the IV. was made to meet what was denominated the errors of Calvin, Luther and other protestants. They were called heretics, and the object was to shut them out from the benefits of Christ's Church, without they entered it through the Roman Catholic organization of which Peter had been the head.

All these changes in the creed did not affect the faith derived from the apostles creed, except by applying the name of a terrestrial organization to Christ's Church, a spiritual kingdom, which gave strength and Divine Power to the priests, bishops, archbishops, to the cardinals and to the Pope. While the laity had nothing to do with the subject, they remained quiet and satisfied, and were even pleased with the idea that their teachers were vicegerents of Jesus Christ and thus stood in the steps of Christ Himself by the assumed apostolic succession. This is the equivalent to a little red blanket held out to the world and which has provoked opposition, discussion and retaliation, crystallizing and strengthening this organization till it has become one solid unit opposed to every other christian organization. This great fire has come from a little spark, and for which the Roman Catholics of to-day are not responsible. That little spark was the assumption of Christ's eleven apostles, that they could continue their succession in Divine appointment and powers by the laying on of hands on whom they might select, and we say distinctly that no such authority, in plain language, can be found in Christ's gospel.

The result is that from its beginning until now, it has taught the true faith derived from the apostles creed, and baptized into Christ's Church millions of human souls, but it has cost by martyrdom and other deaths thousands and thousands of valuable lives. What if the same discipline be continued, it may cost in the future, no man can tell or divine. This has arisen from the two claims set up by the Roman Catholic organization. The first is that it is the exact Church which Christ founded and built and called His Church, of which He was the Lord and Head, and the second is that by reason of Christ having given to His apostles certain Divine powers to make their teachings correspond and be as effectual as His teachings of His gospel after the extinguishment of those powers by death, should be performed by men having the same Divine powers and positions forever.

There is no necessity of making arguments about admitted facts, but consider the facts themselves and what they are. Did Christ found and build His Church or not? It is an admitted fact that He did, and therefore the existence of His Church is an admitted fact. Did the apostle Peter found and build the Roman Catholic organization? Either he did or did not. It is admitted that he did, and that it exists. Then here are two admitted facts; are they one fact as claimed by the Catholics? To determine this we must investigate the construction of each, the object and use of each, and if they differ, the facts differ. Christ's Church is His spiritual kingdom, and extends all over the earth and includes heaven, and is therefore universal. It is a fixed, finished and unchangeable condition and not an entity.

Then what is the Roman Catholic organization? The apostle Peter was appointed by Christ the head of that organization, to do what Christ did in His teachings, and he fulfilled his mission in teaching Christ's gospel. What was the declared object of those teachings? It was to inform the people of the truths of the gospel, that they might prepare themselves by embracing the faith and be baptized into Christ's Church. It follows that Peter's organization was an institution for instruction in Christ's gospel, and they were precedents for faith and baptism. So that the organization was not to reach up to Christ's Church, but was to furnish the material for it. While the appointed apostles followed Christ's directions in teaching, they seemed not to have understood the difference in the object of their teachings and the result of their teachings.

All Christian organizations have the same object, and if they teach the gospel and the true faith and baptism, they produce the same result if they produce any. It then is apparent that the two facts referred to are independent of each other as facts, hence Christ's Church and the Roman Catholic organization are two separate and distinct facts and existences. Christ's Church is a spiritual universal kingdom, while the Roman Catholic organization is a terrestrial corporation, incorporated by the laws of every country where it exists, to enable it to hold property and carry on its teachings of the gospel of Jesus Christ.

Let us examine the bearing which the claimed apostolic succession had upon the reformation. No one will deny the succession as it is called in the ordinary acceptation of the word ; but this is not all that Catholics claim ; they claim that the succession was by apostles, having the same Divine powers as the twelve, and not by the disciples of Jesus Christ. We would be willing, and not only willing, but it would be a christian duty to acknowledge, that the entire succession from the day of Pentecost of priests, bishops, archbishops, cardinals and popes were each and all vicegerents of Jesus Christ and possessed all His delegated powers to the apostles, if such claim could be found in His gospel, not by implication, or by construction, but by language as plain as that used by Him in making His apostles His vicegerents.

The apostolic succession by name, or its equivalent, is not found in the gospel, and hence is not a primary truth of christianity. It is an assumed name not found in scripture. It is a good name, if it only represented the succession in priestly offices of members of Christ's Church, without the claim of being His vicegerents. Names do not prove identities and the name of apostle does not make an apostle, no more than calling the Roman organization Christ's Church. In this connection we would say, that if by any strange construction the apostolic succession with its full catholic meaning be admitted, an indisputable fact arises, that no provision can be found in the gospel giving to anyone the power to revoke the Divine power given to an apostle, or degrade him from the performance of his calling, so that once an apostle always an apostle, until the Divine act of death closes his career.

It therefore follows that all the so-called apostles that seceded from the Catholic organization were still apostles, with all their Divine powers as reformers. Hence Luther and Calvin and others of the reformation were apostles of Jesus Christ with full power, and if they taught the true faith and doctrines of the gospel, they held the same Divine position as though they belonged to the organization under the name of Roman Catholic. If they taught anything different from the gospel, they were responsible to God for the sin, and punishment would await them for that sin. They were responsible by the rules and discipline of the Roman Catholic organization and could be ejected from that organization, and denied the right to preach in that organization.

As an individual opinion, which does not amount to much, we think it a great pity that an organization that has done so much good in the past, by bringing through its teachings millions of human souls into Christ's Church, and has the prospect of doing the same in the future, should be handicapped by a discipline which is repulsive to over half the christian world. There was a time when it might have done good, but that day has passed, and in this enlightened age it certainly does more harm than good, for christianity is a democratic institution, and not an aristocratic one, is a universal one, and is not confined to one particular set of men.

Before the Reformation the Catholics occupied much of the christian ground, and in less than three hundred and fifty years they hold less than one half. From the statistics taken in the United States, the following is the result:

Washington, June 28, 1895. The census report covering the statistics of churches has just been issued. There are 142 distinct denominations in the United States, besides independent churches and miscellaneous congregations. The total number of communicants of all denominations is 20,612,806, who belong to 165,177 organizations or congregations. These organizations have 142,521 edifices, which have sittings for 43,564,863 persons. The value of all church property, used exclusively for purposes of worship, is $697,630,139. There are 11,036 regular ministers, not including lay preachers. There are bodies which have more than 1,000,000 communicants, and ten more than 500,000. The leading denominations have communicants in round numbers as follows: Roman Catholic 6,250,000; Methodist 1,000,000; Baptist 3,725,000; Presbyterians 1,280,332; Lutherans 1,230,000; Protestant Episcopal 500,000. In number of communicants and value of church property New York leads and Pennsylvania follows, but in number of organizations Pennsylvania is first and Ohio second. The increase in the value of church property since 1870 has been $325,146,588, or nearly 92 per cent., while the number of churches has increased 42 per cent. The increase in the number of organizations is 126 per cent.

From this it will be seen that the Roman Catholics have 6,250,000, while five of the leading protestant organizations have 11,375,332.

Let us now examine what the fruit of the claim of the apostolic succession had upon the Reformation. We take the status of things at the time King Henry VIII. of England applied to the

Pope of Rome for a dispensation to put away his wife and marry another. King Henry was a member of Christ's Church in good standing, and had become so through the Catholic organization of which the Pope was the head. The putting away of one wife and marrying of another was a violation of the VII. commandment, "Thou shalt not commit adultery." Christ specifically defined this act as adultery, hence the Pope was compelled to refuse his consent.

When we speak of the Pope being the head of the Catholic organization, we do not mean the head by apostolic succession, but head of the terrestrial organization, and we think for success every christian organization should have a head selected from among the members of Christ's Church, by selection of the fittest. This Pope was the head of the Catholic organization by selection of the fittest from among the members of Christ's Church, and we presume was in the succession line from Christ's apostles by the laying on of hands.

If the powers given to the apostle Peter by Christ, Matt. xvi. 19, "I will give unto thee the keys of the kingdom of heaven, and whatsoever thou shalt bind upon earth shall be bound in heaven. And whatsoever thou shalt loose on earth shall be loosed in heaven," be construed literally, and the Pope had the same power by apostolic succession, then the Pope had the power to loose the bond of marriage between King Henry and his wife, and bind them between him and another woman. This would be defeating Christ's own words, and setting aside in other like cases His gospel.

Admitting by literal construction that Christ did give these powers to Peter while Christ knew the frailities of human nature down the ages, and that good Peter had denied Christ three times, and that Christ had called Peter Satan (Matt. xvi. 23), is it not proof positive that He did not intend Peter's powers to extend beyond his life. At best, under such plain and positive language, if Christ had intended it, he certainly would have given the power to extend Peter's powers to others in equally plain and definite language. No such language can be found in His gospel, nor can it be found by any strained construction, and therefore we say that no such power was given to Peter to extend.

It is unnecessary to say that but for the Pope claiming to be the head of Christ's Church by reason of vicegerent powers derived by apostolic succession, this application of King Henry would never have been made. We do not go too far then in saying that the scenes enacted subsequent to this application would never have stained history but for this claim of the Pope.

We do not know what passed between King Henry and the Pope except his refusal to grant the dispensation. If the Pope had been a little more conciliatory and communicated to the King something in this wise, the result might have been something different.

"It is not in my power to grant you this dispensation, as it would be a violation of the VII. commandment, for Christ said, Matt. v. 32, 'But I say unto you, that whosoever shall put away his wife, saving for the cause of fornication, causes her to commit adultery: and whosoever shall marry her that is divorced shall commit adultery.' God has given you a conscience and free will to sin or not, therefore the sin will be yours, and the punishment be yours without forgiveness." Is it not reasonable to conclude that this reproof, given in a true christian spirit, might have changed the result.

Among the powers given to Peter was that of raising the dead, and every one knows that neither the Pope nor any other man can do that, as if the power was exercised it would defeat the organic laws of God. Is it not therefore worthy of the serious consideration of this powerful and useful organization in a way, to abandon a claim that if exercised would destroy that which by other conceded claims is calculated to build up and beautify for the glory of God. In our humble judgment such a course would remove deep rooted prejudices and would be a great impulse to its extension, and as we look at the question it would undoubtedly be the wish of every true christian.

We now will give some of the effects of the denial of the Pope to the application of King Henry, and the result shows plainly that there was something deeper and stronger in the mind of the English people than a simple denial of a dispensation. King Henry was as bad a man as ever lived, and this feather thrown upon his deep seated prejudices, his passions flashed like dynamite to destroy everthing catholic in his realm. It is unreasonable to suppose that such a trifle in itself could have moved all England to the steps taken against the Catholics, to confiscate their property, burn their churches, seminaries, and murder their people by thousands and tens of thousands, and deprive them of all civil rights. Still this was done through the reigns of King Henry, King Edward and Queen Elizabeth.

We do not pretend to say that all England approved of the course pursued by King Henry, but the scaffold or acquiescence was their choice.

The King assumed the position of self-made Pope to the religion he established, and he had the Parliament at his back to enforce by law his conceptions. The Anglican organization was the result. It adopted the Apostles Creed as its belief and the faith deduced therefrom, and of course adopted faith and baptism as a means of entering Christ's Church, and thus they became a christian organization, having placed itself upon the foundation principles of the christian religion. About its discipline we have nothing to say, being outside the subject matter on hand.

The same spirit of persecution was continued in 1850, by an attempt to pass in Parliament what was called the penal bill. We extract a few passages from the letters of the Rev. D. W. Cahill, D. D., a Catholic Divine, to Lord John Russell, of date November 4th, 1851." We charge you before a revengeful heaven with the exile and death of our people ; both crimes lie at your door, and you have added ingratitude to cruelty ; we honored you, we followed you. You did not so much surprise us by the introduction of your penal bill as by the historical falsehood and insulting bigotry of your speeches. They were unworthy the historian, below the dignity of the statesman and dishonorable to the man. A third rate orator amongst your own party, and a fifth rate speaker in the whole house, you never could lay claim to distinction, except from the supposed honesty and liberality of your political opinions; but now your inconsistency and bigotry have torn from your face the mask which concealed your mediocrity, it is agreed that the foremost leader of the Whigs has been befittingly transformed into the last hack of the tories.

* * * * * * * * * * * *

"Alas! alas, where shall I begin to tell your political career as regards poor trodden down, faithful, persecuted Ireland? Nor is it with ink or paper I would attempt a description of the woes of your rule. No; no! my Lord; the deserted village, the waste land, the unfrequented chapel, the silent glen, the pale face and the mournful national voice, stamp the history of Ireland with the deep, deep impression of your administration; while the ferocity of the unbridled landlord, and the terrors of the uprooted and mouldering cabin, and the cries of the houseless orphan, and the tears of the broken-hearted widow, and the emigrant ship, and the putrid workhouse, and the red oozing pit of the coffinless and shroudless dead, these, these, Oh! all these are all the thrilling and eloquent witnesses, to publish to coming generations and unborn Irishmen the character and laws of the Russell cabinet. Ah ! Sir, when you had read of the terrific facts of the mother living on the putrid remains of her own child ; and when you saw the awful account of several cases of the dead bodies of the poor Irish being exposed for days in unburied putridity and devoured by dogs in this unheard of state, and when you had heard the cries that were wafted across the channel for help, and those that rose to heaven for mercy from Skibbereen, from Ballinasloe, from Kilrush and from Ballinrobe—has your heart, sir, ever smote you with remorse? that you heard this cry of Ireland with a pitiless composure and sent to starving and dying millions a heartless pittance from your overflowing treasury? History tells the remainder, and history repeats itself."

CHRIST'S CHURCH.

We ask the all-important question, was Christ's Mission on earth to establish terrestrial churches, so called, or to establish the christian religion upon the laws of God, and upon the teachings of His gospel? Some may answer this question that His mission was to establish terrestrial churches, but the concensus of opinion we believe would be that His mission was to establish the Christian religion, and His church as the receptacle. We all understand what a terrestrial church is, and a number of them is also called the church of the denomination. For what object are such structures made? They are places made for people to assemble in, and hear the word of God explained and taught; and by such teachings some are converted to the true faith and are baptized into Christ's Church; they are also used by them as places of worship.

Christ gave to His twelve apostles a mandatory law to teach His gospel to all nations, but we fail to find any directions by Him to them to build terrestrial churches, or teach in such churches. The word Church is used to represent so many different entities that there has been great confusion resulting by using the same word to represent these entities. Christ first used it to name His spiritual Church, and many therefore believe that the name governs the entity and not the entity that governs the meaning of the name. To show that the terrestrial churches are not precedents to the achievement of Christ's Church, we refer to Acts ii. 47. "And the Lord added to the church daily such as should be saved."

From which we learn that no one can be saved except they get into the church. The question is, what church was meant, the Church the Catholics call Church, or Christ's Church? Were there two churches, Peter's and Christ's, or was there but one church? If so, who had the title to it, Peter or Christ? Christ spoke of His Church and said He would build it upon this rock, that He was the Son of the Living God and the truths of His Gospel. Peter was simply a teacher of Christ's gospel with permissive powers given him by Christ, but we fail to find any record that he ever used these powers, nor is it evidence that the possession of powers necessarily calls for their exercise.

What is Christ's Church? We answer that it is substantially the Gospel of Jesus Christ and the constitution of the Christian religion, and is not a material entity or terrestrial organization. It is made up of laws of God, reiterated by Jesus

Christ, and those laws are conditional promises of God and Christ to mankind for obedience or disobedience of other laws of the gospel. These promises of God and Christ are the head and controlling laws of the christian constitution.

These laws are the proclamation of Jesus Christ to mankind to show them the road to salvation, and His Church is that road. Then what are the guide boards that He nailed to His cross to conduct the christian into the gates of His church? Belief that He was the only Son of the Living God, and faith in the truth of His gospel. The next is baptism into His church, which is sealing the covenant of the promises of Christ and God to mankind, that thereafter each one covenanting shall live up to the requirements of the gospel. They are then in Christ's Church, where there is One Lord, one faith, and one baptism.

There must of necessity be a clear distinction made between a Divine law and the subject upon which the law operates. As for example, the law of gravity operates universally and always the same, and by its use we are enabled to carry on all the business of life, and without it we could do nothing.

Important and useful as the law is, in the apostolic times the law was unknown, yet the people had the free use of it then as they have now, and so it was with many other laws but lately discovered. The discovery of a law changes nothing, but may explain many things that before were strange and sometimes mysterious. How absurd it would be for any one knowing what the law of gravity is, and how it acts, to call the houses, buildings, and the community occupying them the law of gravity.

Let us then give Christ's Church its proper name and position as the head law of the gospel, governing all its other laws and all terrestrial organizations teaching the gospel. Ten thousand years of teaching an error will never make it a truth, though it may be difficult to acknowledge it.

The gospel record is our christian law, and to it we must refer all our conclusions and differences of opinion. The law has two objects; one of reward in the life to come of a state of happiness for obeying the law in this life, and one of punishment for disobeying it. The gospel plainly sets forth these two positions, and they are confirmed by the word of God and promises of Jesus Christ. These promises are the Grand Magna Charta of the Christian framed in Heaven and sent to earth in escro with Jesus Christ, and He has established His Church to be the dispensary of them to the people of the earth.

What are the conditions under which man can avail himself of the benefits of the Magna Charta and become a party to the agreement? The conditions are so plainly laid down by Christ that there can be no misunderstanding them. These are, belief in Jesus Christ as the Son of the Living God, and of the truths of His gospel, or in other words, that Christ is God's authority. This belief being perfect, involves the faith in the plan of christianity as Divine.

The convert then is prepared on his part to accept the Magna Charta and close the agreement between him and his God to thenceforward follow and obey the teachings of Christ's gospel.

Christ's instructions as to what the converter is to do to accept this agreement and affix his seal. They are—that he is to be baptized into his Church, when the agreement between the parties becomes a binding law, and the accepting party becomes a member of Christ's Church, and this agreement being of Divine authority, no human power can depose him. Once a member always a member, and if he commits sin God will punish him, but no earthly power can do so.

If he belongs to a religious organization, with by-laws as discipline, he can be deposed as a member of that organization, or such other action as the by-laws may designate; but no action of the organization can interfere with any Divine law, or with the agreement between God and Man, the Magna Charta.

This Magna Charta contains all the required relations between God and man on and after its acceptance by any human being. He binds himself, or she binds herself, to obey all the laws of God, material and spiritual. He or she is then in Christ's Church, and this is what the name means. Its institution by Christ was to be universal for the benefit of all mankind, and hence was not to be confined to any section, or to any particular organization. It is more than everlasting, for it will survive all temporal things and all existing laws except itself, and will be co-existent with God.

As faith in the truth of Christ's gospel is an all-important point, it is essential to know just what that faith requires. There are so many constructions of the declarations of Christ, that some may be confused in determining what construction they should follow. It must be remembered that Christ requires faith in the truth of His gospel and not in any particular construction of them; mankind is so peculiarly constituted that they do not all see things alike, and hence draw different conclusions from the same statement. Christ in His wisdom knew this fact, and hence did not state any particular construction of His gospel as the essential to the true faith.

A christian to be eligible for baptism into His church is only bound to have the faith in the truth of His gospel. That truth may or may not be the construction in exactness which he has been taught, or which he has understood from his reading, and if he has used his best intellect in endeavoring to sift out the exact truth, he will not be held responsible if over this he believes in the truth of Christ's gospel. It is the intention and determination to believe the gospel as truth, that is the essential to be the faith, and not in any particular construction. Therefore have charity, and judge not that you may not be judged.

We will now give the mandatory laws of Jesus Christ, which the christian must obey after entering His Church. These consist of God's organic laws which Christ was sent on earth as a Missionary to teach to the world, which He did, and then He appointed twelve apostles with certain Divine powers to teach, as missionaries from Christ, the nations of the earth.

LAWS THAT CHRISTIANS MUST OBEY.

God's Organic Laws.

To accept God as the Creator of all things Visible and Invisible.

To accept Jesus Christ as the Son of God and as His Missionary to the world, to establish the Christian religion and to be the Saviour of mankind.

To accept the Holy Ghost as the mind of God and Jesus Christ.

To accept God's material and immaterial laws, and for obedience of them, rewards of happiness in the life to come, and for disobedience of them, punishment.

Ten Commandments Given to Moses.

I. Thou shalt have no other gods but me.

II. Thou shalt not make unto thyself any graven image nor the likeness of anything that is in the heavens above or in the earth beneath or in the waters under the earth. Thou shalt not bow down to them nor worship them, For I the Lord thy God am a jealous God and visit the sins of the fathers upon the children unto the third and fourth generation of them that hate me, and shew mercy unto thousands in them that love me and keep my commandments.

III. Thou shalt not take the name of the Lord thy God in vain, for the Lord will not hold him guiltless that taketh His name in vain.

IV. Remember that thou keep Holy the Sabbath day. Six days shalt thou labor and do all that thou hast to do, but the seventh day is the Sabbath of the Lord thy God. In it thou shalt do no manner of work, thou and thy son and thy daughter, thy man servant and thy maid servant, thy cattle and the stranger that is within thy gates. For in six days the Lord made heaven and earth, the sea and all that in them is, and rested the seventh day. Therefore the Lord blessed the seventh day and hallowed it.

V. Honor thy father and mother, that thy days may be long in the land which the Lord thy God giveth thee.

VI. Thou shalt do no murder.

Laws that Christians must Obey.

VII. Thou shalt not commit adultery.

VIII. Thou shalt not steal.

IX. Thou shalt not bear false witness against thy neighbour.

X. Thou shalt not covet thy neighbour's house; thou shalt not covet thy neighbour's wife, nor his servant nor his maid nor his ox or his ass, nor anything that is his.

Christ's Two Commandments.

XI. Thou shalt love the Lord thy God with all thy heart and with all thy soul and with all thy mind.

XII. Thou shalt love thy neighbour as thyself. On these two commandments hang all the law and the prophets.

The other mandatory Laws of Christ's Gospel are prayer, faith, baptism, the Lord's Supper, and the most useful and important one given to His apostles was to preach the gospel to all the nations of the earth.

CHRISTIAN ORGANIZATIONS.

These organizations have grown out of the necessity of spreading and teaching the gospel of Jesus Christ. They were unknown in their present shape at the time of the early teachings by the Apostles.

There was then but one embryo organization of which Peter was the head, and no laws existing by which it could be recognized to enable it to hold property and build buildings for places of meeting for instruction and worship. It then did not exist as it now exists, with civil law to enable it to hold property, build cathedrals, seminaries, and various other places for teaching and spreading the gospel. We fail to find anything in Christ's instructions to the apostles directing such organizations or the building of such buildings.

His instructions to His apostles were to teach His gospel to all nations, and that gospel contained everything necessary for faith, morals and practices. Did Christ give His apostles the sole right to teach His gospel? We think not, as that would defeat the very object He had in view of spreading His gospel.

Did Christ direct or empower His apostles to appoint men in His name to teach the gospel? We do not find any such thing in His gospel! Did He deny to any one the right to teach His gospel? We answer most emphatically, No! Then if any one teaches the truth of His gospel with good intent to make converts to the Christian faith, how does his position differ from that of any other teacher of the same things? As teachers both stand on precisely the same footing and foundation, they both teach the essentials for salvation, both are members of Christ's Church, both pursue the same conduct for the Christian prescribed by the gospel.

The question naturally arises in one's mind, why they did not use the name of Christ's Church in the Apostles Creed instead of the "Holy Catholic Church," and why they changed that name in the Nicene Creed to "One Catholic Apostolic Church?" The name "Church" is the noun in the three cases when it is used, and "Christ's," "Holy Catholic" and "One Catholic Apostolic" are the adjectives, making the kind of Church meant in each instance. "Holy Catholic Church" or "Holy Catholic," or "One Catholic Apostolic Church" or "One Catholic Apostolic" are not to be found in Christ's gospel; they are therefore not biblical, and must be treated like any ordinary language as not inspired.

There is one other saying in the Apostles Creed that we do not find in the Gospel, the "Communion of Saints." This with the Holy Catholic Church are subjects of construction, while all the remainder of the Creed is found in the gospel.

As there is but one Church mentioned in the gospel, we are bound to construe Holy Catholic Church as the Holy universal Church of Christ, and the Communion of Saints which at that time referred evidently and of necessity to the apostles agreement in faith.

The Nicene Creed covers considerable more ground than the Apostles Creed, as will be seen by any one reading the two, but cannot be regarded as an abrogation of the Apostles Creed but an extension of it ; so the catholics were sure of being right, and they believe and practice upon the two as one. It is not strange therefore that they should believe in the One Catholic Apostolic Organization which they founded themselves, a privilege which any Christian Organization has as of inherent right. We therefore say distinctly, that the Roman Catholic Organization has the right to make its own discipline, frame its own constitution and practice their own worship, provided they do not interfere, impliedly or otherwise, with the social, political or religious rights of their neighbors or others.

It is well for us to consider the true positions and conditions of religious organizations without any squeamishness as to terms. They are business organizations, having for their purpose the accomplishment of a certain end, and this is the object of every earthly organization and of all individual or collective effort. The object to be obtained by religious organizations is to lay up treasure in heaven, while the object of all other earthly effort is to lay up treasure on earth. No wonder why religious organizations have different discipline and pursue different means of accomplishing the same end. One set of men consider the course they pursue the best to accomplish their object, while another think differently and pursue another course, each finally arriving at the same end. This is a universal rule applied to all earthly efforts.

All business Christian Organizations follow the same general principles in their pursuit that stimulate all other business pursuits, and that is to take such a course of action as to produce the greatest result by taking the best means according to their judgment of conducting the business.

Scarce two farmers ever till their ground alike for the same crop ; scarce two merchants pursue the same course in business, nor any two corporations aiming to accomplish the same end. Yet the two farmers are rewarded with the same crops ; the two merchants make equal amounts of money, and the two corporations serve the community with equal success. It is therefore apparent that it is not the particular manner of doing the business of the discipline of Christian Organization that is controlling and essential, but to accomplish the required result and reach the goal.

As a necessary result for success, every organization and every industrial effort must have a head, and the organization be guarded by conventional rules, and when applied to governments terrestrial, or governments celestial, these rules are called laws. The religious organizations being comprised of part of the people governed, must of necessity come under the governmental law. So that these organizations are recognized as business organizations, and are incorporated like them, with power to transact their business, hold property, and do all other things authorized by their charter.

They then perform all the duties as a citizen required of them by the law. Among those duties are the payment of taxes necessary to the payment of the legal expenses of the government. These taxes are generally remitted on the property of the religious organizations; other taxes however are not, and the money thus obtained passes into the public treasury to be used according to law. The title of the tax-payer to his money ceases on its payment. No one can therefore ask to have the money thus paid returned to him for his uses in promoting his individual interest, or that of the organization to which he belongs, and if he does, it is incipient mutiny against the law of equal rights and equal privileges.

These religious organizations are chartered under the tacit understanding that they will not disseminate among the peoples disintegrating elements, such as the possession of individual powers and distinctions, which they deny to those granting such privileges, or to any one else on the earth. Hence these powers and distinctions should be founded upon plain language in Scripture, and should not be claimed to be derived from deductions and doubtful constructions. In this Government of equal laws, equal rights, and equal privileges, such unequal doctrines must in the end produce conflict. There is conflict now in opinion, and as that strengthens and grows, each party becomes stronger and stronger in their opinions, till history repeats itself.

If these claims of the Catholic organization were necessary to Salvation of Souls, and they were found in plain language as other requirements are in Christ's Gospel, we would ask that they should be posted in letters of gold on every door-post in the country; but they are not claimed to be such, nor are they, but are a discipline of the organization made by individuals and continued by others who were and are alone affected by them directly, while they have a bearing upon the exclusive reception of that religion and go to sustain the Theology that this terrestrial organization is alone the true Church of Jesus Christ.

There is great stress put upon the following passage, to show that the Roman Catholic organization is alone Christ's Church.

Matt. xviii. 15. Moreover if thy brother shall trespass against thee, go and tell him his fault between him and thee alone ; if he shall hear thee then thou hast gained thy brother.

16. But if he will not hear thee, then take with thee one or two more, that in the mouth of two or three witnesses every word may be established.

17. And if he shall neglect to hear thee tell it unto the Church, but if he neglect to hear the Church, let him be unto thee as an heathen man and a publican.

Here was a legal moral question to be decided, and we have Christ's method of deciding it. He told them to refer it to the Church. What Church? This was before the Apostles commenced their ministry and before any organization of the Catholics. At that time there was but one Church, and that was Christ's Church, which He had proclaimed, and He referred this legal question to the law of His Church.

The Church being the head law of the gospel, it was natural that He should refer all moral questions to it for decision.

This principle is more clearly set forth in another passage, Luke x. 25. And behold a certain lawyer stood up, and tempted Him, saying, Master what shall I do to inherit eternal life?

26. He said unto him, What is written in the law? How readest thou?

27. And he answering said, thou shalt love the Lord thy God with all thy heart, and with all thy soul, and with all thy strength, and with all thy mind, and thy neighbour as thyself.

28. And He said unto him, thou hast answered right. This do and thou shalt live.

Christ there approved of the lawyer gaining knowledge by reading the Scripture without the aid of any terrestrial organization, which is a very important point in this discussion.

COMPOSITION OF CHRISTIAN ORGANIZATIONS.

These organizations are composed of three classes of people namely,—Those who attend meetings held for instruction only, those who are legal members of the organization, and members of Christ's Church who have been baptized into it.

The first class are those who are attracted for various reasons, from curiosity, desire to see and be seen, to gain religious information and so on. The second class are the essential material of the organization, are legal members of it and constitute the business portion of the congregation, make the by-laws and assist in establishing the Discipline. The third class occupy in a congregation two positions. One as a member of the business organization, and one as a member of Christ's Church, having accepted the faith that Christ was the Son of the Living God and been baptized in that faith.

All Christian organizations that accept the Apostles Creed as the basis of faith, are entitled to the appellation of Christian Denominations, and all those who do not, are not entitled to that high distinction. That creed embodies the landmarks of Christ's Gospel. The manner of organization of these denominations being mainly done by business men having business views of things, they naturally mix up terrestrial matter with the principles of religion, and hence they have disciplines which are not contained or to be found in Christ's Gospel. Still the teachers teach the principles of the gospel in addition to the carrying out the required discipline, and as far as they teach Christ's Gospel, they are teaching Christianity; but if the discipline does not bear directly upon it, they are talking to the wind about subjects not connected with the Christian religion.

The machinery of discipline in some organizations is so cumbersome and onerous, that it discourages the layman from undertaking it, instead of inviting him by the simplicity of Christ's teachings. This state of things involves the necessity of laymen thinking for themselves and striking out to discover the simple kernels of Christianity. It now takes a candidate for the ministry to go through a regular course of Seminary Studies to find out what he is to teach of the gospel and discipline of his denomination, for we call discipline all that is preached in the pulpit outside the gospel of Jesus Christ.

Most of the quarrels within denominations and betwixt denominations are due to points of discipline, and these are generally called heresies. They are simply differences of opinion as to whether the teacher is following the discipline or not. There are very few cases of heresy upon the fundamental doctrines of Christianity. The greatest Christian quarrel of the world, which resulted in the Protestant Reformation, was caused by a point of Discipline of the Roman Catholic organization by reason of King Henry VIII. being a catholic; the question at issue had to be referred to the Pope.

There is nothing in the Christian world that requires so rigid an examination and amendment as this subject of Discipline. The gospel of Christ and the principles of Christianity will take care of themselves, but the main machinery of the mode of this dissemination requires revision because it is continually changing.

That the layman may be relieved of responsibility of errors of construction and general teachings outside of the gospel, he must himself know what the requirements of that gospel are for his salvation. If he can by any means arrive at that information, he can discard all teachings inconsistent with it.

Accident, education, association and various other causes bring him into attendance of a given denomination of Christians, and he becomes a member of that denomination, without, as a general rule, being able to assign any reason for doing so. He has a responsibility of his own, as well as the ministers who teach him. He should first ascertain whether that denomination accepts the Apostles Creed as the basis of faith, which is that Christ was the only Son of the Living God and that Christ's Gospel is truth, and that the true faith and baptism are essential to become a member of Christ's Church, and as a member he is bound to live according to the requirements of the Gospel.

Every layman taking an interest in his salvation should know these Basic principles of Christianity, and it is easy for him to ascertain whether these are the acknowledged principles of the denomination to which he proposes to belong, and if his enquiries are assured in the affirmative, it is a Christian denomination and safe for him to trust himself and his salvation to its teachings and instruction. The community of interests between the teacher and the layman are such that enquiries by the layman should not be considered as an interference with the prerogatives of the teacher, but should be evidence to him of a deep interest in the subject.

The responsibility for digressive preaching from the Gospel in pulpits, is not alone the responsibility of the preachers, for the layman should inform himself so as to be able to check such digressions by conciliatory objections. This would have the effect of doing away with much of the useless and often damaging harangues frequently heard from itinerant preachers in pulpits consecrated to the service of God. If the Christian literature and pulpit oratory of the day could be infused with more Christian Charity and love, they would all come nearer obeying the Eleventh and Twelfth Commandments of Jesus Christ.

GOD'S ORGANIC LAWS.

The great scheme of existence of all things which culminate in the establishment of the Christian religion should be considered as a unit, and that religion and the acts which brought it into existence as the crowning factor. Without this view, Christianity standing alone upon its merits even, fails of the proofs and support which it has when linked into the chain of events which led up to its establishment. In fact it is impossible to see how a full and clear conception of Christianity can be arrived at by any reflecting mind, without a knowledge of every preceding element upon which it depends for its existence. We do not wish to be understood as saying that a person cannot be a sincere christian and enjoy all the benefits resulting therefrom, without the knowledge of every preceding step in this chain of events.

How is a knowledge of these events to be obtained? As the first and all important requisite at least, the enquirer must believe in God the Author and Creator of all things, visible and invisible, and believe in the inspired record of the Creation and the Jewish religion in the original

Hebrew of the Old Testament, and in Christ's Gospel in the original Greek in the New Testament. Without this belief the enquirer would be limited to what he sees in nature, and what he could hear of Jesus Christ as a man and not as man and God in combination. Even this knowledge should be sufficient to lead his mind on to investigate the further and loftier subject, but with this limited belief and knowledge he would be unqualified to reach the true name and position of the Christian. Assuming then that the enquirer believes in God, in Jesus Christ, in the inspiration of at least that portion of Scripture relating to the Creation, to the Jewish religion, to the Christian religion, and that God and Christ have the same mind usually called the Holy Ghost, he is prepared to enter upon the facts of God's Organic Laws.

The Creation and the Organic Laws resulting for the regulation of all things, is the normal idea that presents itself to the reflecting mind. Following the Creation in the order given in the Genesis, we see the controlling principle that governs all things, namely, the dependence of one thing upon another. Thus the order of Creation begins by God creating space or room to put His other Creations in, and called in the Hebrew heaven or expanse, and then the Creation of primordial matter, (earth without form and void), then the light, then the waters, then the dry land (earth primordial matter combined), then the gathering together the waters to make seas, lakes and rivers, then the planting of the Vegetable Kingdom, then giving motion to the Heavenly Bodies to give us days, nights and seasons, then to create the inhabitants of the waters and the animal kingdom, and finally to make Adam (incorrectly translated in all Bibles "man"), because in Gen. v. 2, Adam is specifically defined as "male and female" created in the day of creation and named Adam, and then created The Adam (mistranslated man) the husband of Eve, and then another class of male and female, making in all of human beings created one class of male and female under the name of Adam (the Gentile race) and The Adam the husband of Eve and the other class of male and female being Hebrews.

The first chapter of Genesis in our judgment *is the most important one of the entire Bible*, as it is the history of the foundation of all God's works, and of all His laws, material and immaterial, and is of necessity the ground work of the Christian religion, and still it is the most neglected portion of Scripture, and probably for the reason that there are so many mistakes of translation that have run so long, no one is desirous of being the first to rectify them. It has thus become the least understood of all the Bible.

The Creations, the establishment of the Organic Laws of God, the creation of mankind, the establishment of the Jewish religion, the sending of Jesus Christ as a Missionary from God to the world, His teachings, His examples, His crucifixion, His rising from the dead, His ascension, leaving behind Him His established Church, are links in the great chain that bind man to his God. Each link is of equal binding strength upon humanity, and the Christian's education should embrace them all equally.

The importance of each link in the chain can be readily seen by asking the question, what would the Christian religion be if any one of them was eliminated?

The question answers itself and shows the importance of each and every one of them to finish the beautiful structure for the instruction and admiration of the Christian student. Independent of the information as to the God plan of Christianity, these links will serve a double purpose as elucidations of the main subject and as coincident proofs of the record where they are found, for the scientific proposition is that when two straight lines coincide in two points, they coincide throughout. The one straight line being the inspired portions of the Old and New Testament, and the other straight line being the Organic Laws of God, and by comparing the two any number of coincidences can be found.

It is well then to see what the Organic Laws of God are as defined in nature, and in the Scripture Inspiration, both natural and spiritual.

THE ORGANIC LAWS.

God the Creator of all things, visible and invisible.

Jesus Christ the Son of God and Saviour of mankind.

The Holy Ghost the mind of God and Jesus Christ.

The material and immaterial Laws of God governing the Universe and mankind.

Obedience of mankind to these laws.

Rewards in the life to come to mankind for obedience to them, and punishment for disobedience.

The Ten Commandments delivered by God to Moses.

These laws were all established within the six days of Creation, and have continued unchanged to the present time, and will continue so to the end. Is it then of consequence that the Christian should understand the first chapter of Genesis, which, when investigated, clearly and accurately gives the full account of the bringing into existence by the fiat of God every conceivable entity with its qualities as a first form, and as a necessity of Divine Laws for their continuance and regulation.

We look with amazement and wonder at the Sun, the Moon, the Planets and the Stars in Space, and why? Because of their immensity, and of their value to mankind. Each creation is dependent upon another, and all centre in use in support of the human races, and thus they become the avowed objects of creation. The more closely and minutely we examine all these things, the more the investigator becomes convinced that the design of God was to place man at the pinnacle, and all else under him. To illustrate this idea and show its magnitude, thereby to gain some conception of man's importance in the Universe, we quote an article from Chamber's Journal:

"The Distance to the Stars."

"Astronomers agree in fixing the distance of "the nearest star at 22,000,000,000,000 miles,

"and we are probably not far from the truth if
"we set the distance of Sirius at about 100,000,-
"000,000 miles. It is calculated that the ball
"from an Armstrong 100-pounder quits the gun
"with the speed of about 400 yards per second.
"Now, if this velocity could be kept up it would
"require no fewer than 100,000,000 years before
"the ball could reach Sirius."

WHAT WE SEE AND KNOW.

It is admitted that there are now and have been since the establishment of the Christian era, six distinct races of humanity upon the earth, and if they are reproduced in purity of type without hybridity, the reproduction will be the same in each race. These races are the Caucasian, the Mongolian, the Malay, the Indian, the Negro, and the Hebrew. At the time of the establishment of the Christian religion, these races were all on the earth, and are now here, and the Christian is bound to acknowledge and not deny this Organic Law of God. True science and an every day observation have developed and traced in action the laws of reproduction in these races, while the Theologians have battled with these scientists on the theology of the unity of the race in Adam and Eve.

The churches by their teachings, and all orthodox sacred writers have maintained that Adam and Eve were our first parents, from whom all humanity on earth have been produced. Such is the strength and depth of this education, that whenever reference is made to the subject, they throw aside the Organic Law of God, and insist upon calling Adam and Eve our first parents.

At this point arises an important question: Are we to take as our guide in reading the Genesis, the original Hebrew, which gives us a diversity of origin in the human family, or shall we take as our guide the theologians translation of it, which makes or endeavors to make the human family to have come from Adam and Eve? As the Hebrew is the admitted and undoubted inspiration of God, and as it differs widely from the English and other translations to which we refer, we adopt the Hebrew as our guide in the account of Creation in the Genesis.

It may be a surprise to some readers of the English Bible, that Adam in the Hebrew was not the name of Eve's husband, nor was Eve created in the six days of creation, but was made from the rib of The Adam, the name of her husband, sometime after he had been put into the Garden of Eden. And although the name of Eve's husband, The Adam, appears in the first Eleven Chapters of Genesis in the Hebrew forty-seven times by name and identity, her husband's name has never yet appeared in any translation of the Bible.

St. Paul was the author of the Theology of the Unity of the race in Adam. That dogma is not found either in the account of Creation in the Hebrew, or in the Jewish religion in the Old Testament, or in Christ's Gospel in the New. Still it has been taught in the early Churches following the lead of St. Paul to the present time as Church discipline. As that dogma has no foundation in truth now, nor had it at the time the Christian religion was inaugurated, the Christian must reject it and cling to the Biblical record in the Hebrew as an Organic Law of God.

It is difficult to determine exactly where the error arose, but as the present Hebrew is from the Hebrew manuscripts from which the translation into the Greek was made, it is reasonable to suppose that the mistake occurred in Septuagent in the Greek, as from this translation was made into the Latin, and from this all other translations have been made. It was a very natural mistake as the material laws were not well understood, and the tradition of that day was that all humanity had sprung from a single pair.

In the King James Bible the translators, in order to make the account correspond with the unity of the race, were compelled to drop these important Hebrew words, namely "Adam," "The Adam," and the word "And," at the head of Genesis i. 27, and substitute "man" for "Adam" and "The Adam," and "so" for the Hebrew word "And." Further in the account, by interchangeably using "Adam" for "The Adam," and translating "The Adam" "the man," and leaving out of sight the name The Adam, the husband of Eve, they made out the unity of the race in Adam and Eve.

This being a very important point for the Christian to understand, we give the two verses in the Genesis which is all that relates to the creation of mankind, and also give the Genesis v. 2, which clearly defines the name Adam in the day of Creation.

Genesis i. 26. And God said, let us make Adam in our image, after our likeness, and let them have dominion over the fish of the sea, and over the fowl of the air, and over the cattle, and over all the earth, and over every creeping thing that creepeth upon the earth.

Gen. i. 27. And God created The Adam in His own image, in the image of God created He him; male and female created He them.

Gen. v. 2. Male and female created He them, and blessed them, and called their names Adam in the day when they were created.

From this it will be seen that Adam was the name given by God to a class of male and female created, and hence could not be the husband of Eve, while The Adam was an individual man created, and after he was put into the Garden of Eden to dress it and keep it, the following took place:

Gen. ii. 21. And the Lord God caused a deep sleep to fall upon The Adam and he slept, and He took one of his ribs and closed up the flesh instead thereof.

Gen. ii. 22. And the rib which the Lord God had taken from The Adam made He a woman and brought her unto The Adam.

This settles definitely some important points. First, that The Adam, not Adam, was the husband of Eve. Second, that Eve was not created on the day of creation among the females then created. There having been others created and living before she was made, about which there can be no question, the translation or construction of unity of the race in the following verse, is a bold error.

Gen. ii. 20. And The Adam called his wife's name Eve, because she was the mother of all living.

If the construction of this verse is that Eve was the mother of all living of the Jewish line that was to evolve Jesus Christ, then it is correct.

Gen. i. 26, is the record of the Creation of the Gentile races, namely, the Caucasian, Mongolian, Malay, Indian, and Negro, while Gen. i. 27, records the creation of the Hebrew race which includes the Jews. This is proven by the word dominion in Gen. i. 26. The five Gentile races have held dominion of the earth during all history, while the Hebrews, in part the Jews, attempted to build the Tower of Babel and become a nation, but God frustrated their design and scattered them among the Isles of the Gentiles and nations of the earth by confusing their language. They made a second attempt in Babylon, with the same result.

The drift of the account and history goes to show that the earth was peopled in numbers substantially as they now exist. The Caucasians having been created in Europe, the Mongolians and Malays in Eastern Asia, the Negroes in Africa, and the Indians in America. This requires the necessity of the creation of the Vegetable Kingdom substantially as it now exists, for food of the animal kingdom, and for humanity. In short, that this earth and all upon it was created substantially as it now exists, and has been continued by the never varying law of God by reproduction in type.

The reading world requires to be electrified and amused, hence we see how readily it snaps at any theory of creation.

Geology came forward with a very plausible theory, having for its foundation that God could not create a fossil as well as any other reproduced thing that had parents. The parents of the fossil are the previous existence of plants or animal life and necessary food for its formation. The fossil is the completed result from existing parents, and so is man, and every other reproduced thing. In the creation it was results that were created and not the parents, hence the fossil was created as a result the same as all other things were created. The geologists deny this and say that God could not create a fossil, and this is the foundation stone of their theory. We ask, how do they know that God could not create a fossil?

Geology is the old science of mineralogy electrified with the denial that God could not create a fossil.

The Mineralogical arrangement of the various rocks, minerals, &c., corresponding with the similar arrangement of parts of the human system, have the same general arrangement of parts to make a whole. Having given any particular part we are enabled at once to tell its location in the completed body. Evolution is another theory that is attracting much attention from our pulpits. We do not intend to discuss the merits of this theory, but dismiss it with all other theories of Creation, as they are anti-biblical and anti-christian.

So far as they are anti-biblical, we need not give arguments. We have a plain, simple and truly scientific account of the Creation in the Genesis, and Christians believe and assume it as the work of God and His inspiration.

As far as we have seen of any theory of creation, nothing has yet appeared to overthrow that account. To deny the Genesis account of Creation, we must set aside a part of the Fourth Commandment, " For in six days the Lord made Heaven and Earth, the sea and all that therein is, and rested the seventh day." It is also part of Christ's teaching in His Gospel.

All these theories which go to illustrate a different mode of creation from the one laid down in the inspired Scripture, tend to bring Christianity into bad repute. They certainly do no good and no one can point to any good result that has come from them. When God abandoned His protection to the Jews and the Jewish religion and established the new Dispensation of the Christian religion with Christ as the Head, every element of the earth and all upon it and every natural law was in complete order. These with mankind were turned over to Christ as a new Creation, with all the advantages of past experience and knowledge.

Neither Christ nor His religion was called upon to defend any theories of creation or dogmas of religion. He had a free and open field and was alone to be guided by the laws which he found in operation at that time. There was nothing to interfere with Christ's Gospel and the new principles which it inculcated; all was a new, bright and plain road.

The Organic Laws of God, together with the mandatory laws which He was to lay down in His Gospel, were the only restraint upon His teachings. It was to be a new world, a new departure and a new revelation.

We cannot be too emphatic on the point as to the responsibility of the Christian in accepting, obeying and teaching, that the material laws of God in operation at the time of the establishment of the Christian Religion, were the laws of God to be recognized as part of Christianity, and binding upon it. At that time six types of humanity existed upon the earth in numbers and have been uniformly reproduced in type from that time to the present. About this there can be no difference of opinion, it is an established historic fact. The Christian abstractly has nothing to do with theories, mistakes, mistranslations or traditions on this point ; he has the laws of God in operation before his eyes daily and a knowledge that these laws of reproduction have never changed during the Christian Era. This definitely settles for the Christian the question of the unity of the races from a single pair of human beings, and confirms the account in the original Hebrew in Gen. i. 26, 27, and Gen. v. 2, of a diversity of people created.

We will now endeavor to show that the Organic Laws of God are all paralleled in the inspired record. The first laws named as organic were the existence of the Father, Son, and Holy Ghost (the mind of God and Christ) as the Creator of all things visible and invisible and of mankind one of those specific acts. The specification of His being the Creator of all material things is found in the Genesis commencing with heaven (space) and then earth without form (primordial matter) and then light and then waters and then dry land (earth combined of primordial matter) then the gathering together the waters to make seas, lakes, rivers, &c., and then planting the earth with the Vegetable Kingdom, then giving motion to the Heavenly bodies to make day, night and the seasons, then creating the fishes to populate the waters, and then the fowls to fly in the air, and then the animals of the earth, and lastly creating mankind. This is so clear and marvelously connects the Creator with the created, that words cannot improve the condition.

The proof of the God Head being paralleled in the Genesis is found in the creation of Adam.

Gen. i. 26. And God said, let us make ADAM in OUR image after OUR likeness, and let THEM have dominion, &c.

While it is evident and plainly expressed that the creation of Adam was the act of the God Head, there is a singularity at first thought that the creation of The Adam was executed by God alone.

Gen. i. 27. And God created The Adam in His OWN image; in the image of GOD created He him.

There would seem to be about as much mystery in the language of these two creations as there is in the Creation itself. But a scrutinizing investigation will change that supposed mystery into a most interesting and valuable Biblical lesson.

On the intelligent reading of these two accounts of creation rests the whole structure of the Biblical account of the Christian religion. We do not wish to be understood as saying that the Christian religion depends upon the correct reading of these two verses, or upon the correct translation of any particular passage ; but as mankind is the subject of religion, it is at least pleasant for the Christian to know that his creation from the hand of God is correctly given to him by teachers supposed to know what they are teaching.

All the Organic Laws of God are universal in their action over the subjects to which they apply respectively, and the law of obedience is the next in order for consideration.

The parallel of this law is found in the inspiration when God commanded The Adam not to eat of the tree of Life. Still he did eat of it through the persuasion of his wife Eve, and punishment immediately followed the disobedience. The cases of The Adam and of his daughters marrying into the Gentile races were the first and only ones recorded in the early history of disobedience; but they accumulate as the history goes on.

All Christians acknowledge that obedience to the Laws of God and punishment for their disobedience are the two great boundary lines of the Christian religion, and were equally so for the Jewish religion, and have been universal laws from the creation of mankind, and equally binding upon all men. We cannot understand how a pious good man who obeys all the laws of God, and loves Him, and whose conduct fulfills all the requirements of Gospel, should be held responsible, and be punished for the sins of another. The only exception made by God is found in the Fifth Commandment, where He declares that "He is a jealous God and visits the sins of the fathers upon the children unto the third and fourth generations of them that HATE Me and show mercy unto thousands that LOVE Me and keep My Commandments." This is a mandatory law and controls all theologies and suppositions as to the transmission of sins, or responsibility for the sins of another, as the class to which the exception applies is only those who HATE God, and its continuance only for a limited period.

This theology of responsibility for sin committed by another has been as fruitful of discussion as the unity of the race on which it has been founded. The Organic Law is that sin against God's laws will be punished. Now sin is an act, mental or otherwise, and if there is no act committed, according to this Organic Law there can be no punishment to follow.

The theology of original sin in Adam requires sin in all of his descendants even beyond the third and fourth generations, even though they had committed no sin themselves. We say that the Organic Law of punishment for sin committed controls this question, that no one can be punished for sin of another because he does not commit an act of sin which the Organic Law requires for punishment.

We now come to the concluding Organic Laws of God. His Ten Commandments given to Moses, which ratify and confirm into mandatory laws all the previous ones we have considered. "I am the Lord thy God," confirms the law of the God Head, for if it be admitted that there is a God, then it follows that there was a Divine Christ, and the Holy Ghost the mind of God and Christ, "And show mercy unto thousands that love Me and keep My Commandments." To love God is thus a mandatory law. Not to take the Lord's name in vain, keeping the Sabbath day holy, working six days and resting on the Sabbath, are each mandatory laws. "For in six days the Lord made the Heaven and the Earth and all that in them is," confirms the literal account of Creation in the Genesis, and the material laws connected therewith. "Honor thy father and thy mother," "Thou shalt not kill," "Thou shalt not commit adultery," "Thou shalt not steal," "Thou shalt not bear false witness against thy neighbour," "Thou shalt not covet any of thy neighbour's possessions," are each and all mandatory laws.

A question may be asked of what utility to the Christian are all these ancient laws, as old things have passed away and Christ declared the Scriptures fulfilled. The Christian should know that the Organic Laws are God's platform, are fixed and immutable, and are the same from their inception through all ages to the end. When God sent His Son Jesus Christ upon earth as a Missionary to give to all the people the new dispensation, these laws were then in full force and operation, and formed part of His teachings. Reverencing these laws and the subjects upon which they act, from the uniform action of the heavenly bodies to the blade of grass in the field, a stupendous plan reaching from the creation to the establishment of the Christian religion is presented for the contemplation and acceptance of mankind.

On what does this acceptance depend? We answer that it depends upon our own knowledge, belief and faith. Then the question arises, what portion of that acceptance is covered by our knowledge, what portion by belief, and what portion by faith? To arrive at a correct conclusion, we must understand what is knowledge, what is belief, and what is faith. We answer that the establishment and action of material laws is knowledge, and belief is what may be called secondary knowledge which we derive from the inspired word of God, and faith is the acceptance of the whole plan of the Christian religion as recorded in the gospel as truth. So that faith, if it is strong enough, takes rank with the Christian as a material law.

It must be remembered that material laws never conflict with the true Word of God, and therefore we are justified if we always construe that Word as in harmony with these laws. Some claim that the making of Eve out of the rib of The Adam, and the creating of Christ in the womb of a Virgin, were violations of His material laws. Such people do not understand what a material law of God is. A material law is the continuance of reproduction in state or in kind of any entity. We have no account of any other human being made from the rib of a man, or any other child being created in the womb of a virgin, and hence there never has been any reproduction of the kind in the human family, and therefore this making and creation were not violations of material laws, but were bringing into existence humanity by different processes, never again used.

If the professing Christian believes in a God, and that He created the infinite number of subjects for material laws to act upon which come within His knowledge, why should he reject the creation in the Conception of Mary the Mother of Jesus, when after that Conception the child grew and was born in accordance with the material laws governing the birth of all children. The Conception of Mary was a single act of Creation by God among millions, yes countless creations, which all professing Christians willingly admit to be the Act of God, while some reject all rules of logic and evidence, and deny that God could have done this one act, and for so slight a concession endanger their happiness in the life to come.

As the Inspired Word of God is the foundation of our belief, all can see the necessity of a correct translation from the original into the various languages which are made for the education of the Christian World.

How little attention apparently has been given to this subject we have fully explained. What can we expect from such deviations from the true Word except confusion and false deductions. First let the foundation be made correct and deductions of truth will follow.

THE CATHOLIC AND PROTESTANT LAYMEN.

The layman of any true Christian Organization founded upon the Gospel of Jesus Christ, has two different and distinct relations in the terrestrial organization to which he may belong. The one may be, and often is, before baptism and entering Christ's Church, and the other is after entering Christ's Church by taking the vows of baptism. In the first condition he is bound to obey the laws of the land and the specific laws of the organization to which he belongs, which is a corporation, and its by-laws and discipline are enforced by the same means, in a general way, as the laws of the land. On being baptized and on entering Christ's Church through a Christian Organization by making the baptismal vows, the member accepts the offer of God and Jesus Christ to reward him or her in the future life with happiness, if they thereafter live a life in conformity with the laws and requirements of the Gospel, or punishment for non-compliance.

There is no terrestrial law that can reward or punish a member of Christ's Church for compliance or non-compliance with the laws of the Gospel, but he or she can be rewarded or punished for compliance or non-compliance with the laws of a Christian Corporation. It is therefore idle to say that a terrestrial Christian Organization is, or can be, Christ's Church, for the one can exist without the other, which is dependent upon discipline of the Christian organization. So too by by-laws and other regulations a Christian Organization can be incorporated to receive and include only members of Christ's Church, and not to admit any others within their doors; but this would not be Christian, as these organizations are for the double purpose of teaching the gospel to make converts to faith, and furnish a place for the members of Christ's Church in which worship and other requirements of the gospel can be performed.

From this it will be seen that a terrestrial organization, with a multitude of places for teaching and worship, which are usually called a Church, is not the same Church as Christ's Church, one being governed by terrestrial laws, while the other is governed by the laws of God. Every layman who is deeply interested in his religion, should not fail to acquaint himself with the gospel. It contains less reading than most novels, and when one is acquainted with the laws of God, material and immaterial, the reading and understanding of the truths of the Gospel are as simple and plain as any other reading.

The Christian religion is conduct spiritual or otherwise, guided by the laws of God, and following the example and teaching of Jesus Christ. These are all contained in the Gospel. These teachings and examples are all consistent and governed by the organic laws of God, so that it is easy to determine what are the foundation principles of the Christian religion. From want of Gospel knowledge by the layman, Christianity is generally regarded as a huge, mysterious cloud, which cannot be penetrated by human knowledge. Scraps of light are presented here and there, and duties defined here and there, but the mysterious cloud in its wholeness still remains to many.

There is some trouble and some uncertainty in reading the Gospel in the present day, as given to us by the Apostles in the various languages into which the original has been translated. But while there may be errors of translation, and errors of interpretation, we believe the essential points of the Gospel still survive ; and all sincere and devoted christians should accept it as such. Christ said :

John iii. 5. Verily, Verily, I say unto thee, except a man be born of water and of the Spirit he cannot enter into the Kingdom of God.

This is the alpha and omega of the foundation of the Christian religion, and contains all of faith or of conduct required by God or Christ. First as to Faith. On the faith of Peter that Christ was the Son of the Living God, Christ said He would build His Church on this rock, and the gates of Hell should not prevail against it. This is the foundation of the Church of Christ, instituted for the benefit of those who accept the faith and are baptized into it. The baptismal vow completes the faith in the truths of the gospel and closes by its acceptance the contract between man and God, that he will thereafter comply by his conduct with its requirements.

This is all as we understand it of the Christian religion. There is no directions who, where, or when baptism shall be performed, so that it is done in the name of the Father, the Son, and the Holy Ghost. Can there be anything simpler and easier of understanding, done by God or man?

Every Christian heart should overflow with gratitude to God for His promises so easily grasped and complied with. There can be no mistaking the simple and compact Words of Christ, reinforced by other passages of the Gospel.

The next question in order is whether these representations of Christ's teachings, that the Apostles did perform their required duties with fidelity and accuracy in this respect? If the answer be in the negative, those must abandon the Christian religion. If on the other hand they admit that the eleven Apostles did give us a true record of Christ's gospel in simple, plain and understandable words, in the language in which they recorded them, we have the reliable Word of God, and an enduring Christian religion.

Did Jesus Christ give us by His Apostles a record that could be understood by the nations of the earth, according to His mandatory law of teaching, or did He give instructions to these Apostles to make a record that could not be understood except by the interpretation of somebody who would assume to make the gospel what it should be, according to their conclusions of what was really the intention of Christ and His Apostles?

Interpretation of Divine laws is a monstrous assumption, and has been the direct cause of most of the dissentions, quarrelings and disputes between Christian Denominations. Civil laws, sometimes the imperfections of humanity, require higher wisdom for interpretation, but these are all the workings of weak humanity. Not so with Divine laws ; they are made by perfect wisdom, where the mind of man cannot reach, follow, or fathom.

We therefore say that the Gospel of Jesus Christ is the offspring of Divine wisdom. If there be some weak minds that cannot understand it without substituting human for Divine wisdom, those would do well to follow such portions as they can understand, for there are enough of those for all practical purposes of salvation.

Now let us examine the organic laws of God, the mandatory laws of Jesus Christ as additions to the organic laws, and see if we find anything that cannot be understood by the simplest mind when they are taught orally or by reading. We mean by understanding to accept them as truth. Then, do christians accept as truth that there is a God ; that Jesus Christ was the Son of God, created in the womb of the Virgin Mary to be human form with Divine mind ; that the God Head is composed of these two and is guided by the common mind of both, usually called the Holy Ghost ; that the material or Natural Laws of God in operation at the time of establishing the Christian religion are in unchanged operation now and are binding upon Christians ; that

God requires of man recognition and obedience to all His laws, material and spiritual; that He will reward men for obedience of them, and punish them for disobedience; to accept as the laws of God, the Ten Commandments given to Moses, and which Christ made part of His Gospel; to accept as mandatory laws the XI. and XII. Commandments of Jesus Christ, and the other mandatory laws of prayer, faith, baptism, and the Lord's Supper; and to the Apostles, the mandatory law of teaching His Gospel to all nations?

We have been unable to discover in all Christ's Gospel teachings, any new principle of morals or duty, which has not its root in some one of the above laws, except the mandatory law to His apostles to teach His Gospel to all nations. We now ask the pertinent question: Is there any one of the above laws of God or of Jesus Christ, which are requirements of Christian duty, that cannot be understood and accepted as truth? Then where is the necessity or excuse for interpretation? Without it be, to bend the Gospel to the support of some Theology, an idea of a man?

All should accept the writings of the good men who wrote of matters supporting the principles of the Gospel, but should reject any doctrines, if there be any, that are antagonistic to God's laws, whether material or spiritual.

Miracles performed by authority of God are limited acts for the time being.

THE APOSTOLIC ERA.

Jesus Christ laid down in His personal teachings the entire foundation of the Christian religion with every law governing it. The first great point then was to adopt a means of circulating these principles to the knowledge of the world. Twelve of His adherents, or disciples, were selected as apostles, each to represent Him, to deliver His Gospel to the nations of the earth. Each was to have the same Divine powers to perform miracles as He used, so that the people would more readily believe. Each of the eleven apostles was for the purpose of teaching the gospel, to be (for this purpose) a Christ for life.

Accordingly the day of Pentecost was appointed as the time to commence these apostolic teachings, and throw open the doors of Christ's Church to the world. Peter's first effort was rewarded by the conversion of three thousand souls to the faith, that "Jesus Christ was the Son of the Living God" and of the truths of His Gospel, and were baptized into Christ's Church. The question here arises, were these converts baptized into Christ's Church, which He founded upon the faith that He was the Son of the Living

God, and on the truths and requirements of the vows of baptism to lead a life according to its requirements, or were they baptized into the Roman Catholic Organization, of which Peter was the head, and vowed on baptism to obey its by-laws and discipline in addition to those required by Christ's Church?

To belong to the Catholic, or any other Christian Denomination, a member of that organization must bind himself to obey the discipline of the organization, and if he does not, he can be suspended or dismissed, or otherwise dealt with.

The position of a member of Christ's Church is very different. Once a member, always a member, and no human power can displace him, or interfere with him. If he is a member of Christ's Church, and also a member of a Christian organization, he can be dealt with by it for any violation of baptismal vows or violation of any discipline of the organization. His baptismal vows are with God, to accept His promises of reward for good conduct, or to be punished for sin for deeds done in the body.

This is the contract between the members of Christ's Church and God, and is the Magna Charta of the Christian, and God will hold him responsible for any violation of that contract. The Gospel does not confine the making of this

Contract to any particular Christian Organization, to any particular men, or to any particular person, or any particular position, nor does it specify the drops of water to be used in baptism, so that the using of a drop, or more, or an ocean, complies with the requirements of the Gospel.

If every Organization had confined itself to the teachings of the eleven apostles in the Apostolic Era, there would be no necessity to-day to make an appeal for Christian unity, as there would be in that event, unity upon the Gospel, as taught by Christ, of one Lord, one Faith, and one Baptism. There are Christian Denominations, so-called, which do not accept all of God's Organic Laws, and the entire of Christ's Gospel, and such cannot be called Christian; but there are very many that do, and they are Christian, and if they had followed the teachings of the Apostolic Era, without any further disciplines in their organizations, peace and Christian love would have distinguished them to-day from the quarreling, bickering sects which now disturb the Christian World.

Nineteen-twentieths of all the differences between Christian Denominations arise out of Discipline and not from the Gospel. Some Denominations are so hampered by cumbersome discipline, that the principles and requirements of the Gospel are lost sight of, and the discipline has sometimes become their religion, instead of the Gospel. There is altogether too much machinery in discipline, and without the layman is a scholar in the gospel, it is difficult for him to distinguish between discipline and gospel.

This muddles up Christianity to such an extent, that it is not surprising that complications that now exist have good grounds for their existence.

Creeds as such, are not found in the Gospel, but are compilations from it of its salient points. The Apostles Creed, as it is called, was the first one adopted by the Roman Catholic Organization. The Gospel reader is surprised not to find in it the keystone of the Christian Religion, while that is set forth prominently in the Gospel, namely, faith and baptism as requirements to enter upon a Christian life, and further, that the name given by Christ to His Church* (Christ's Church) is entirely ignored by name in that Creed, and another name not found in the Gospel (Holy Catholic Church) used in its stead. This latter is an indefinite name, while Christ's Church is a definite one, which all can understand that read the Gospel.

It is probable that this may have been the reason why the same Catholic Organization found it expedient to make another Creed called the Nicene Creed, in which the name Holy Catholic Church was dropped, and the name One Catholic Apostolic Church was used instead. Still no reference was made in this Creed to Christ's Church, or to faith and baptism as a means of enjoying its blessing. Time and discussion no doubt suggested the fact that the name in the Nicene Creed was too great a departure from the Apostles Creed by having dropped the word Holy, so the Pope approved of a later Creed where the name One, Holy, Catholic Apostolic Church was adopted. Still no reference was made in this Creed to Christ's Church, or to faith and baptism, the Key-Stone of Christianity.

It is upon this Creed that the Catholic Organization found their claim of being the only Christ's Church, from which it will be seen that the claim is based upon the discipline of their organization, and not upon the gospel. We make no comments upon these facts, leaving every one to draw his own conclusion from them, so that every layman in any Christian Denomination can see that he can belong to any one of them, and receive the benefits promised, without being compelled to belong to this Catholic Organization, which claims to be the exclusive and only Christ's Church. We conclude that it will be a long time before Christian unity will be accomplished on this basis, if ever.

The Gospel teachings of the Catholic Organizations, as far as we are acquainted with them, are upon the foundation principles of the Christian religion, and it has done vast good in the past in making converts to the true faith and baptizing millions into Christ's Church, and its vast Organization promises equally great and good work for the future, but its discipline, teachings that the Pope, the Cardinals, Archbishops, Bishops and Priests are Vicegerents of Christ, with permissive powers to heal the sick, cast out devils, raise the dead, and forgive sins, powers given by Christ only to His twelve Apostles, and that it is the only Christ's Church, are claims that excite the worst passions of half the Christian world that is not Catholic.

If we are rightly informed, the Pope approves of every Article of Faith and every point of discipline, and the laity accept them as the requirements of their religion. Is it then surprising that the Catholics are all bound together in one solid phalanx against all other differing opinions. From this cause they are a devoted and sincere people, complying with all the requirements of faith and discipline. The requirements of discipline are so numerous and extensive, that the subject of these religious duties is kept constantly in their minds. The teachings begin in the cradle, all catholic mothers being engaged in this occupation until the children are old enough to attend the higher teachings in the houses of the organization.

This is but a fraction of their teachings; the numerous orders, societies, priests and nuns, almost beyond computation, complete an army of devoted christian teachers. Hence it is not surprising that through this rigid attention to the whole subject, they have accepted as faith the discipline of the apostolic succession with Divine permissive powers, and the misnomer of Christ's Church for the Roman Catholic Organization. There may be found some excuse for this anomalous condition. The Catholic laity, as a rule, do not study the gospel much from the record of it given to us in the New Testament, but accept all of their teachings without a thought of reservation.

When the Apostolic Era was ended in the establishment of the principles of the Christian religion, it was A FREE FOR ALL, because Christ's Church was to be and is universal, and it was natural that the Catholic Organization should follow the teachings of the gospel, as the apostles had done, and strive to make their converts believe that this was the only true Christ's Church, without very close investigation. No doubt their zeal overcame their absolute knowledge of the Gospel, and they fell into a rut that all subsequent Catholics have followed.

If they had investigated closely, they would have found that the original number of Christ's Apostles with Divine powers was twelve, and after Judas killed himself, there were eleven. Now it is claimed that there were twelve, Matthias having been chosen by the Eleven as the Twelfth to fill the place of Judas. In the first place, there is nothing in Christ's Gospel that gave the living apostles power to fill vacancies. This is simple assumption. There were two candidates for the place of Judas, Matthias and Barsabas; the lot fell upon Matthias and he was selected.

There not being a word in the Gospel that Christ made any provision for giving any one the Divine permissive powers that He gave His twelve apostles, nor allowing them to do so, these powers ceased at the death of each apostle.

Will any one pretend to say that Christ's mandatory law to the twelve apostles to teach the

Gospel to all nations, applied to any persons except those named?

It was a specific command, with a specific object, and that object was that His gospel should be made known to all nations. The acceptance of His gospel after the Apostolic Era, and the teachings that would and did naturally result, is quite a different mode from the Apostolic teaching.

Suppose the Apostolic teachings had convinced no one in the nations of the earth, did Christ in His gospel make any conditions or arrangements for such a contingency? By no means; all was centered upon the Apostolic teachings of the eleven, and no one can gainsay that proposition. Still Christ spoke many times of the acceptance by the world of His Gospel, and that the gates of Hell could not prevail against His Church, and the course of events goes to prove His words as true, as all others of His declarations.

Succession of good teachers by the laying on of hands is a valuable discipline, as it holds responsible the ordainer to select the fittest for the work. The eleven apostles established this discipline as outside the gospel, as Christ never ordained any of His Apostles by any such form, but simply by selection, and the form cannot be found in His Gospel. In like manner, the Apostolic succession with Divine powers forms no part of Christ's Gospel.

Christ's Church was established by Him, and He was and is the only true Head. Peter was the first head of the Catholic Organization, and was the first one occupying the position of Pope, and that Organization has continued to have a Pope ever since, and to this, in a great measure, can be referred the continuance and great success of that Organization.

www.ingramcontent.com/pod-product-compliance
Lightning Source LLC
Chambersburg PA
CBHW051724300426
44115CB00007B/447